Art Deco Jewellery

1920 – 1949

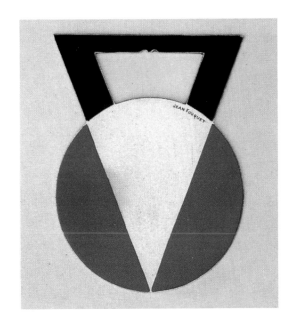

Melissa Gabardi

THE ANTIQUE COLLECTORS' CLUB

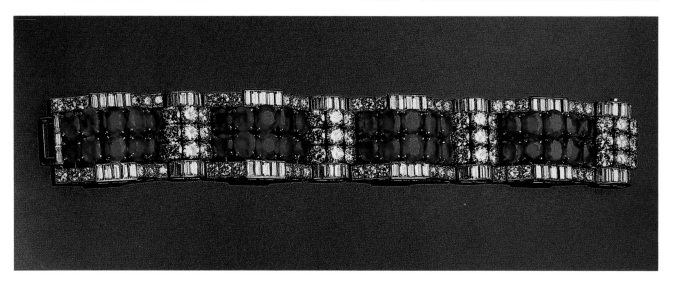

Art Deco
Jewellery
1920 – 1949

© 1989
World copyright reserved
First published 1989

ISBN 1 85149 065 5

Published for the Antique Collectors' Club
by the Antique Collectors' Club

British Library CIP Data

Gabardi, Melissa
    Art deco jewellery 1920-1949
    1. Jewellery. Art deco style
    I. Title [Bijoux de l'art deco aux annees 40.
    English]
    739'.27

Printed in England by the Antique Collectors' Club Ltd.,
5 Church Street, Woodbridge, Suffolk.

Frontispiece: Invisibly set ruby and diamond holly leaf clip and the original design by Van Cleef et Arpels, 1936.

A ruby and diamond bracelet by Van Cleef et Arpels, 1936. The original design for this bracelet is shown on page 3.
From the collection of the Duchess of Windsor. Photos: Sotheby's.

Jewels shown at the bottom of page 3: A gold, coral, emerald and diamond clip, designed as a butterfly perched on a cabochon coral flowerhead. Cartier, 1946.

A gold, enamel and emerald panther clip. Cartier, 1948. Original design for a ruby and diamond bracelet. Van Cleef et Arpels, 1936.

All from the collection of the Duchess of Windsor. Photos: Sotheby's.

Opposite: Pendant in silver and red and black enamel signed by Jean Fouquet. Private collection. Photo: Thomas Heuer. (Inset). Photograph by Man Ray (1926) showing a selection of bangles.

Contents

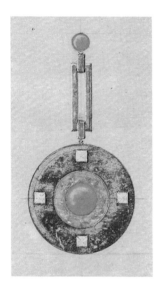

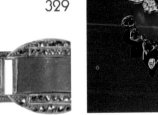

Acknowledgements

The author wishes to thank all those who assisted in the creation of this book, for the loan of documents and photographs as well as for their very useful advice.

Above all, thanks to the great jewellery houses of Paris who gave her access to their archives: Maison Cartier, especially Mme Betty Jais; Maison Boucheron, Mme Laure de Fels; Maison Chaumet, Mme Néret-Minet; Maison Mauboussin, M. Michel de Robert; Maison Mellerio, M. Mellerio; Maison Poiray; Maison Van Cleef et Arpels, M. François Canavy.

Also, thanks to M. and Mme Barlach-Heuer, M. Martin du Daffoy, M. Félix Marcilhac, M. Michel Perinet. In Germany, Frau Erna Zarges Dürr (Murnau) and the house of Oscar Labiner (Munich). In England, the house of Garrard (London). In Belgium, M. Fredy Wolfers (Brussels). In Italy, Umberto Accenti (Milan), Daniela Balzaretti (Bergamo), Franco Bernardini (Milan), Rinaldo e Floriana Cusi (Milan), Nella Longari (Milan), Gianni Bulgari (Rome), Carlo Fleuteri (Rome), Stella Cesare Settepassi (Florence), Claudio Zanettini (Cortina).

Finally, the author would like to thank the following salerooms and galleries for the use of photographs: Christie's Geneva, M. Hans Nadelhoffer; Milan, Signora Giorgina Venosta; Rome, Signor Francesco Alvarà; Finarte Milan, Signora Daria Porro and Signora Anna Negrisoli. Sotheby's London, Zurich and Geneva, Mme Myriam Laurié, Mr Nicolas Rayner, Mr David Bennet, Daniela Mascetti, Brigitte Blangey and M. Bernard Berger.

THE ANTIQUE COLLECTORS' CLUB

The Antique Collectors' Club was formed in 1966 and now has a five figure membership spread throughout the world. It publishes the only independently run monthly antiques magazine *Antique Collecting* which caters for those collectors who are interested in widening their knowledge of antiques, both by greater awareness of quality and by discussion of the factors which influence the price that is likely to be asked. The Antique Collectors' Club pioneered the provision of information on prices for collectors and the magazine still leads in the provision of detailed articles on a variety of subjects.

It was in response to the enormous demand for information on "what to pay" that the price guide series was introduced in 1968 with the first edition of *The Price Guide to Antique Furniture* (completely revised, 1978), a book which broke new ground by illustrating the more common types of antique furniture, the sort that collectors could buy in shops and at auctions rather than the rare museum pieces which had previously been used (and still to a large extent are used) to make up the limited amount of illustrations in books published by commercial publishers. Many other price guides have followed, all copiously illustrated, and greatly appreciated by collectors for the valuable information they contain, quite apart from prices. The Antique Collectors' Club also publishes other books on antiques, including horology and art reference works, and a full book list is available.

Club membership, which is open to all collectors, costs £17.50 per annum. Members receive free of charge *Antique Collecting*, the Club's magazine (published every month except August), which contains well-illustrated articles dealing with the practical aspects of collecting not normally dealt with by magazines. Prices, features of value, investment potential, fakes and forgeries are all given prominence in the magazine.

Among other facilities available to members are private buying and selling facilities, the longest list of 'For Sales' of any antiques magazine, an annual ceramics conference and the opportunity to meet other collectors at their local antique collectors' clubs. There are over eighty in Britain and more than a dozen overseas. Members may also buy the Club's publications at special pre-publication prices.

As its motto implies, the Club is an amateur organisation designed to help collectors get the most out of their hobby: it is informal and friendly and gives enormous enjoyment to all concerned.

For Collectors — By Collectors — About Collecting

The Antique Collectors' Club, 5 Church Street, Woodbridge, Suffolk

1920-1930-1940
THREE STYLES: ONE PERIOD

If jewellery is a reflection of the tastes and tendencies of the society which created it, then it is also true that it cannot be dissociated from the period of its origins.

Thus the jewellery of the twenties necessarily reflects the many contradictions of that post-war decade.

In fact, French jewellery of this period corresponds precisely to the Art Deco revolt against academicism. The formal freedom which this movement represents was fully understood and perfectly translated into their own medium by the innovatory artist-jewellers, of which the most outstanding were Jean Fouquet, Gérard Sandoz and Raymond Templier — to quote only a few names of incomparable stature.

In their hands, the traditional article of jewellery underwent a fundamental change. It became a completely new kind of ornament, an object more closely related to the machinist painting of Fernand Léger, or to the geometrical forms of Mondrian or Malévitch, than to the classical adornment of the eighteenth and nineteenth centuries. There appeared, for example, bracelets directly inspired by ball-bearings, and rings unequivocally referring to the big ends of motor-car engines. There is even an example of the bicycle chain being elevated to the status of feminine ornament. Jewellery, so far always thought of as the tangible expression of wealth, suddenly became a symbol of the age of technology.

In parallel with this activity on the part of the artist-jewellers, the high fashion jewellers of the rue de la Paix and the place Vendôme interpreted the geometrical rigour of Art Deco with a profusion of precious stones, expressing the luxurious magnificence of the Roaring Twenties.

F. Solar wrote at the time: 'Talking of modern jewellery, it seems provocatively young. It is made for the modern woman of today, and is in harmony with the simple line of her dresses, the pure and unfettered curves of her body.'

Nevertheless, Art Deco jewellery was not destined to live a long life. It was, in fact, to disappear at the end of the decade, although it left the indelible mark of its geometrical forms on the jewellery of the years to come.

The first to show the influence of Art Deco was the white jewellery of the 1930s, with its geometrical structures studded with diamonds. The polychromatic jewellery of the same period, on the other hand, was primarily inspired by Oriental influences, particularly by Indian art. A new tendency in jewellery was initiated towards the end of the 1930s. Yellow gold replaced platinum: new combinations of precious and semi-precious stones took over from the lavish displays of pavé set brilliants. What caused this change of direction?

Economic, political and social factors are never far from the vicissitudes of taste and fashion. The economic and political crisis of the 1930s almost certainly encouraged the triumph of gold which, as well as conceding to the notion of innovation, had a number of indisputable advantages. The Second

World War accentuated this movement towards a certain severity, in fashion as well as jewellery.

This is the source of the development of the 1940s style in jewellery, in which gold was of primary importance. To compensate for the shortage of precious stones, also difficult to find in the trade, articles of jewellery became larger and took on a plasticity resembling sculpture.

The formal characteristics of jewellery were no longer related to those of Art Deco. Nevertheless, looking carefully at many of the models created in the following thirty years, it is possible to detect the influence of the geometrical style of the artist-jewellers referred to above.

Unfortunately, the classification of these various strains of jewellery design, which co-existed, were interlinked, and influenced by each other, remains very confused. Today, the generic term 'Art Deco Jewellery' is used, quite arbitrarily, to qualify a piece of jewellery of abstract design signed by Raymond Templier, a polychromatic brooch of vaguely Oriental style, or a brooch representing a stylised vase of flowers executed in platinum and diamonds. But one might equally well find the term used to refer to a piece in yellow gold representing a bow or a bouquet of flowers.

In the attempt to shed some light on this rather confused subject, which covers the production of thirty years or so, we have chosen a classification by decades — although this is admittedly often arbitrary: 1920s jewellery; 1930s jewellery; 1940s jewellery.

It is evident that a specific style does not emerge spontaneously at a precise date, and it is also clear that it does not equally suddenly disappear. Before being universally recognised, a style derives from experimental work on the part of a small number of innovators, placed in particular circumstances. It is maintained on the initiative of a host of nostalgic imitators long after it has stopped being fashionable. The chronological division into decades is far from being precise. Our intention is simply to define the period during which styles in jewellery coincided with specific fashions, were most widespread, in most general use, and found unquestioning favour with the public.

Thus our system of classification should be seen as an indication rather than an absolute rule. But it does seem to clarify the history of a form of jewellery deriving from a period characterised by an impulse which, in its beginning, as revealed in the work of the artist-jewellers, was more intellectual than aesthetic, and came to an end just after the war, that is, with the end of 1940s jewellery.

CHAPTER I
THE EXPLOSION OF ART DECO

The rigorously geometrical style of Art Deco derives its name from the famous Exposition Internationale des Arts Décoratifs et Industriels Modernes held in Paris from April to October, 1925.

'This exhibition', wrote Pierre Kjellberg in *The Masters of Art Deco Furniture*, 'was originally intended to take place in 1916 and, contrary to what has often been thought, the style to which it gave its name came into being well before the Roaring Twenties. Its true origins should be sought in the reactions of the beginning of the century against the excesses of Art Nouveau.'

One hundred and thirty lavishly decorated pavillions, spread from the Esplanade des Invalides to the Grand Palais and along the banks of the Seine, took in a variety of products of the artist and artisan. There were sections for architecture and town-planning, interior decoration, furniture, knick-knacks, vases, book-binding, fabrics, dresses, and of course, jewellery. The jewellery section took up five hundred square metres of the Grand Palais and included nearly four hundred exhibitors.

According to the jeweller Georges Fouquet, the exhibition was 'seeking objects deriving from new and entirely original ideas, excluding imitation and inspiration from traditional styles'. If he is to be believed, the gemstone and jewellery exhibition opened its doors to a fairyland setting, designed by the architect Eric Bagge. It revealed a glittering display of new jewellery, shimmering with various colours. Precious and semi-precious gemstones and hard stones were all there. This dazzling symphony caught the eye, and visitors to the exhibition retained in their memory the vision of an Aladdin's cave...

But what objective description can we give of the new style, known as the '1925 style' by reference to the year of the exhibition?

Art Deco is primarily characterised by prismatic surfaces, geometrical forms and the general stylisation of decorative motifs borrowed from nature (animal or vegetable). The 1925 exhibition was the fullest expression of this artistic movement of the inter-war period.

Leaving aside aesthetic considerations, the event had loftier aims. Its ambitious project was to promote a form of social art, or rather to link art with the imperatives of modern industry. The express intention of the promoters of the exhibition was to prove to those abroad that the French were capable of enhancing all of life's luxuries with a quality of superior taste and perfection.

The problem of the interaction between art and industrial technology (with the aim of lending a new aesthetic quality to all aspects of practical life) had already been posed in the first three decades of the century by various movements concerned with the plastic and applied arts in Austria, Germany and Holland, as well as in Scandinavia. The 'Viennese Secession', for example, a movement which flourished between the end of the nineteenth century and the First World War, had tried to associate the fine arts with decorative art and interior design. The major artists associated with this movement were the painter Gustav Klimt, the painter and architect Joseph Hoffmann and the draughtsman-designer Kolo Moser.

Fernand Léger
Costume designed for the
Ballets suédois
(1922).
Private Collection.

Obviously the mass-production of everyday objects tended towards the suppression of ornamental elements, now an unnecessary encumbrance.

'With the development of culture, ornamentation disappears from everyday objects', wrote the Austrian architect Adolf Loos in *Ornament und Verbrechen* (Ornamentation and Crime), published in Vienna in 1908. Later the Viennese

Workshops tried in their turn to create everyday objects which satisfied the new aesthetic criteria while remaining strictly cost effective.

Under the aegis of the architect Walter Gropius, founder and director of the German Bauhaus school, there developed from 1919 to 1932 (years which mark the beginning and the end of the Weimar Republic) an extraordinarily important movement, which was the leading example of these new practical tendencies in art. It tried to respond to the demands of a new consumer society by bringing together creative talent and manufacturing techniques, and promoting a rational art, based on simple, sparse lines.

Gradually, the notion of functionalism extended itself to the arts. Walter Gropius's Bauhaus had brought together artisans, artists, engineers, industrial designers and architects, all engaged in the same search for purified forms, and trying to apply them to mass-produced consumer items. The introduction on to the market of new materials and revolutionary techniques allowed, in architecture, the development of a new dynamic style and the creation of streamlined buildings offering maximum comfort in living areas, while reducing wasted space and trimming building costs (the finest of the New York skyscrapers, the Seagram building, a steel and glass structure, was conceived by Mies van der Rohe, who taught at the Bauhaus). These were the 'cultural politics' of an enlightened bourgeoisie trying to extend the benefits of progress to the widest audience. But the roots of Art Deco are also buried elsewhere, in a whole series of disparate phenomena which are worth referring to here. The end of the First World War marks the decline of the predominant style of the last years of the nineteenth century and the first two decades of the twentieth century, that is, Art Nouveau (sometimes referred to as the New Century style because it characterised the Exposition Universelle de Paris of 1900).

The new generation set itself up in revolt against the arabesques, the floral and vegetable forms, the excessive and oneiric decorative motifs of the Art Nouveau aesthetic, and exhibited unanimous enthusiam for the geometrical, the functional and the abstract.

In 1918, Le Corbusier and Amédée Ozenfant launched the purist movement, the rational and applied expression of cubism. Two years later they founded the review *L'Esprit Nouveau* (The New Spirit), which proclaimed the need to replace the ornamental with pure lines corresponding to functional criteria.

Cubism, which refused decoration in favour of an analytical, realist and objective vision of form, can doubtless be seen as one of the principal sources of inspiration for Art Deco's extreme fascination with the geometrical.

At the same time, the influence of other important movements in painting, like fauvism, suprematism, futurism and Orphism, should not be forgotten.

Oriental art also left a strong imprint on the new style. Its influence is particularly strongly revealed in the intensity of colour and the importance of colour contrast which characterises the Art Deco palette.

Pendulette in the shape of a Japanese temple gate, in rock crystal, onyx, black enamel, gold and diamonds.
Van Cleef et Arpels (1926).
Photo: Christie's.

It is worth quoting, amongst other sources of the movement, the famous 'Ballets russes' of Serge Diaghilev, which from 1910 onwards were all the rage in Paris, beginning with the *Schéhérazade* of Rimsky-Korsakov. The bold chromatics of the décor and costumes unleashed the enthusiasm of the audience. The influence of these choreographies on fashion, jewellery and interior decoration was so great that, at the time, people talked about a 'Ballets russes' style. Serge Diaghilev had gathered around him a galaxy of leading artists and intellectuals: Max Ernst (originator of the idea for the scenography of *Romeo and Juliet*), Alexandre Bénois (who designed the costumes for *Giselle*), Pablo Picasso, Georges Braque, Larionov, Miro, Juan Gris, Léon Bakst and Sonia Delaunay.

As this suggests, painters of the period were happy to work on set design and costumes. Stravinsky and Prokofiev were also friends of the Russian choreographer. In 1922, Fernand Léger designed the highly acclaimed horizontally striped costumes of the *Skating Rink*, a choreography on ice by Jean Borlin, put on within the scope of the 'Ballets suédois', for which Picabia and de Chirico also worked.

Other artistic events also contributed to the birth of Art Deco. Amongst these was Negro art, whose decisive role made itself felt after the two Colonial Exhibitions in Marseilles and Paris, in 1922 and 1931 respectively. Picasso, of course, had already felt the impact of Negro art in June 1907, when first visiting the Ethnographic Museum at the Trocadéro. The result of this confrontation was to be a painting which has to be thought of as the first cubist manifesto, *Les Demoiselles d'Avignon*.

Josephine Baker's *'Revue nègre'* had a noticeably similar influence to that of the 'Ballets russes' fifteen years earlier.

The development of archaeological research in the field of Mayan art also had its effect — in the plastic arts — in terms of the introduction of new linear motifs (concentric square structures and stepped pyramids). The discovery by Howard Carter and Lord Caernarvon, in 1922, of the tomb of Tutankhamun, inaugurated a passion for Egyptian decorative motifs.

Thus scarabs, hieroglyphs and spread-winged falcons, came in *en masse* in the decoration of jewels, furniture and knick-knacks. It is worth mentioning here the major influence exerted by the ancient arts of China, Japan, India and Persia, which opened up to the creators of Art Deco an enormous iconographical repertoire as well as a wide range of new materials. Thus lacquers, carved jade, pearls, ivory, coral, agate, malachite and lapis lazuli were widely used. In what is only an apparent contradiction with its definition of beauty as functional, Art Deco showed a predilection for all kinds of precious raw materials: exotic woods (Macassar ebony, palm wood, sycamore, mahogany, Brazilian rosewood), lacquer, hardstones, marble, mosaics, bronze, speckled lacquer, mother-of-pearl marquetry, silk brocades... The decorative use of these sophisticated artisanal techniques helped give a new impetus to a whole series of crafts which had fallen into disuse. With this renewal of the decorative arts cabinet-makers, glass-blowers, goldsmiths, ceramists, jewellers, book-binders, upholsterers, makers of bronzes, gilders, lacquerers, creative artists and simple artists, all rediscovered the importance they had been losing at the end of the nineteenth century.

The same decorative motifs were taken up in all fields. These were, as we have already seen, usually 'geometrical abstracts'. Sometimes, however, they were inspired by naturalist themes. But if this was the case, they were always geometrically stylised. Whereas Art Nouveau had favoured exotic and imaginary animals (a fantastical bestiary in which, for example, a dragonfly had a woman's torso) or frightening creatures like reptiles and spiders, Art Deco offered, in contrast, a selection of wild and domesticated animals (panthers, tigers, gazelles, antelopes, birds, greyhounds, cats). Whereas in the flora of Art Nouveau irises, lilies and orchids had occupied pride of place, Art Deco preferred roses (the famous cubist rose of Iribes), camellias, baskets of flowers and fruit, all highly stylised and highly coloured. In ornamentation the fountain theme and the motif of stepped pyramids also took pride of place. In architecture, mass and volume replaced decoration, and large, flat surfaces were emphasised. Rationalism, simplicity, correctness of proportions were the characteristics of the architecture of the period. This was a severe but imposing aesthetic, based on the new principles of functionalism.

But it is essentially in the field of interior decoration that Art Deco found its highest form of artistic expression, and displayed the most refined sense of luxury. Pure, sober, refined lines, clean surfaces, perfect curves: these were the principal elements of decoration and the basis of modern taste and design.

Design for a pendant earring in platinum, onyx and brilliants (1925). Cusi di via Clerici Archives (Milan).

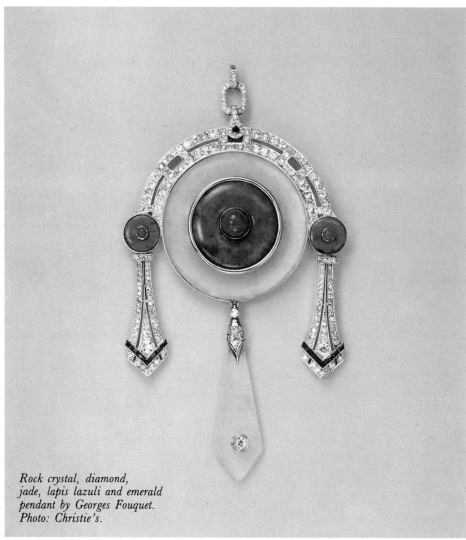

Rock crystal, diamond, jade, lapis lazuli and emerald pendant by Georges Fouquet. Photo: Christie's.

Glass and metal were widely used. In decoration, metal took pride of place, as an element of stability, and for the cool quietness of its texture and the cleanness of its lines. Metalwork was sometimes so light and airy that it came to resemble wickerwork and lace.

Furniture — usually produced in one-off models — was sober and structured, sometimes enriched with parchment, ivory and mother-of-pearl.

Emile-Jacques Ruhlman (1879-1933) was the great cabinet-maker of the period. He created simple, elegant, perfectly finished models in rare woods, sometimes decorated with sumptuous inlays of ivory, morocco and *galuchat* skin.

Other distinguished figures in the creation of the new style in furniture were Marcel Coard (1889-1974), Paul Follot (1877-1941), Armand-Albert Rateau (1883-1938), André Groult (1884-1967) and André Mare (1887-1932).

In this rapid survey of Art Deco we cannot overlook the decisive role played by the great Parisian designer Jacques Doucet, who quickly revealed himself to be an adept of the new style. After collecting eighteenth century furniture all his life, he suddenly decided, in 1912, to sell it all in order to live surrounded by objects of his own time. The decoration of his new apartment in the avenue

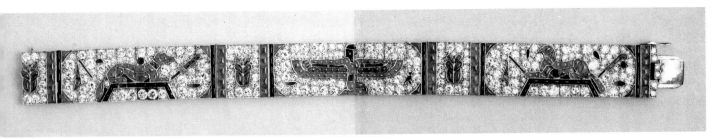

Egyptian inspired bracelet in diamonds, rubies, emeralds and onyx.
Van Cleef et Arpels (1925).

Article of Egyptian jewellery discovered by Mariette Vautour. Ram's headed vulture in gold
and coloured glass. Musée du Louvre.

Jabot pin in onyx, diamonds, pearls
and coral.
Photo: Sotheby's.

Make-up case in diamonds, lapis lazuli, onyx, pearl and jade.
Photo: Sotheby's.

Brooch in diamonds and sapphires.
Photo: Sotheby's.

du Bois was entrusted to another eclectic figure of the time, Paul Iribe. Iribe was both a caricaturist and an interior designer, and distinguished himself by the creation of textiles, jewels, wallpapers, décor and furniture, working with the assistance of Pierre Legrain.

The world of fashion was particularly sensitive to the fascination exercised by this new style. We have only to think of Paul Poiret, a glittering star in the firmament of Parisian fashion design, who was also involved in interior design. Indeed, Poiret had already, in 1912, founded the 'Atelier Martine', a design school based on innovatory ideas, which made an important contribution to the renewal in furnishings and to the motifs used in wallpaper and textiles.

Unlikely as it may seem, the decline of Art Deco began immediately after the 1925 Exhibition which marked its apotheosis. In 1920 Le Corbusier had already announced, in the first manifesto of *L'Esprit Nouveau*, that 'A house is a machine for living'. Advocating simplicity — as a basis for the functional structuring of modern life — he was trying to eliminate all useless ornament. He wrote: 'In the machine age design should express function; modern life imposes its style by creating its own objects... its typewriter, its telephone, its admirable office furniture... the steamship and the aeroplane.'

Design should be the expression of what is rational and functional. Like German Expressionist painting, he sought to create archetypes. In his review *De Stijl,* Théo van Doesburg wrote: 'We must arrive at a universal and collective mode of expression.'

Towards the end of the 1920s, modernism grew up as a reaction to Art Deco. This international style banished any form of decoration. Articles of furniture were very simple, with no mouldings, edgings or decorative motifs. They represented the full development of tubular metal. Their vast polished surfaces, often in dark colours, had as their sole ornament the glittering of chrome and metal.

Moreover, these simplified structures presented the advantage of being economical which, in the period following the 1929 crash, was not a negligible argument in their favour.

Modernism marked the end of a period stamped with a taste for luxury, sumptuousness and distinction — in short, an aesthetic emblem of wealth.

CHAPTER II

THE EMANCIPATION OF WOMEN'S FASHION

In all periods the evolution of women's fashion has had an effect on the creation of jewellery. Clearly, the success of certain articles of jewellery has often been conditioned by dress and by the shape of the female silhouette, which seems always to have been naturally adapted to the demands of fashion.

The 1900s style corresponded to the rounded and affected silhouette of the woman who had a decorative taste in jewellery. The 1920s marked the triumph of the androgynous woman, the slender, flat-chested form. Opulent curves gave way to strongly-marked bone structures. Long luxuriant tresses, the eternal symbol of femininity, were sacrificed on the altar of fashion. And so the famous bob-cut was born: the hair worn short, sleek and smoothed down, with a rounded fringe and kiss-curls touching the cheeks. But short hair could also be curled in gentle waves.

Skirts became shorter, revealing legs which, thus liberated, could bend themselves to the frenetic demands of the Charleston or to the more langorous pleasures of the tango. Women began to enjoy active participation in sports, and to acquire a new freedom of movement, in both the figurative and literal senses of the word.

Trousers, which had traditionally been outlawed in polite society for the fair sex (one fine morning in 1911 women in trousers made the newspaper headlines), became the symbol of the emancipated woman. The First World War hastened the movement. Women took the place of men away at the front, and went off to the building site, the factory or the office. This new professional activity on the part of women had a strong influence on dress, and played a part in emphasising the distinction between day-clothes and evening-wear.

The former, simple and functional, had to comply with the practical demands of the working day, whereas the increasingly sophisticated and feminine evening attire represented a need for compensation.

The post-war period was characterised by a very understandable sense of euphoria — the Roaring Twenties. And the exuberant women's fashions then in mode were a faithful reflection of the period.

Paul Poiret (1879-1944) was the uncontested leader of Paris fashion design in the pre-war period. He got rid of corsets and launched a new style based on the creation of clothes which no longer imprisoned the body in a rigid strait-jacket but, on the contrary, liberated it and gave room for movement. Initially installed in the rue Pasquier, before moving to the faubourg Saint-Honoré, Poiret is remembered for the ostentation of his legendary and exotic hospitality, for the creation of highly coloured dresses inspired by the Orient and the 'ballets russes', as well as for clothes influenced by the First Empire style.

Albums of drawings by Paul Iribe and Georges Lepape, entitled respectively *Les Robes de Paul Poiret racontées par Paul Iribe* (1908) and *Les Choses de Paul Poiret vues par Georges Lepape* (1911) give an idea of his work.

Leading artistic figures worked with Poiret. Raoul Dufy, for example, created textile designs for him.

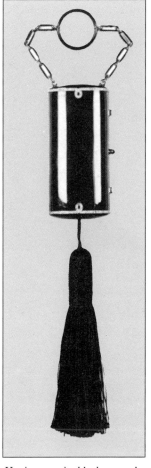

Vanity case in black enamel edged with small brilliants. Boucheron (1925). Boucheron Archives.

Evening bag in black
velvet, decorated with
diamonds and onyx.
Janesich.
Photo: Sotheby's.

MISTINGUETT

Mistinguett by C. Gesmar.
Musée de la publicité.

Here it is worth mentioning Romain Tirtoff, better known by his pen-name 'Erté'. Arriving in Paris from Russia in 1912, he was taken on by Paul Poiret in the following year as a fashion designer. Erté's imagination was unbridled. His many designs for jewellery, of an extravagance and an elegance rarely equalled, are sufficient proof. His sautoirs and his famous hair jewellery of 1922 are spectacular cascades of jade pearls and Oriental pearls.

From about 1920 onwards, for almost a decade, fashion deprived women of their 'attributes'. Again, it was Poiret who, in 1922, in the Roaring Twenties, helped to launch the mode for more or less rectangular clothes: breasts disappeared, and the waist dropped to hip level.

The painter Sonia Delaunay, one of the most representative protagonists of artistic research in the twentieth century, was also to be responsible for important innovations in fashion. In 1914, her 'Poem dresses' caused a sensation. Later, in her studio on the boulevard Malesherbes, she astonished an increasingly large audience by her creation of multicoloured, exclusively

'Les choses de Paul Poiret'
vues par Georges Lepape
(1911).
Musée de la mode et du
costume. Photo: E. Hubert.

A 45 carat claw set emerald pendant, hanging from a necklace of brilliants set in platinum.
Cartier Archives (1926).

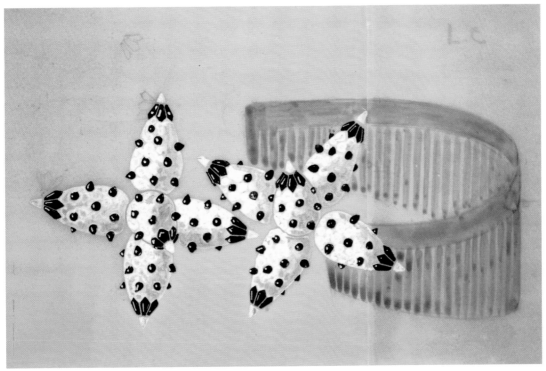

Comb decorated with platinum picots, pavé set with brilliants and onyx.
Cartier Archives (1925).

geometrical textile patterns, which introduced Orphism into fashion.

Sonia Delaunay is also known for having taken up unusual materials, like raffia and oilcloth, never previously used in dressmaking. Obviously her models were aimed at a limited clientele, partly on account of their price, but also because they were extremely difficult to wear. Sonia Delaunay dictated a lifestyle rather than a fashion. And this is why Tzara always wore cravats, which she particularly liked, since for him this was a mark of recognition. Together with his monocle, it defined him as belonging to an *avant-garde* club.

Although Sonia Delaunay's works often displayed an astonishing range of violently contrasting colours, it remains true that one of the key harmonies of 1920s fashion was black and white.

The collective hysteria represented by the passion for modern dance styles (tango, charleston, foxtrot) imposed a new style of clothes which seemed to have been specially designed for dancing: sleeveless evening dresses with soft low fronts, straight or flared skirts, usually slit at the side for freedom of movement. All these outfits had as accessories a long scarf and and the inevitable low-slung belt.

1923 was the year of the cloche hat, with turned-down brim, worn very low over the forehead.

In 1924 more or less shapeless clothes were the most fashionable. 1925 was the year in which skirts were drastically shortened, showing the knee.

Writing about fashion, Bruno du Roselle remarked: 'The Archbishop of Naples has no hesitation in announcing that the Amalfi earthquake is the result of divine wrath against the indecency of this fashion.'

Head-band with Egyptian motifs. Cartier Archives.

Bag decorated with diamonds and precious stones.
Cartier. Photo: Sotheby's

Earrings in diamonds and onyx mounted on platinum.

This 'lascivious' mode had its counterpart in exaggerated make-up: a scarlet mouth and black-rimmed eyes drawn on a deathly-pale face created by the application of a series of layers of rice-powder.

The ancestor of the mini-skirt obviously demanded increasingly diaphanous stockings, predominantly in greys and beiges, with seams alluringly dividing a well-shaped calf.

Shoes were mainly open and pointed, with lots of straps, designed to show off a slender ankle.

Gabrielle Chanel, known as Coco, represented another myth of the 1920s, which lived on through the whole of the following decade. The Chanel style, simple, almost stark, met with unexpected but unconditional success. The tailored costume was indisputably the keystone of her collection, and this basic item of dress was interpreted in a completely new way, filtered, so to speak, through the sensibility of the great Parisian designer. It was adaptable to all occasions, and thus ideal for the working woman who wanted to remain elegant from morning to night.

The Chanel line, soft and slender, and in 1927 fundamentally sporty, became the rule. Almost all the designers of the period were conquered by it.

In the 1930s Coco gave free rein to her fantasy, finding an outlet for it in the most extravagant discoveries — inlaying, for example, woollen chemisiers with costume jewellery.

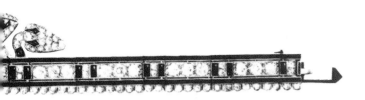

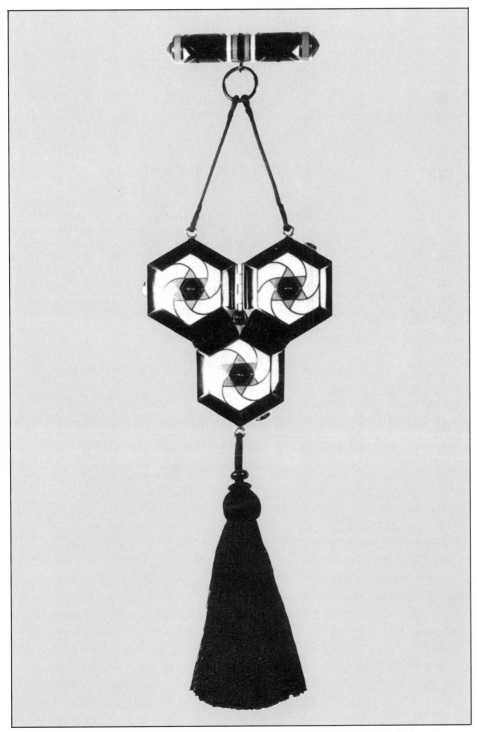

Vanity case in gold and onyx decorated with black and coloured enamel and finishing in a black tassel (1925). Boucheron Archives.

Pendant consisting of a jade disc decorated with onyx and brilliants, finishing in a black silk tassel.
Boucheron (1925).
Boucheron Archives.

Pendant consisting of a jade disc decorated with diamonds and onyx, and finishing in a black silk tassel.
Boucheron (1925).
Boucheron Archives.

23

Pendant watch in diamonds and onyx, mounted on platinum.
France. Photo: Sotheby's.

Illustration for the last of the lettres persanes *by Edouard Garcia Benito.*
'Diane' (1920).

Lesley Blanch wrote, in 1938: 'Chanel showed that grey flannel slacks and a simple woollen pullover were nothing without a mass of pearls, and wrists loaded with barbarous bracelets.'

The birth of a style is never a sudden event. Styles are always preceded by a period of gestation which hints at the future.

Thus, what was to be the prevailing fashion of the 1930s was already perceptible in 1928 and 1929. The waist began to return to its natural place, and shaped bodices started once more to reveal the delicate curves of the breasts. In short, the fashion which developed out of the financial crisis of 1929 excluded the exaggerated styles of the Roaring Twenties (very short skirts, bob-cuts, shapeless dresses), and returned, with good sense and balance, to a kind of conformity.

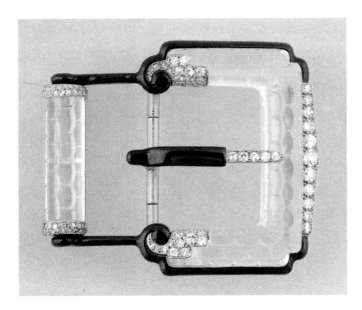

Left: Belt buckle in rock crystal, black enamel and diamonds. Cartier. Photo: Sotheby's.

Right: Pendant watch in brilliants and emeralds mounted on platinum. Mauboussin. Photo: Sotheby's.

So there triumphed a classical modernity which allowed femininity to blossom, while managing to reconcile it with the natural.

The waist, which in the 1890s had been situated just below the bosom, and in the 1920s went down as far as the hips, finally regained its rightful position in the 1930s. Elasticated corsets gave a graceful line to the female silhouette. The disastrous cloche hats were succeeded by flat, three-cornered, round or turban-shaped models.

Morning and afternoon, women wore the ubiquitous tailored costume which allowed full freedom of movement.

Trousers, very wide around the hips, finally became acceptable. Floor-length evening dresses often moulded the curves of the body, but gently, thanks to the judicious use of crepes, wool, silk and satin. These materials benefited fully from the famous 'cut on the bias' invented by another representative of high fashion design, Madeleine Vionnet. They were particularly suited to the 'drapes' characteristic of Madame Grès's studio.

Costume jewellery in enamelled metal, bakelite or paste became more important day by day. The fashion for this kind of jewellery increased as pieces became larger.

The Italian, Elsa Schiaparelli, is universally considered to be the most outstanding talent in Parisian fashion design of the 1930s. Whereas her great rival, Coco Chanel, is remembered for her sobriety of line, Schiaparelli (Schiap as she was then known) imposed herself by the excesses of her lively imagination and the chromatic extravagance of her creations, which poured out at an astonishing rhythm: prints, patchwork and *trompe-l'oeil*, joke hats, culotte skirts, sports outfits. She launched bizarre spectacle frames and the famous telephone bags. She was the first to set up a boutique selling accessories and jewellery under her own label. The jewellery was often signed by the most illustrious names of the period: Christian Bernard, Jean Cocteau, Salvador Dali, Van Dongen, Alberto Giacometti, Man Ray and many others. These creations were assuredly influenced by surrealism which, in certain ways, made common cause with her innovatory mind and non-conformist aesthetic ideas. She wanted, in her own terms, to create 'a new elegance in accord with

A collection of round bracelets of different diameters and in different colours. Photo: Man Ray (1926).

the brutal rhythm of modern life, while not excluding the eternal feminine, the body, which alone dictates the structures of a dress.'

All the aesthetic upheavals brought in by changes in fashion necessarily influenced the production of jewellery, which was expected to be in harmony with the varying styles of dress.

In the December 1927 issue of *Vogue*, we find the following remark: 'Apart from the classical piece of jewellery, which is separate from the dress, we are

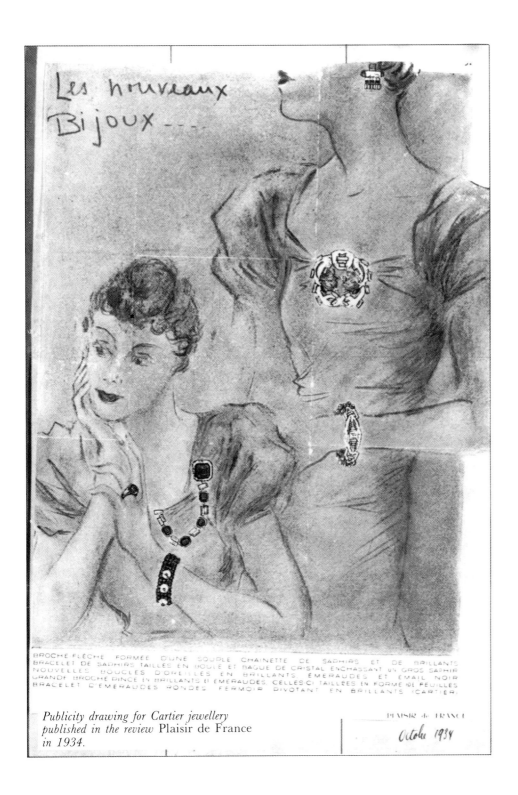

Les nouveaux
Bijoux...

BROCHE FLECHE FORMEE D'UNE SOUPLE CHAINETTE DE SAPHIRS ET DE BRILLANTS
BRACELET DE SAPHIRS TAILLES EN BOULE ET BAGUE DE CRISTAL ENCHASSANT UN GROS SAPHIR
NOUVELLES BOUCLES D'OREILLES EN BRILLANTS EMERAUDES ET EMAIL NOIR
GRANDE BROCHE PINCE EN BRILLANTS ET EMERAUDES CELLES-CI TAILLEES EN FORME DE FEUILLES
BRACELET D'EMERAUDES RONDES FERMOIR PIVOTANT EN BRILLANTS (CARTIER)

Publicity drawing for Cartier jewellery
published in the review Plaisir de France
in 1934.

PLAISIR de FRANCE
Octobre 1934

starting to see jewellery deliberately designed to set it off.'

The best example is the sautoir or long necklace, usually completed by a pendant, falling onto the breasts or thrown over the back but with the aim, in both cases, of setting off a low neckline.

The new hairstyles made redundant accessories like combs, tiaras and diadems (traditional allies of long flowing hair). But, on the other hand they called for the creation of headbands, which were the ideal complement to the

27

Brooch in diamonds and onyx mounted on platinum. Photo: Sotheby's.

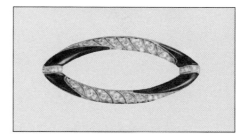

Brooch in diamonds and onyx mounted on platinum.

Wristwatch in diamonds, cultured pearls, onyx and coral, mounted on platinum. Cartier (1920). Photo: Sotheby's.

bob-cut. Headbands, ribbons worn low on the forehead, could also, if necessary, be decorated with aigrettes.

The headband, the cigarette holder and the sautoir represent an identikit image of the *femme fatale* of the 1920s. The fashion for the cloche hat, also well-suited to the bob haircuts of the period, limited the use of hairpins, which had been indispensible for fixing floppy Romantic hats in heavy coils of long hair. To provide an elegant decoration for the ear-lobes, which were now revealed by short hair, earrings tended to become longer and longer, and to be equipped with pendants. A new screw-in system was developed to fit them, and this was gladly taken up by all the women who had fiercely refused to have their ears pierced.

'The more women's clothes become revealing, the more they feel the need to beautify themselves with large pieces of jewellery,' declared Pierre Contreau in 1932.

Bare arms — denuded by fashion — stimulated the imagination of jewellers, who set for themselves the task of showing them off. They created gold or silver bracelets, either articulated or in the form of bangles, sometimes set with precious or semi-precious stones. It was usual to wear a number of them on the same arm, and this Oriental jangling also became a fashion.

Bracelets were made of ivory, jade, coral, lapis lazuli, agate, onyx and — why not? — plastic! There were models which could be linked together to form a collar or necklace, known in fact as a 'dog-collar'. The fore-arm was often set off by narrow bangles in ivory, tortoiseshell or plaited elephant hair (held together with gold or silver), or even by simple enamelled, lacquered or painted bracelets.

Brooches were not reserved exclusively for the bosom. They were also used to decorate hats, shoulders, belts or hips (where they were used, for example, to hold together drapes). Clips remain perhaps the most characteristic jewels of the period. they began to acquire importance at the end of the 1920s. Worn together, they served as pins. On their own they were used to modify a low neckline. Used on the belt, they could be buckles in precious stones.

As early as 1926, according to *Vogue*, 'Worth launched a typically Art Deco jewelled buckle in brilliants and onyx, worn behind the neckline of a black velvet dress. Its function was to hold together the close collar.'

The article of jewellery the least subject to the whims of fashion is perhaps the ring, which almost always retains its classic form. But rings too adapted themselves to the style of other ornaments, and began to be decorated with cabochon-cut precious stones. The solitaire, every woman's dream, was never to be dethroned.

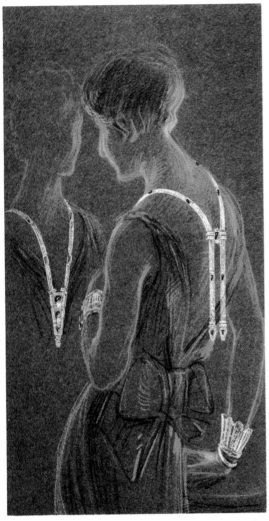

Pendant watch in diamonds and onyx mounted on platinum.
France. Photo: Sotheby's.

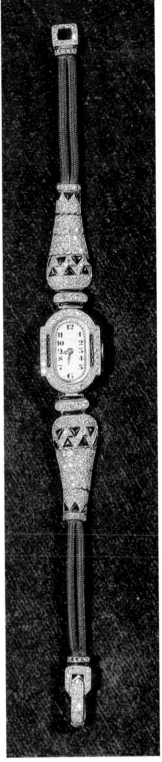

Diamond and emerald parure, created by Chaumet in 1920.

Right: Pendant watch in diamonds and calibré-cut sapphires, mounted on platinum and hung from a black silk ribbon.
France. Photo: Sotheby's.

With the appearance of the sporty style, watches, symbols of an active and dynamic life, became important. A wide variety of models appeared. Wristwatches fitted in well with other articles of jewellery. From 1925 onwards, in conformity with the black and white style, they tended to have a platinum or white gold case, set with diamonds, with very delicate decorations in filaments of onyx. At the same time, other models were highly coloured, heavily decorated with precious stones. Pendant watches, hung from ribbons or chains, should not be forgotten. They were often heightened with enamel, or with semi-precious stones engraved with decorative motifs.

This new complicity between dress and jewellery, much desired by the jewellers, was also the dream (made true) of the famous dress-designers of the period. Georges Fouquet wrote a long article to this effect, entitled 'Modern Jewels and Jewellery', published in January 1942 in the review *L'Orfèvrerie, la*

Wrist watch in diamonds and onyx, mounted on platinum.
Van Cleef et Arpels.
Franco Bernardini Collection.

Wristwatch decorated with diamonds and onyx mounted on platinum. Photo: Sotheby's.

Joaillerie, where he said: 'the article of jewellery is part of the décor of women's dress. It complements it, and cannot be worn indiscriminately by one woman or another... We have always reacted against jewellery which looks as though it has been mass produced according to the same model, in different sizes, and which you come across, in social gatherings, worn by several women at the same time.'

The woman's figure and silhouette, the colour of her hair and the way she does it, the colour of her eyes and the vivacity of her gaze, are so many parameters which determine the creation and choice of a piece of jewellery. If these different elements are given careful consideration, it is always possible to find the personalised article of jewellery, in which is affirmed — by the choice of model — the taste of the person buying or giving it, to which the jeweller must lend the assistance of his art.

The decorative article of jewellery consists of lines, planes, open-work. The architecture of the ensemble must be harmonious, free of those details which complicate manufacture without adding anything to the work.

Georges Fouquet continued: 'The quality of an article of jewellery does not reside only in its manufacture, but also in its artistic value. But it is not enough that the piece should be pretty in itself, seen in isolation; it must also be in harmony with the setting in which it is called upon to live. And that setting is the woman who wears it, the dress to which it is pinned, the neck from which it is hung, the head on which it is set. That is why we have always thought that it would be interesting to make a presentation, not only of dresses, but also of the jewellery which should complement the outfit. Our idea found someone to carry it out in Jean Patou, the famous dress-designer who, in 1927, decided to show his collection in conjunction with jewellery which we had chosen together. On this occasion, rare to be true, Jean Patou invited to his gala evenings the whole of Paris society and visiting foreign personages. In the midst of flowers, the so far unrevealed creations of the coming season were paraded. Slim volumes indicating the names of the dresses (there were almost four hundred of them) and the imperatives which had presided over their creation were given to the invited guests. And within these notices our two names were printed together, linked in what he referred to as a "close collaboration".' This famous example of a symbiotic relationship between a dress-designer and a jeweller is illustrative of a predominant tendency of the period. The decisive importance of the choice of the article of jewellery is confirmed by the April 1926 issue of *Vogue*: 'The choice of the least accessory is just as important as that of the dress. Daytime rings are emeralds or sapphires; evening rings are diamonds. To a whole series of the most refined bracelets, women will prefer a single large bracelet in diamonds or in diamonds and onyx. The hat-pin or bodice-pin is a circle in onyx and diamonds. The tiny watch, framed by small diamonds, is slipped over a double round layer of rubber on platinum claws. A flat, round toilet case, in jade and black enamel inlaid with gold, is the most chic of accessories.'

CHAPTER III

Art Deco Jewellery by Artist Jewellers

Clearly the fundamental principles of Art Deco are to be found in jewellery: linearity, geometrical forms, emphasis on stylisation, sharp edges and chromatic audacity (lots of colour contrast). The present enthusiasm for Art Deco is quite recent. It was confirmed in 1966, at the exhibition 'Les Années 1925', organised at the Museum of Decorative Arts in Paris, and given the sub-title 'Art Deco — Bauhaus — De Stijl — Esprit Nouveau'.

A considerable number of pieces of Art Deco jewellery derived from the artistic endeavour of a small circle of creative avant-garde jewellers. The great merit of these innovators was to have created modern jewellery inspired by contemporary aesthetics. Although these authentically new articles of jewellery are completely free of earlier influences, they nevertheless bear the indelible mark of geometrical abstraction, the contemporary movement in painting. As a rule, the applied arts usually lag a few years behind the schools of painting or sculpture which inspire them. Today these jewellers' creations are classified according to different categories. They have been defined as constructivist or cubist jewellery, by analogy with the movements in painting which influenced them. And sometimes they are known as modernist jewellery or even, simply, artistic jewellery. It is true that such jewellery was usually the work of artists. But the high degree of technical excellence in its production excludes it from the category of artistic jewellery in its true sense, in so far as the latter usually implies an artisanal mode of production. Thinking, for example, of the definition 'constructivist jewellery' — so named because of the link between the motifs used and the pictorial themes of the famous Russian painters — it might be more accurate to speak in terms of suprematism. For the jewellery in question more clearly reflects the geometrical designs of Malevitch and his school than constructivist or cubist forms. Moreover, Art Deco jewellery had the enormous merit of putting artistic content above mercantile value. This consideration is most significant in the case of the artist jewellers. Their work in fact represents the freest form of creative expression. Aesthetic concerns took precedence over the richness of metals and precious stones. Materials were chosen for their decorative quality and not simply for their intrinsic value. Artists of this period were susceptible to the wide variety of influences of science and technology, — the cinema, electricity, aviation and other important achievements of modern engineering — which exercised an undeniable fascination over the wider public.

But what were the particular features of this first category of Art Deco jewellery? The pieces were characterised by squared volumes, sharp edges, simple geometrical forms, abstract decorative motifs and broad plane surfaces, sometimes superimposed. Some of the creations made full use of the three dimensions, and this tended to assimilate them to sculpture. Squares, circles, triangles, rectangles and semi-cylinders were the forms most frequently used in design. Metallic plane surfaces were created in platinum, gold, silver and steel, or even in new alloys like 'osmior' or 'platinor'. Metal could have either a matt or a polished finish. It could be coloured in lacquer or enamel with

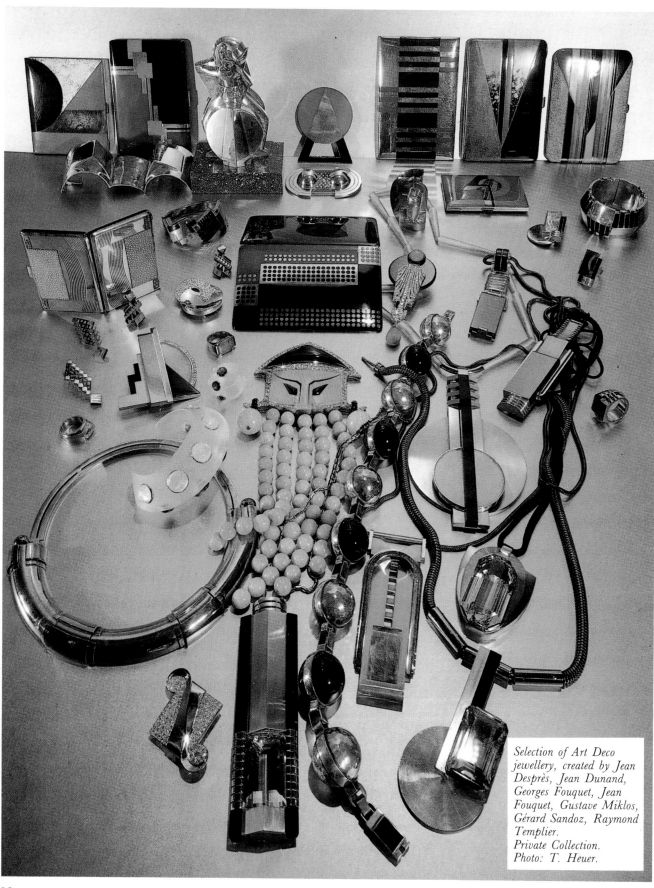

Selection of Art Deco jewellery, created by Jean Desprès, Jean Dunand, Georges Fouquet, Jean Fouquet, Gustave Miklos, Gérard Sandoz, Raymond Templier.
Private Collection.
Photo: T. Heuer.

bright, contrasting tones (black, white, green, blue), or sometimes more delicate hues (cream, periwinkle blue, almond green). Plane surfaces were also made out of plaques of hard gemstones like onyx, jade, rock crystal — translucent or frosted — coral, turquoise or lapis lazuli. Very often a large stone (artists had a predilection for aquamarine, topaz, amethyst and citrine) would occupy the centre of a geometrical composition.

In general the use of brilliants for decoration was discreet, and took the form of lines, or segments of small diamonds used as an edging, or as a means of creating a break in the design, as for example with the motif of crossed sabres. Sometimes surfaces were decorated with pavé set diamonds.

Particularly noteworthy within the repertoire of the most fashionable models were pendants, hung either on chains or silken cords, necklaces sometimes completed by a pendant, and bracelets, rings and brooches.

It is interesting to note that within this new perspective the article of jewellery almost took on the status of a work of art. The critic Emile Sedeyn draws attention to the permanence of this tendency in Georges Fouquet's

Design by Raymond Templier, heightened with gouache, for a fastener to be made in jade and coral. L. and B. Heuer Archives.

33

monograph, *La Bijouterie, la Joaillerie, la Bijouterie fantaisie au XXe Siècle* (1934): 'The ones most likely to endure are not the ostentatious displays, but those in which the metal is associated with raw materials of a financial value less than their beauty, like aquamarine, amethyst, topaz, or tourmaline. Art, which never ages, will prolong the career of these jewels. It will endow them with their true character. They will never be disassembled so that the materials can be used in a different form. They are, first of all, works of art rather than financial investments.'

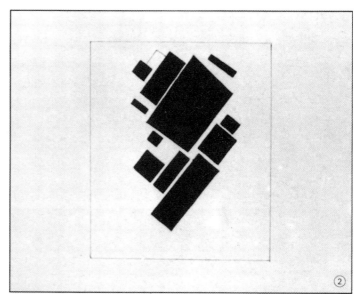

1. Silver cup with enamelled cubist design, created by Jean Goulden in 1929.
Photo: Sotheby's.

2. 'Suprematist Composition', one of the thirty-four drawings done in 1920 by Kasimir Malevitch for the book Suprematism.
Photo: Sotheby's.

3. Pair of appliqués *in chrome metal and glass by Damon, designed in 1929 by Boris Lacroix.*
Photo: Sotheby's.

Panel in black, beige and brown lacquer with speckled lacquer inlay, created by Jean Dunand according to a drawing by Gustave Miklos based on geometrical design: signed Miklos (1925). Photo: Sotheby's.

THE CREATIVE ARTISTS

JEAN DESPRES (1889-1980)

Jean Desprès was born at Sauvigny in 1889 into a family of stained glass artists. After serving an apprenticeship as a goldsmith in Avallon and Paris, he was employed during the war in an aircraft factory. In this way he gained familiarity with industrial design and the working of metals. This experience left its mark on his jewellery, which can be seen to have been clearly influenced by engineering. In 1925, Jean Desprès took part in the Exhibition of Decorative Arts in Paris, at which he showed articles of toiletry. A year later, he exhibited at the Salon des Indépendants. Towards the end of the '20s and at the beginning of the '30s, he worked with Etienne Cournault creating a series of surrealist jewels decorated with engraved glass.

In general, his creations in gold and silver use geometrical forms with a sober background. Usually they are subdued in colour. Several pieces very

Pendant in silver, gold and lapis lazuli, created by Jean Desprès between 1928 and 1930.
Photo: Sotheby's.

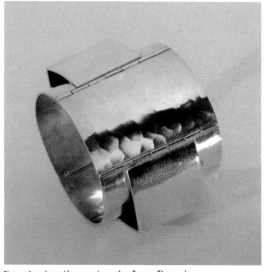

Bracelet in silver, signed: Jean Desprès.
Private Collection.
Photo: Tomas Heuer.

representative of his work were on show at the 1975 exhibition at the Schmuckmuseum in Pforzheim. One of these was a large silver bracelet, signed and dated 1925. It is composed of three motifs. The central part, in beaten silver, is linked to the rest of the bracelet, which is in burnished silver, by two rows of hinges in high relief.

The collaboration between Desprès and Etienne Cournault gave rise, in 1927, to the creation of a silver brooch consisting of a disc decorated with two horizontal filaments in black lacquer. On one side two rectangles, superimposed but staggered, are partly supported by the circular plaque, while on the other side three truncated cylinders are butted on to each other. A stylised lizard motif is engraved on the glass plaque which forms the uppermost of the two rectangles.

The solid three-dimensional ring created in 1925 is in the same style. The same elements are to be found: staggered, superimposed rectangles. One of these, in gold, is decorated with segments of red lacquer. The other, enamelled in black, is decorated with two truncated cylinders in gold.

Brooch in silver, black lacquer and glass engraved by Etienne Cournault, signed Jean Desprès in 1927. Private Collection. Photo: Tomas Heuer.

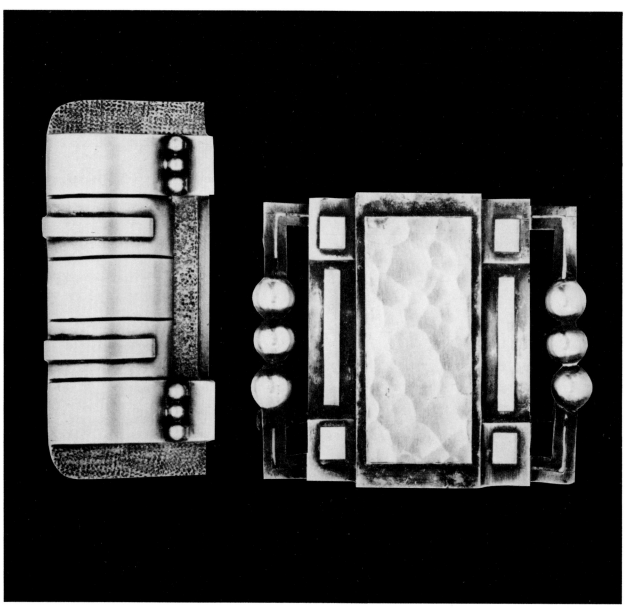

Left. Brooch in silver and gold, created by Jean Desprès around 1930. Photo: Sotheby's.

Right. Brooch in silver and three colours of gold, created by Jean Desprès around 1930. Photo: Sotheby's.

At the 1925 Exhibition the artist displayed a necklace that he was to show later at the Paris International Exhibition of 1937. This piece of jewellery consists of nine silver spheres. Four of them are lacquered in black. The nine elements are disposed in alternation. Each sphere is surrounded by a flat band in gold and silver which allows it to be fixed to a system of interconnecting rectangular links.

Another brooch, produced by Desprès in 1929 and 1930, consists of two half-spheres joined to a plaque of pearls, flanked by two strips of lapis lazuli.

Finally, the ring presented by the artist in 1930 to the Pavillon de Marsan is clearly inspired by aeronautics. Its shape recalls the turning propellor of an aeroplane.

JEAN DUNAND (1877-1942)

Jean Dunand was born near Geneva, where he attended the Ecole des Beaux-Arts. On his arrival in Paris, in 1897, he studied wood-carving in the studio of Jean Dampt. Sculpture remained his principal activity until 1902. Then he spent some time making vases in copper, steel and silver, with typically Art Nouveau decorations. From 1912 onwards the study of the techniques of Japanese lacquerwork and its applications monopolised his attention. His son-in-law, Jean Goulden, a doctor working in Paris hospitals, closely followed his father-in-law's experiments·before actively and enthusiastically participating in them.

The surprising effects obtained by Dunand in lacquerwork assured him fame and a place in posterity. He skilfully applied this personal technique to the decoration of furniture, screens and other objects, always using a stylised design. His astonishing smoking room in black lacquer, shown in 1925 at the Paris International Exhibition, remains a masterpiece. In 1927, Dunand was made president of the Association des artistes décorateurs (Association of Decorative Artists).

Flower-shaped appliqué brooches in German silver with cloisonné work in speckled lacquer, created by Jean Dunand circa 1925. Photo: Sotheby's.

Copper vase with geometrical pattern in red and black lacquer Created by Jean Dunand circa 1925. Photo: Sotheby's.

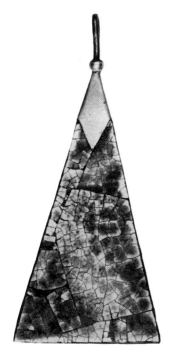

Triangular pendant in red lacquer with speckled lacquer inlay. Attributed to Jean Dunand. Circa 1925. Photo: Sotheby's.

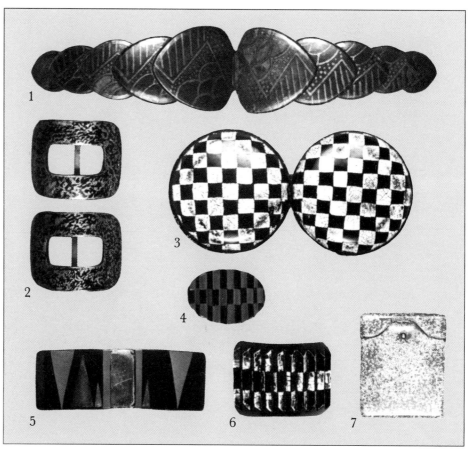

1. *Two-piece copperwork buckle. Created by Jean Dunand in 1925. Photo: Sotheby's.*

2. *Pair of shoe buckles in lacquered wood, created by Jean Dunand in 1925. Photo: Sotheby's.*

3. *Two-piece buckle in lacquered metal with speckled lacquer design. Created by Jean Dunand circa 1925. Photo: Sotheby's.*

4. *Buckle in lacquered metal. Created by Jean Dunand circa 1925. Photo: Sotheby's.*

5. *Two-piece belt buckle in lacquered metal. Created by Jean Dunand circa 1925. Photo: Sotheby's.*

6. *Wooden buckle in speckled lacquer and black lacquer. Created by Jean Dunand in 1925. Photo: Sotheby's.*

7. *Match case in aureum, red lacquer and speckled lacquer. Created by Jean Dunand circa 1925. Photo: Sotheby's.*

Copperware bracelet with geometrical design. Metal band decorated with chevrons, triangles and rectangular blocks inlaid in white metal on a black patinated background. Created by Jean Dunand circa 1925. Photo: Sotheby's.

Between 1928 and 1935, he was concerned with the now legendary interior design of the liners *Ile-de-France* and *Normandie*. At the same time he was producing his famous *rayonniste* vases, lacquered in red and gold, black and white.

Although the creation of jewellery represented only a fairly minute fraction of Dunand's varied activities, it nevertheless offers a dazzling reflection of his great artistic sensitivity. He began designing jewellery from 1924 onwards, in a style related to his other polychromatic creations. As a base he used above

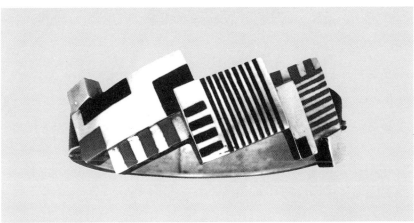

Earrings in silver and black and red lacquer, created by Jean Dunand circa 1925. Private Collection. Photo: Tomas Heuer.

Vase in patinated copper and lacquer. Created by Jean Dunand circa 1925. Photo: Sotheby's.

Silver bracelet with geometrical design in lacquer. Created by Jean Dunand circa 1925. Photo: Sotheby's.

all silver and aureum (an alloy of silver and brass), which seem admirably suited to the use he made of them, heating and lacquering them.

Bangles in lacquered silver, created around 1925, were decorated all over with alternating segments in black and red, interwoven with black triangles. A pair of elongated earrings of 1925 also bears his unmistakable stamp. They consist of a network of silver squares lacquered in red and black. Tiny silver squares embellish the chequer-board surface, and the composition is completed by a red lozenge decorated with three segments in black.

Another pair of earrings, also dating from 1925, consists of an alternating combination of parallelograms suspended from a lozenge in lacquered silver, with polychromatic geometrical motifs.

GEORGES FOUQUET (1862-1957)

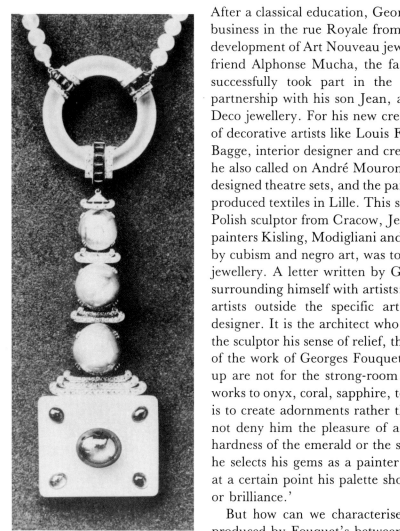

Necklace with balls, ring and plaque in frosted rock crystal with a pendant of three cabochon cut sapphires. In the centre of the plaque a cabochon sapphire, and in the corners four calibré cut emeralds and brilliant cut diamonds. Archives Fouquet (1924). Musée des Arts décoratifs (Paris).

After a classical education, Georges Fouquet took over the well-known family business in the rue Royale from his father Alphonse. He played a role in the development of Art Nouveau jewellery and produced, following a design by his friend Alphonse Mucha, the famous ring bracelet for Sarah Bernhardt. He successfully took part in the 1900 Exhibition. In 1919 he entered into partnership with his son Jean, and soon launched into the production of Art Deco jewellery. For his new creations, he surrounded himself with a number of decorative artists like Louis Fertey, designer and studio overseer, and Eric Bagge, interior designer and creator of furniture, wallpapers and textiles. But he also called on André Mouron, known as Cassandre, who drew posters and designed theatre sets, and the painter of cubist tendencies, André Léveillé, who produced textiles in Lille. This small group of artists was joined in 1937 by the Polish sculptor from Cracow, Jean Lambert-Rucki, who was friendly with the painters Kisling, Modigliani and Soutine. Lambert-Rucki, strongly influenced by cubism and negro art, was to give a new direction to the style of Fouquet's jewellery. A letter written by Georges Fouquet bears witness to his taste for surrounding himself with artists: 'I have always spoken in favour of calling on artists outside the specific art of jewellery, leaving aside the specialised designer. It is the architect who can bring in his knowledge of mass and line, the sculptor his sense of relief, the painter his awareness of colour...' Speaking of the work of Georges Fouquet, Emile Sedeyn adds: 'The jewels he dreams up are not for the strong-room in the bank, and the place he gives in these works to onyx, coral, sapphire, topaz and aquamarine proves that his intention is to create adornments rather than investments. Moreover, his subtlety does not deny him the pleasure of associating with these secondary materials the hardness of the emerald or the sumptuous display of the diamond. Above all, he selects his gems as a painter chooses his colours. What is essential is that at a certain point his palette should provide him with the necessary harmony or brilliance.'

But how can we characterise the development of the Art Deco jewellery produced by Fouquet's between 1920 and 1930? Until about 1924, Fouquet created articles of jewellery in the tradition of the high class Parisian jewellery of the rue de la Paix: pendants, brooches, buckles, bracelets, rings in platinum and diamonds, often exploiting the opposites of black and white. Later he became interested in hard stones, in coral and in the carved jade of ancient Chinese figurines, as well as semi-precious stones like aquamarine, topaz and amethyst, preferably used in significant proportions. Often chromatic contrasts were achieved by opposing the opacity of hard stones with the transparency of loftier stones like the emerald, sapphire or diamond. Rock crystal, always appreciated for its limpidity and its brightness, was frequently used by Fouquet. Sometimes he would frost its surface. The plaques which made up his geometrical motifs were usually framed or intersected by inset lines of tiny brilliants. Sometimes pavé set brilliants added an element of ostentation to the composition. It was possible to see a number of specimens of his work at the 1975 Pforzheim exhibition and at the 1983 exhibition, entitled 'Les Fouquet', at the Museum for Decorative Arts in Paris. His 'Devant de robe' (Dress Front), produced between 1920 and 1925, is inspired by a Chinese mask. The face, in green enamel, adorned with a triangular hat in onyx, finishes with a cascade of five *pampilles* in jade beads.

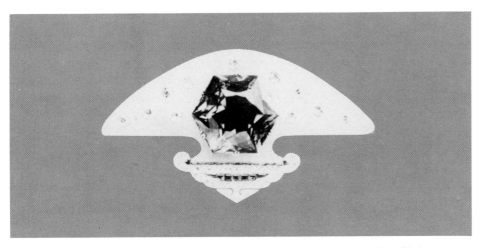

Brooch in frosted and engraved crystal with aquamarine, diamonds and small calibré cut coloured stones. Archives Fouquet (1924-30). Musée des Arts décoratifs (Paris).

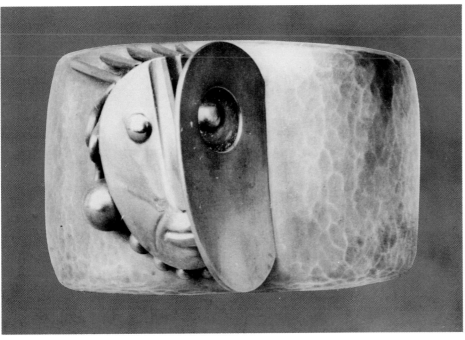

Bracelet in beaten silver and gilded silver. Archives Fouquet (1936-7)
Musée des Arts décoratifs (Paris).

Brooch in platinum, diamonds, onyx, cabochon and coral drop, created by Georges Fouquet circa 1925. Private Collection. Photo: Tomas Heuer.

Fouquet took up the same subject in 1924-25 to make a pendant. But this time the mask carved in frosted rock crystal was topped by a glittering hat in platinum and diamonds. Three large cabochon emeralds were suspended from the ear-lobes and the lips.

A triangular brooch in ivory, hollowed out in the centre, inset with three cabochon cut turquoises, with tiny squares in onyx and small gold balls, dates from 1922-23. A drop-shaped turquoise completes the piece.

A platinum brooch was composed of a sort of triangular frame, edged with brilliants, sapphires, calibré cut emeralds, and decorated at the corners with three large cabochon cut sapphires. Another remarkable pendant was composed of a disc in frosted crystal, decorated in the centre with a button in lapis lazuli, surrounded by a jade circle. The platinum setting, corresponding to the upper part containing the disc, was delicately worked and inlaid with brilliants. It was completed by two small green jade discs, from which hung two pendants in emeralds and brilliants. The main disc was also completed by a lance-shaped pendant in frosted rock crystal. Three pendants dated 1922-23 were strongly influenced by the vogue for 'black and white' jewellery. They were made up of plaques in onyx (one triangular, one rectangular and one hexagonal) decorated with geometrical motifs in diamonds. The pendants were always hung from black silk cords.

Taking up the current fashion for tassels, Fouquet created several designs in this style around 1922-24. The composition of the fringe varies. One contains tiny coral pearls; in another fragments of coral alternate with tiny coral balls. Yet another is made of silken threads decorated with jade pearls.

A sophisticated brooch of 1924 is composed of an onyx disc mounted on platinum, with a coral drop and a cabochon, and between the latter a cascade of brilliant cut diamonds.

Another brooch of 1924, which can be converted into a pendant, is clearly inspired by the Chinese style. A plaque in pale green carved jade hangs by extremely delicate links of platinum, brilliant cut diamonds, and black enamel, from a ring in the same tone of jade, decorated with two small rings in black enamel.

After 1925 the contribution of artists to the creation of Fouquet's pieces became more marked.

Eric Bagge left his mark on two pendants dated 1925, both of which are hung on silken cords. The first, suggesting two beams of light in the darkness, consists of a large onyx disc, crossed by two rays surrounded by tiny brilliants. The other, more rigorously geometrical, is formed of a frosted rock crystal rectangle, inlaid with onyx triangles and framed with brilliants and onyx. The upper edge is of red enamel set with brilliants.

*Study for a pendant created by
Cassandre circa 1924-5.
Musée des Arts décoratifs (Paris).*

*Design for earrings. Georges Fouquet
circa 1923-4.
Musée des Arts décoratifs (Paris).*

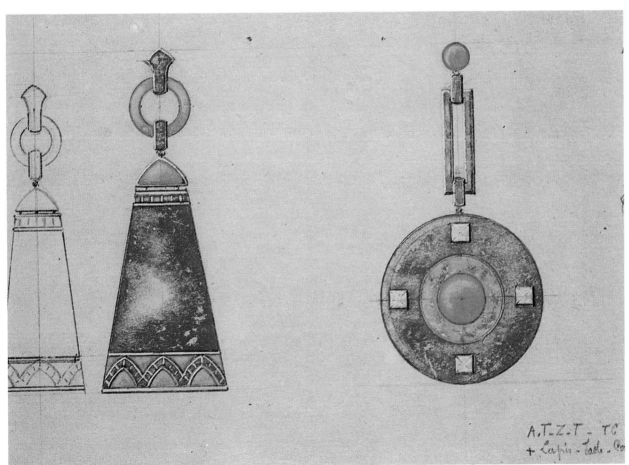

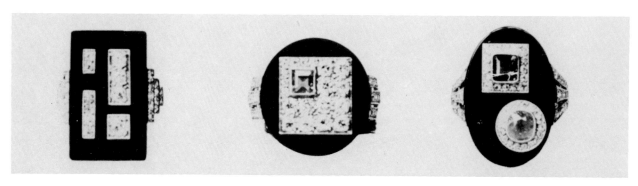

Rings designed by A. Léveillé, produced in frosted crystal or onyx inlaid with coloured stones and diamonds. Archives Fouquet. Musée des Arts décoratifs (Paris).

The pieces designed by André Léveillé in 1925 are of a different concept, but retain a geometrical structure. One pendant of cubist inspiration is made of frosted rock crystal fixed to a hexagonal plaque in onyx. Another is composed of an octagonal plaque in frosted rock crystal, decorated with a superimposed design executed in large hardstones.

Another example, in the form of an oval plaque, is inlaid with geometrical

Bracelet in black enamel, jade and diamonds. Archives Fouquet. Musée des Arts décoratifs (Paris).

designs in onyx, coloured calibré cut stones and scatterings of brilliants.

A final pendant consists of a disc of frosted crystal, decorated with an abstract design in onyx, sapphires and cabochon cut emeralds, surrounded by lines of brilliants.

The bracelets bearing the stamp of Léveillé are extremely original. Their base is a trelliswork in gold with decorations made up of lines of diamonds and geometrical motifs in coloured hardstones or precious stones. There is also a *Manchette* bracelet (cuff-bracelet), comprising a gold band streaked with black enamel lines, in turn decorated with a row of brilliants. Léveillé's rings, made of frosted rock crystal or onyx, take the form of broken geometrical designs (squares, circles, segments) in hardstones and diamonds.

In 1925, a pendant in the shape of a frosted crystal disc decorated with two semi-circles studded with diamonds and coloured stones with, in the centre, a half-moon in onyx, was created after a design by Adolphe Mouron, known as Cassandre.

After obtaining the collaboration of the sculptor Jean Lambert-Rucki, Georges Fouquet produced, from 1936-7 onwards, a series of solid, sculptural pieces of jewellery, inspired by industrial design. A cubist decoration was displayed on bands of gold or beaten silver. The 1983 Paris Exhibition devoted to his work showed a number of jewellery designs deriving directly from the archives of the rue Royale. Particularly remarkable were two sketches for bracelets for the upper arm, open at both ends, to be produced in platinum (1922). One finished in two semi-spheres in coral, and was set with tiny brilliants and onyx. The other finished in two stylised heart motifs, set with brilliants and edged with emeralds and calibré cut sapphires.

There wre also two designs for pendant earrings dated 1923-5. One took the form of a trapezium in lapis lazuli decorated with geometrical designs in sapphires and coral. The other, circular in shape and made of lapis lazuli, was decorated with concentric circles in jade and coral, and hung from a rectangular link in jade.

There was also a design for a pin which could be worn as a pendant, after a drawing by Cassandre dated 1925. This was to be composed of superimposed geometrical plaques (rectangles, triangles, segments of circles) in rock crystal, onyx, lapis lazuli, coral and topaz. Another design, by the same artist (1925) consisted of a lozenge-shaped pendant in burnished platinum, divided by clusters of brilliants on a background of lapis lazuli and topaz. It was decorated in the centre with a large emerald.

Yet another design by Cassandre, also of 1925, was of purely cubist inspiration. It was for a guitar-shaped clasp, composed of superimposed geometrical designs, and was to have been made of onyx, aquamarine, frosted crystal and translucent crystal.

Finally, a sketch for a bracelet, conceived by Cassandre in 1925, presented a series of links in different colours, to be made in coral, lapus lazuli, amethyst and aquamarine, framed by two parallel rows of brilliants.

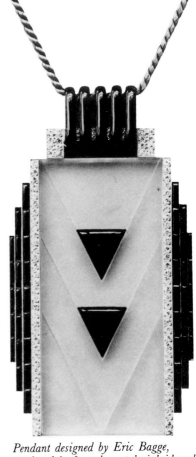

Pendant designed by Eric Bagge, produced in frosted crystal, inlaid and edged with onyx, platinum and brilliants, with red enamel in the upper part.
Archives Fouquet (1925).
Musée des Arts décoratifs (Paris).

Bracelet and ring in rock crystal, decorated with amethysts and moonstones, mounted on platinum, created by Jean Fouquet circa 1930. Private collection. Photo: Tomas Heuer.

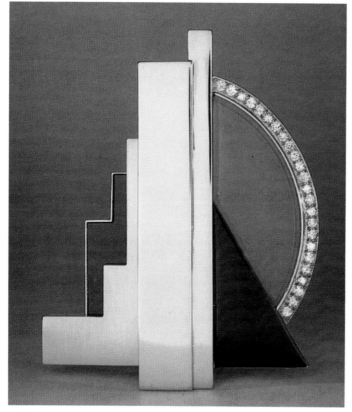

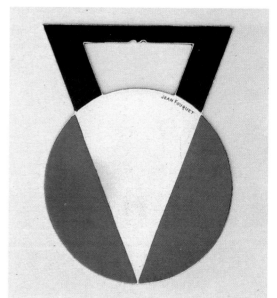

Above. Pendant in silver and red and black lacquer, signed Jean Fouquet. Private Collection. Photo: Tomas Heuer.

Left. Brooch of white gold, yellow gold, rock crystal, onyx, black lacquer and brilliants, created by Jean Fouquet circa 1925-9. Private Collection. Photo: Tomas Heuer.

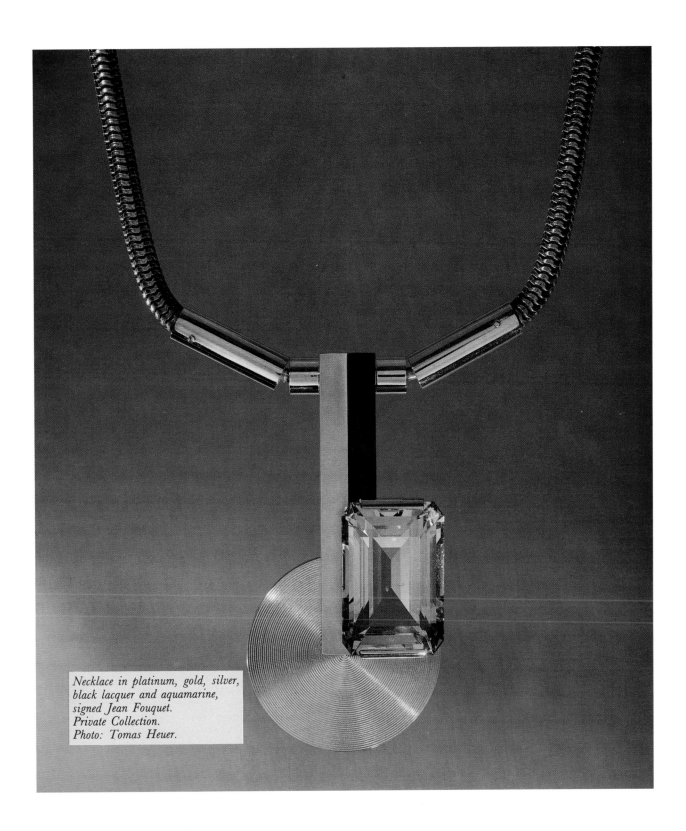

*Necklace in platinum, gold, silver,
black lacquer and aquamarine,
signed Jean Fouquet.
Private Collection.
Photo: Tomas Heuer.*

JEAN FOUQUET (BORN IN 1899)

After studying Classics and Literature, Jean Fouquet became involved in the family business, and quickly achieved success. He was a friend of the surrealist poets Louis Aragon and Paul Eluard, and wrote for Le Corbusier's review *L'Esprit Nouveau*. He developed a discerning taste for abstract composition. His articles of jewellery were genuine masterpieces, and were characterised by simple, pure forms. Large flat surfaces were often decorated with big stones and lines of brilliants. He preferred grey gold to platinum and lacquer to enamel, and never scorned the effects which could be obtained with chromed steel.

Having created an extensive series of flat objects prior to 1930, he began to make, after that date, jewellery of a considerable degree of plasticity. To this end, he used large volumes of gold and rock crystal. He exhibited regularly at the *Salon d'automne*, and showed at the 1928 and 1937 Exhibitions. The latter year saw the publication of his monograph *Bijoux et Orfèvrerie* (Jewellery and the Goldsmith's Craft. In 1930, he was a founder member of the *Union des artistes modernes* (Union of Modern Artists). In 1958, he took part in the Brussels Universal Exhibition. He retired for reasons of health in 1964 and so brought to an end his creative activity.

To give some idea of the extensive innovations introduced by Jean Fouquet into Art Deco jewellery, it is worth mentioning the famous brooch, conceived between 1925 and 1929, which was used as cover illustration for the catalogue to the Pforzheim Exhibition of 1975. The strictly geometrical composition consists of two very elongated rectangles in white gold. On the right, these are juxtaposed to a semi-circle in frosted rock crystal edged with small brilliants

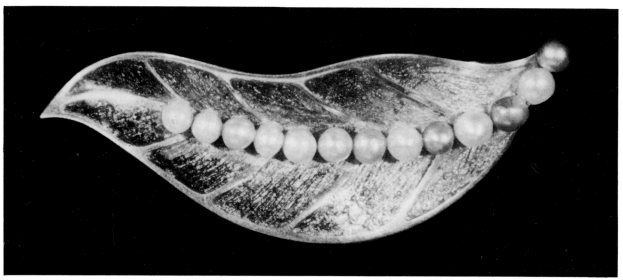

Leaf-shaped gold brooch by Jean Fouquet covered with pale blue and aubergine enamel, set in the centre with small pearls circa *1920. Photo: Sotheby's.*

and overlaid with a right-angled triangle in black lacquer. On the left, the brooch presents two flat, interlocking, stepped motifs, one in yellow gold and the other in black lacquer.

The very famous necklace of 1925-30 is also worthy of mention. A large pendant consisting of a white gold disc with concentric ridges, decorated with a large aquamarine, hangs from three hinged motifs in burnished silver. The disc and the necklace are joined by a two-coloured bar in gold and black lacquer.

The series of pendants created between 1927 and 1929 do undoubted honour to Jean Fouquet, and are worthy of our attention. One of these consists of five parallel vertical bars in burnished grey gold, decorated with a topaz framed by a line in black lacquer and a row of brilliants. Another pendant, known familiarly as *l'Obus* (the Shell), is composed of two half cylinders in frosted rock crystal, pointing downwards (like the shell of a gun), slightly staggered, and laid onto a vertical rectangular bar in burnished platinum. Another is in grey gold. It is in the form of a shield cut in two by a horizontal line of diamonds cut as brilliants, framed by two narrow bands of black lacquer. A remarkable pendant, dating from 1930, is composed of seven concentric rings in grey gold, set out like a halo round a large citrine.

For Jean Fouquet, rings are the most important form of jewellery. The examples produced by him between 1927 and 1937 completely sum up his creative concept. They are simple, solid, square in shape, and precious stones progressively give way to hardstones.

A *demi-parure* produced in 1930 is also a remarkable creation. It consists of a bracelet and brooch in rock crystal with amethysts and moonstones set in platinum.

The so-called *roulement a billes* (ball-bearing) bracelet in chrome steel of 1931 bears witness — to say the least — to the influence of technology on Jean Fouquet's art. The same might be said of other creations of extremely simplified design by the same jeweller — for example a matching bracelet and ring in rock crystal and platinum, decorated with moonstones, amethysts and diamonds, or the bracelet and ring in yellow gold, set off by pavé set topazes in a convex rectangle.

Brooch in yellow and white gold, the only piece by Gustave Miklos discovered to this day, produced in 1927 by Raymond Templier. Engraved signature: 'G. Miklos'. Stamped: Raymond Templier 16484. Private Collection. Photo: Tomas Heuer.

GUSTAVE MIKLOS (1888-1967)

Miklos was born in Budapest, where he studied painting at the School of Art and Design. Arriving in Paris in 1909, he attended the art schools and showed at the *Salon d'automne*. He volunteered for the Foreign Legion in 1914, and served for a considerable time in Greece, where he became fascinated by Byzantine art. He acquired French nationality in 1923. At about this time he made the acquaintance of the dress designer Jacques Doucet, who employed him to carry out the internal decoration of his house. Miklos designed carpets and silver plate for him, and also produced articles in gold plate and enamel. In 1925, he showed his work at the Paris Exhibition. This is the period during which he began to design pieces of jewellery. Although his eclectic creativity found expression in all fields of art, his particular predilection was for sculpture, which he took up in 1923 (in 1928 he organised a one-man show of sculpture at the *Galerie de la Renaissance* in Paris). He also showed at the International Exhibition of 1937 in the pavillion of modern artists.

In 1940, he left Paris permanently, to go and live in the country, where he devoted himself to teaching. Miklos's jewellery is essentially the expression of his sculptor's temperament. An excellent example of this is the brooch he designed for Raymond Templier in 1927, representing a mask influenced by negro art. It is in yellow, sculpted gold. The stylised woman's face is surrounded by geometrical motifs and topped by a half-moon in white gold.

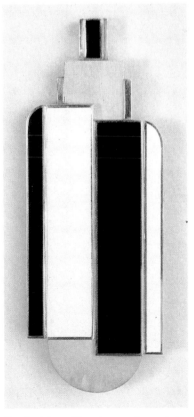

GÉRARD SANDOZ (BORN IN 1902)

Gérard Sandoz was born into a family of jewellers from the Jura. His grandfather Gustave had set himself up in Paris in 1865. From his earliest youth he liked to draw and paint. After pursuing traditional studies at various art schools, he went into the family business and worked with his father Gustave-Roger. He was introduced to contemporary decorative art by his uncle, Paul Follot. From the age of eighteen he was designing articles of jewellery and pieces of gold already distinguished by a rigorously geometrical style. His work was shown at the Paris Exhibitions of 1925 and 1937. As a painter, he exhibited at the *Salon d'automne* and the *Salon des artistes créateurs*. His aesthetic is clearly revealed in the article he published in August 1929: 'La Renaissance de l'Art francais' ('The Renaissance of French Art').

'It is a matter of re-establishing everything in its rightful place, with precision and originality, not deliberately assuming that art is everywhere or

Pendant in gold and enamel, created by Gérard Sandoz between 1937 and 1938. Photo: Sotheby's.

nowhere, but thinking that it is often very simply and very naturally there, without necessarily always needing a décor,' he wrote. 'The article of jewellery,' he concluded, 'should be simple, clean, constructed without flourishes.'

His creations, the conception of which very noticeably suggests engineering, are structured on several different planes, made of gold and silver, usually associated with haematite, labradorite, onyx and citrine.

The vigorous, elemental character of his forms is revealed in a series of pendants created around 1928. One is composed of a rectangular plaque in haematite, mounted on silver, and linked to the chain by a motif in fluted citrine. Another, in three linked parts, consists of a vertical rectangular haematite plaque, joined to the chain by two motifs, one of which is square, the other rectangular, and fluted at the edges. Another pendant is in the shape of a double arc, in white and red gold, with a matt surface. It is decorated with a rectangular plaque in labradorite and small segments in white gold. A famous piece by Sandoz is the brooch known under the name 'Semaphor'. In the centre of a strictly geometrical composition a plaque in brilliant coral is strikingly juxtaposed to a jade plaque. It is also worth noting a remarkable pendant, created in about 1927-28, consisting of two discs of different diameters. The smaller of the two, composed of two plaques in rock crystal, is joined to the larger one by a facetted link, inlaid with, amongst other decorative motifs, an onyx baguette. It is suspended by means of thirteen cones in rock crystal.

Brooch in gold, frosted crystal and onyx following the design of the Gérard Sandoz pendant of 1928. Photo: Sotheby's.

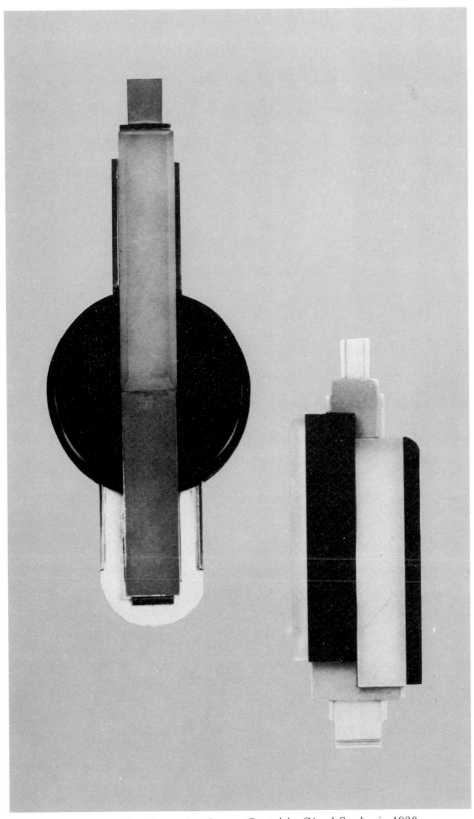

*Left. Pendant in gold, frosted crystal and onyx. Created by Gérard Sandoz in 1928.
Photo: Sotheby's.*

*Right. Pendant in gold of two colours, onyx and rock crystal, created by Gérard Sandoz
between 1928 and 1929. Photo: Sotheby's.*

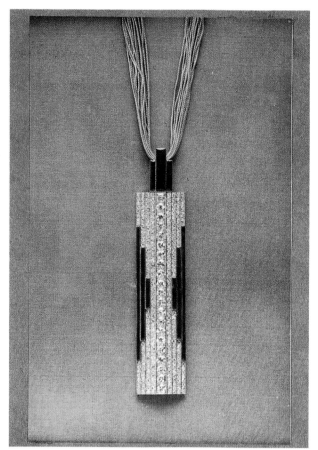

Pendant produced by Raymond Templier.
L. and B. Heuer Archives.

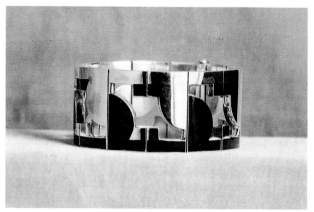

Bracelet created by Raymond Templier in 1928.
L. and B. Heuer Archives.

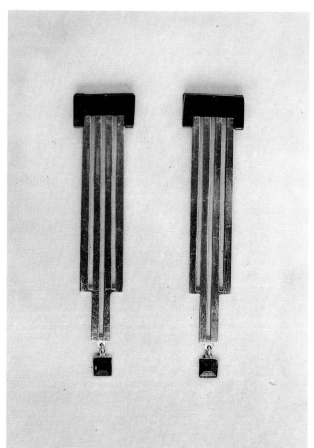

Wrist-watch in platinum and brilliants, created by Raymond
Templier in 1929. L. and B. Heuer Archives.

Pendant earrings created by Raymond Templier in 1928 for
the film 'L'Argent' by Marcel Lherbier.
L. and B. Heuer Archives.

RAYMOND TEMPLIER (1891-1968)

Raymond Templier belonged to a dynasty of Parisian jewellers, Maison Templier, founded by his grandfather in 1849. In 1919, after studying at the *Ecole des Beaux-Arts*, Raymond went into the family business, which was at that time directed by his father, Paul Templier.

As early as 1911, he exhibited at the *Salon des artistes décorateurs*. Afterwards he regularly contributed to similar exhibitions, both in France and abroad, and was a founder member of the *Union des Artistes Modernes*. In 1929, he took on the designer Marcel Percheron, who was to remain his faithful collaborator for nearly thirty years. In about 1936 he became his father's partner, and their two christian names, Paul and Raymond, were henceforth to figure together on the firm's letterhead.

In general, Raymond Templier's creations were free of decoration. His jewellery, executed in a variety of materials, was characterised by a rigorously geometrical design, as austere as it was complicated. The Templier style was particularly suited to women leading a sporty, dynamic life. In 1928, he created the famous *parure* worn by the actress Brigitte Helm in Marcel Lherbier's film *L'Argent* (Money). Reproductions of this *parure* were to appear in all the books and articles devoted to Art Deco. His spectacular diadems, half-crown, half-turban, and his pendant earrings, their shape suggesting Manhattan skyscrapers, became almost symbolic of Art Deco. But other, rather different creations, still bear the stamp of Raymond Templier's resolutely Art Deco style. For example, the silver bangle of 1927, composed of a fairly wide convex band, decorated on the surface and at the notched edges, with eight alternating sets of motifs in black lacquer. This model was infinitely reproduced in different colours and with different decorative motifs. A pendant created in 1928 is also of remarkable purity. An oval plaque in matt platinum, decorated in the centre with a large aquamarine, is applied to a polished platinum base in the form of a shield. Still using geometrical forms, a bracelet of 1928, made in polished and matt platinum, presents a succession of square and rectangular motifs, decorated with regularly disposed rows of aquamarines.

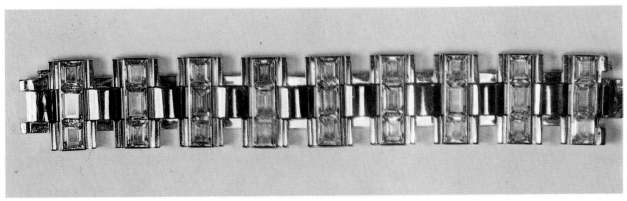

Bracelet in platinum and aquamarines. Signed by Raymond Templier. Private collection.

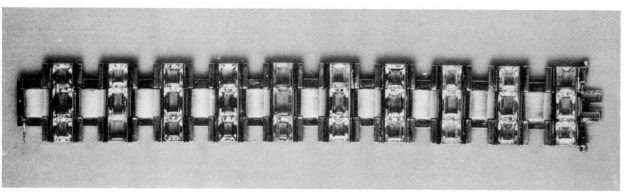

Design for the preceding bracelet produced by Raymond Templier in 1928.
L. and B. Heuer Archives.

The work of this great artist-jeweller also includes a whole series of clips and brooches designed between 1930 and 1936. Using strictly geometrical forms, he contrasted white gold and platinum (circles, triangles, spirals) with pavé set brilliants. It is also worth mentioning a whole panoply of brooches and pins in platinum enhanced by a dazzling decoration consisting of superimposed enamelled triangles.

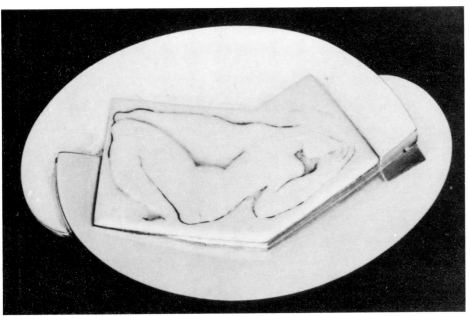

Pendant in silver, gold and carved ivory. Created by Raymond Templier and Csaky circa 1930.
Photo: Sotheby's.

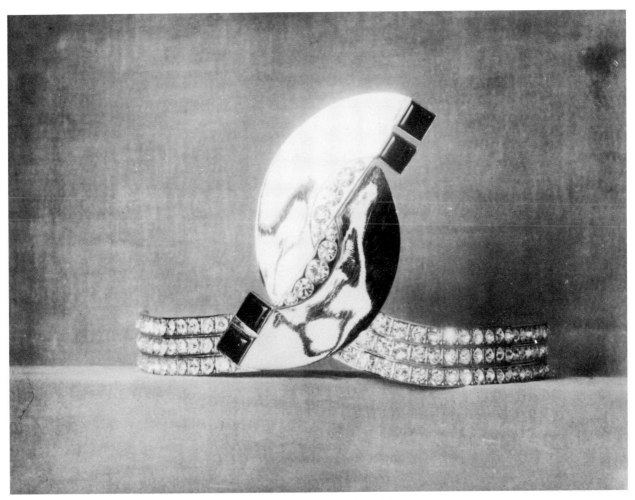

Diadem created by Raymond Templier in 1928 for the film 'L'Argent' by Marcel Lherbier.
L. and B. Heuer Archives.

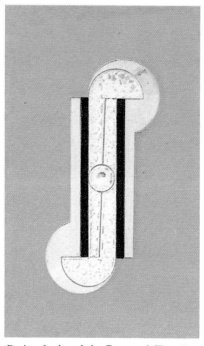

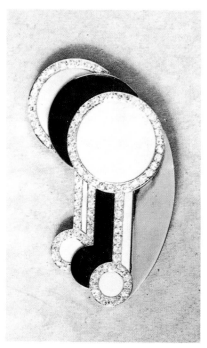

Brooch created by Raymond Templier in 1928. L. and B. Heuer Archives.

Design for brooch by Raymond Templier created in 1932. L. and B. Heuer Archives.

Brooch created by Raymond Templier in 1929. L. and B. Heuer Archives.

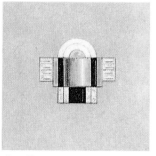

Ring in platinum and peridot. Created by Raymond Templier circa 1930. Photo: Sotheby's.

Jewellery designs by Raymona Templier. L. and B. Heuer Archives.

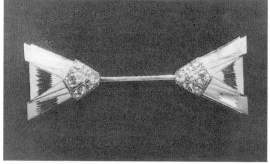

Design for brooch by Raymond Templier created in 1932. L. and B. Heuer Archives.

Jabot pin in platinum, enamel and brilliants, created by Raymond Templier in 1925. L. and B. Heuer Archives.

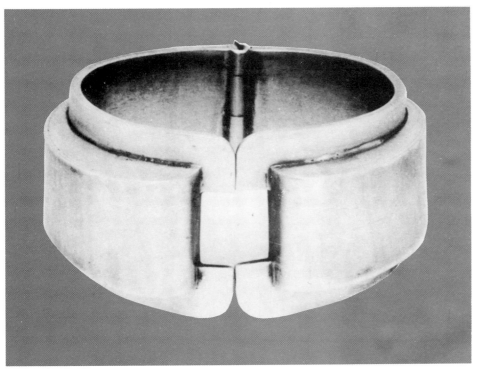

Silver bracelet with band in relief on flat cut-out base, created by Raymond Templier   circa 1930. Photo: Sotheby's.

Brooch produced by Raymond Templier in 1929. L. and B. Heuer Archives.

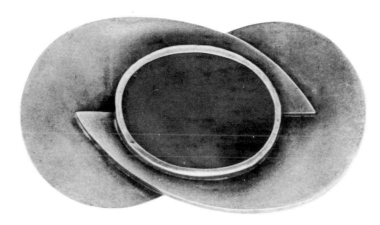

Brooch in gilded silver and amber-coloured agate, created by Raymond Templier circa 1930. Photo: Sotheby's.

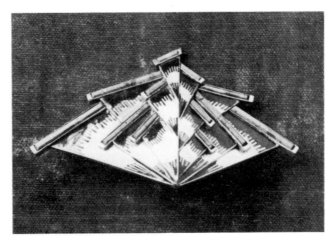

Brooch in platinum, enamel and diamonds, created by Raymond Templier (1924). L. and B. Heuer Archives.

PAUL BRANDT

Paul Brandt was already designing jewellery during the Art Nouveau period, but it was after the First World War, in the twenties, that his sketches began to reflect the strict geometrical forms which governed the creations of Jean Fouquet, Georges Sandoz or Raymond Templier. He achieved perfect harmony and balance by the simultaneous opposition of forms (rectangles, triangles and circles) and different materials (black enamel, matt or polished platinum, onyx and pearls).

Amongst his many creations is a brooch created in 1930 of white gold, diamonds, onyx and cut rock-crystal. Two staggered, superimposed circles are inlaid with diamonds and decorated with two cabochons of facetted crystal. We should also mention a pair of clips in white gold, diamonds and onyx, both square in shape, with perforated geometrical motifs and triangular motifs in onyx inlaid with diamonds. Finally, a bracelet in silver and speckled lacquer, composed of rectangular motifs decorated with chevrons and semi-circles in black and green lacquer on a background inlaid with speckled enamel.

Alongside these pioneers of the years around 1925, other artist-jewellers, perhaps less well-known, but equally endowed with genuine talent and fantasy, produced important work in the purest Art Deco style.

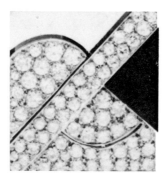

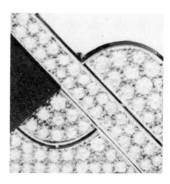

Pair of clips in white gold, diamonds and onyx, created by Paul Brandt in 1930. Photo: Sotheby's.

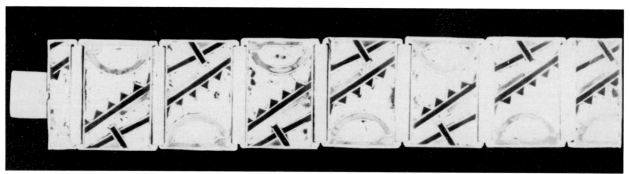

Bracelet in silver, lacquer and speckled lacquer inlay, attributed to Paul Brandt (1925-30). Photo: Sotheby's.

Other Creative Jewellers

It is difficult to recall all of the distinguished great names in the fabrication or design of Art Deco jewellery without making omissions. It would, however, be unforgiveable to leave in the shade the designer Charlotte Perriand, whose *Roulement a billes* (ball-bearing) necklace is related to the bracelet of the same name in chrome steel by Jean Fouquet; the architect Robert Mallet-Stevens, who distinguished himself by the creation of earrings and cigarette cases decorated with square mirrors; René Robert who, after training at the *Ecole professionnelle de bijouterie-joaillerie-orfèvrerie*, distinguished himself by creating a series of necklaces, mostly in silver, ivory, coral and ebony.

Of course, the list could be much longer. We will restrict ourselves, however, to noting the substantial contribution of the U.A.M. (*Union des Artistes Modernes*) to the creation and development of a non-elitist modern art, aimed at the widest possible audience, in which jewellery evidently played an integral part. Founded in 1930, the association was directed by leading personalities like the architects Chareau, Le Corbusier, Robert Mallet-Stevens, Hélène Henry, René Herbst, Charlotte Perriand and the artist-jewellers Jean Fouquet, Gérard Sandoz and Raymond Templier. The group exhibited for the first time at the Pavillon de Marsan in 1930. This exhibition

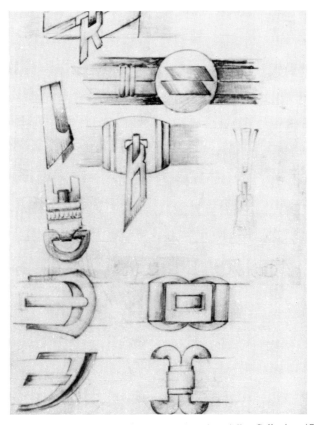
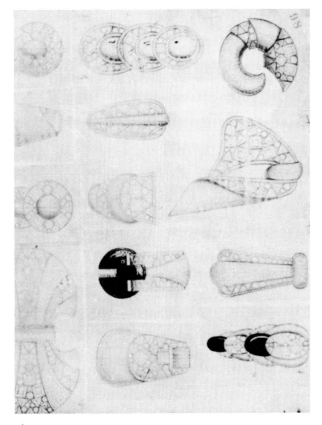

Workshop drawings from Adler's, Istanbul.   Adler Collection (Geneva).

63

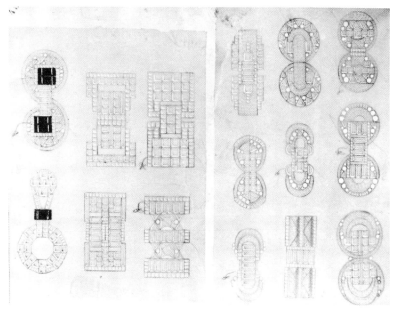

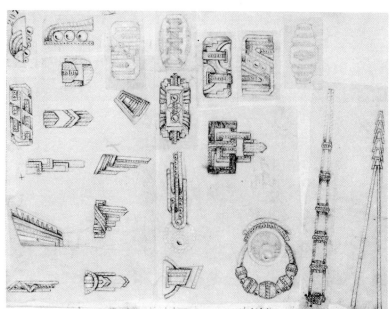

Workshop drawings from Adler's, Istanbul. Adler Collection (Geneva).

Brooch in white gold, diamonds, onyx and crystal, created by Paul Brandt in 1930. Photo: Sotheby's.

included the jewellery with which we are concerned, inspired by the contemporary aesthetic in the plastic arts, involving rigorous design and irreproachable construction. France and its workshops undoubtedly had a leading role in the production of Art Deco jewellery which, elsewhere, usually took the form of replicas of designs deriving from the high-class French jewellers who will be the subject of our next chapter.

It should be noted, however, that the Adler Company of Geneva kindly allowed us to consult its albums of original designs for the 1920s and 1930s. These articles of jewellery were produced by their parent firm in Istanbul, which was flourishing during this period. The sketches show a number of models of rigorously geometrical design, with matt or polished surfaces, decorated with brilliants, either pavé set or in rows, clearly very similar to the work of Raymond Templier.

CHAPTER IV

HIGH FASHION JEWELLERY IN THE 1920s

Alongside the work of the Art Deco artist-jewellers, the great Parisian jewellers, principally set up in the rue de la Paix and the place Vendôme, were also creating new designs, striking in their boldness and brilliance of colours. But a wealth of decoration in precious stones was the constant common denominator, the golden rule which these prestigious firms, with their unequalled techniques of execution always followed.

In their interpretation of the new stylistic language of the period, the big jewellers nevertheless took the risk of making unusual associations of materials, bringing together in the same piece of jewellery materials of widely different commercial value. Thus, in the series of black and white jewellery, diamonds and pearls were happy to mingle with onyx, black enamel and rock crystal. Similarly, in their polychromatic creations, coral, jade and lapis lazuli were juxtaposed with emeralds, sapphires, rubies, engraved or not. It should also be noted that in the case of the polychromatic jewellery — which often represented baskets of fruit, vases of flowers, etc. — they used a profusion of coloured precious stones from India, unusually worked, with a concave cut (the intaglio technique) to reproduce leaves, flowers, fruits, and a whole exotic menagerie of birds and fish. Diamonds were necessarily the basic element. When used on their own, they were of exceptional size or colour. To the classical styles of cutting (round, rectangular, oval) was now added a whole variety of new cuts (baguette, pampel, pear, briolette, etc.), lending themselves to the creation of geometrical motifs. Another fundamental change affected the metallic structure of the article of jewellery. Platinum, a metal which is both precious and extremely strong, was often used instead of the gold and silver employed up to that time.

Thanks to platinum important changes in the setting of jewels occurred. Settings became lighter, more refined, acquired what one might call an airy grace. It is to Louis Cartier that is to be attributed the great merit of bringing platinum into general use.

In an article entitled 'La Joaillerie française à l'Exposition des Arts décoratifs' ('French Jewellery at the Exhibition of Decorative Arts'), published in *Vogue* in September 1925, the jeweller Robert Linzeler confirmed this tendency, revealed in the work of the great creative jewellers of the period. He claims that Raymond Templier said to him, on the day of the opening of the jewellery exhibition: 'What an influence Paul Iribe will have had on jewellery!' And he continued in the following terms: 'This influence has been brought to bear in two ways. First of all the sense of dimensions. In all the drawings he made showing women's hands, the rings were composed only of large stones. Secondly, the decorative value of the jewel... He saw straight away what could be made out of the combination and mixing of different coloured gems by the contrast of opaque and transparent stones, and he played with these contrasts as a painter plays with colour. The art of the cutter is one of the great innovations of modern jewellery. Diamonds are no longer simply round, oval, or rectangular, as they used to be. They are now cut in all shapes and sizes, which is what creates such curious and special effects, with lines, triangles, hexagons, and even trapeziums. Jewellery is acquiring from this use of stones a fantasy and a variety which it has never before attained... So what were the stones in fashion? There no longer seemed to be any particular stones in fashion, at least not in the context of the exhibition.' If emeralds were very widely represented, sapphires were equally so, and rubies were used with all the latitude that could be allowed for a stone red in colour, and thus relatively difficult to harmonise with the other colours in the pieces presented.

If the Paris International Exhibition of 1925 revealed the inventive genius of French jewellers and goldsmiths, we should not forget that it was not the first of its kind. A year before, another important exhibition had been held at the Grand Central Palace in New York. This exhibition established the importance of French taste and elegance in fashion and jewellery. Among the exhibitors were Boucheron, Cartier, Mauboussin and Van Cleef et Arpels.

But how can we define the distinctive features of the different categories of Art Deco jewellery produced by the high-class French jewellers of the 1920s?

Consulting the archives of the leading Paris houses reveals a kind of common fund, within which the most typical models of Art Deco were specific to the production of each of the firms. Certain parallel developments are perceptible at the same time amongst the big jewellers, although they each retained their own specific characteristics and individuality — as we shall see after looking briefly at the history of the leading firms, most of which are still trading today.

Evidently there are certain features common to all high-class Art Deco jewellery: 'For evening wear black and white are extremely distinguished,' was a slogan chorused by all the women's fashion magazines. And of course the theme was taken up in jewellery, which rendered, with the means at its disposal, the same basic contrast, and expressed it in terms of rock crystal, onyx, platinum and brilliants, where necessary enlivened by an occasional patch of red coral. This fashion, derisively nick-named the half-mourning fashion, favoured, perhaps excessively, brooches made of platinum and decorated at the ends with small plaques of geometrical form in onyx or rock crystal, as well as brooches and bracelets whose Art Deco design was to be composed of cloisonné motifs in onyx outlined by lines of brilliants.

From 1922 onwards, most brooches took the form of links of circular, square or hexagonal section, in onyx or rock crystal, with a symmetrical lateral decoration of motifs worked in platinum and set with brilliants. The article which appeared in the August 1926 issue of *Vogue* expresses quite well the passion for crystal jewellery: 'Thus we have seen amber, jade and onyx successively in vogue, and now the fashion for crystal: frosted or polished. Necklaces, sautoirs, bracelets, pins, belt-buckles, hand-bag fasteners, cigarette-holders, pendant earrings. The fantasies born of this craze are innumerable... This fashion sums up, in fact, one of the aspects of the period in which we are living... in which so many things are artificial.' Not mentioned are the rings decorated with coloured precious stones using this unusual material as a basis.

There was also the fashion for tassels, deriving from upholstery trimmings, pendants hanging from silk cords or small chains. Art Deco invented the pendant brooch, attached to the lapel. From such brooches were suspended the various decorative motifs for which the period had a predilection: vases of flowers, bowls of fruit, geometrical designs, Egyptian motifs, etc.

Rings usually took the form of stepped platforms, with a large stone in the centre.

It was in 1925 that Art Deco jewellery became openly polychromatic. Brooches representing bunches of flowers or baskets of fruit were the characteristic expression of this form of jewellery. Bouquets in engraved or cabochon cut rubies, emeralds and sapphires, usually with platinum and diamonds as a base, carried all before them. Polychromatic Art Deco jewellery was particularly inspired by the decorative motifs of Oriental figurative art — Chinese, Japanese, Persian, Indian and, above all, Egyptian.

If works of this kind were typically Art Deco, the decorative motifs themselves remained intrinsically exogenous, or characteristic of these distant and ancient civilisations. This kind of decoration was typically used for objects like powder compacts or cigarette boxes, whose flat surfaces lend themselves to designs in lacquer-work or inlays of semi-precious stones. It was really from 1920 onwards that accessories — boxes, cigarette-cases, powder compacts, lipstick-holders, vanity-cases, smoking articles — acquired a considerable importance, and were treated in the same way as jewellery. The art of the functional became deliriously imaginative, both in form and decoration, and the iconographical repertoire brought into play made these articles even more precious. In terms of Oriental inspiration, Persian hunting scenes alternated with Chinese or Japanese landscapes and Egyptian motifs. Purely geometrical designs in a strictly Art Deco style always served as a framework. But there were also simpler models in gold, usually enamelled in black or red with small geometrical decorations in brilliants or coloured stones. In certain cases the surfaces of the box were composed of plaques of semi-precious stones (lapis lazuli, agate, rock crystal, jade) always framed or decorated with Art Deco motifs.

The most spectacular creations of this kind were produced by artists like Paul Brandt, Gérard Sandoz, Raymond Templier, and then by the great jewellery houses like Boucheron, Cartier, Janesich, La Cloche, Mauboussin, Van Cleef et Arpels.

Other specifically Art Deco motifs, like fountains, provided variations for jewellery design. Moreover the new interest in sport, and the beauty of speed proclaimed by the Italian futurists, were a fresh source of inspiration to jewellery designers, who flooded the market with series of brooches representing, not only motor-cars and aeroplanes, but also sailing boats, skaters, tennis rackets, etc.

Until about 1920 fine pearls fetched astronomical sums, and were of inestimable value on the jewellery market. At that time they were as highly coveted as diamonds. But, in about 1930, the market for pearls suffered an unprecedented upheaval, partly occasioned by the appearance of cultured pearls, which were soon to invade the European market-place. The original producer of cultured pearls was the Japanese, Kokiki Mikimoto, although Mikimoto was not the only one, or the first, to exploit this line in Japan. Nevertheless, Mikimoto had the merit of creating, with undeniable skill, a commercial network for cultured pearls. According to some authorities, cultured pearls were responsible for dethroning fine pearls. However, this merely points to the historic crash of 1930. It is true that at this date the price of pearls dropped to a tenth of their 1928 value. But 1928 was the eve of the Wall Street crisis, which was the real culprit in this collapse. It is interesting to note that it was cultured pearls, despised by reputable jewellers when they first appeared, which encouraged — for obvious reasons of price — the proliferation of the sautoirs which so clearly characterise the elegance of the period around 1925.

BOUCHERON

Boucheron was the first jeweller to set up in the place Vendôme in 1893, in the building in which the celebrated and beautiful Countess of Castiglione, the favourite of the Emperor Napoleon III, had lived. But the foundation of the firm predated this. Indeed, Frederic Boucheron had already opened his first shop in Paris in 1858, in the Palais Royal, the quarter which at that time had the monopoly of the luxury trade in the capital. An expert in precious stones, he was also known as a creator of genius and an unrivalled jewellery technician (he had learned his trade from the greatest jewellers of his time). Success was not slow to come. The international exhibitions, which were very frequent at that period, were a trampoline for his fame. He won a first prize at Philadelphia in 1875, another at Paris in 1889, yet more in 1900.

He opened a branch in Moscow (which was closed at the beginning of the Revolution), and another in London, which still exists.

His son, Louis, took over the running of the family business, and his sons Fred and Gérard continued his expansionist policies. The house of Boucheron is naturally the supplier of an elite clientele: the English and Saudi-Arabian

Bracelet consisting of small plaques of coloured hardstone with engraved stylised floral designs and a surround of small brilliants. Boucheron (1925). Photo: Sotheby's.

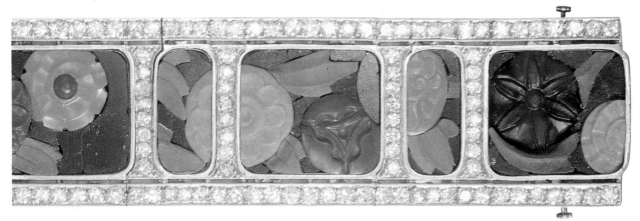

Detail of Boucheron floral bracelet shown above.

Large devant de corsage *pin in lapis lazuli, onyx, coral, jade and diamonds mounted on gold. Produced in 1925 for the Exposition des Arts décoratifs. Boucheron Archives.*

Large devant de corsage *in lapis lazuli, coral, jade, onyx and diamonds on a gold mount. Produced in 1925 for the Exposition des Arts décoratifs. Boucheron Archives.*

Necklace of jade and onyx pearls, ending in a tassel-shaped pendant in onyx and jade pearls. Boucheron (1925).

Royal families, as well as famous names in banking and the arts.

In 1930, Louis Boucheron was summoned to Teheran on a highly important secret mission: to estimate the value of the fabulous treasure of 'The Arabian Nights', the exchange value for the Iranian currency in circulation. After several months of study, working with the assistance of three experts, Louis Boucheron was able to indicate to the Shah the precise value of the throne covered with precious stones, of the terrestrial globe on which a single emerald represents Iran, and of his extraordinary mantles for state occasions.

Since the 1970s, the house of Boucheron, directed by Alain Boucheron, the great-grandson of the founder, has opened new branches all over the world — in Japan, Switzerland, the Middle East and the Far East, to name only a few. The Boucheron archives, in their chronological presentation, give a precise idea of the evolution of style between 1920 and 1940.

The album containing the collected iconography of the jewellery produced between 1923 and 1925 shows a series of rectangular or oval brooches, and even circular or hexagonal ones (with cut-off corners). They are in onyx or rock crystal, sometimes frosted, decorated with geometrical motifs in platinum or white gold. These models were to be produced without interruption until about 1927. A famous specimen in this series — composed of an oval central element in onyx, flanked by two loops in coral and diamond segments — is now in the Musée des Arts Décoratifs in Paris. During the same period are to be found, alongside brooches of geometrical design, a whole series of objects with black and white stylised floral motifs. These are flower compositions in brilliants, surrounded by a filament in black enamel. The sharp contrast between the dazzling white of the brilliants and the black of the enamel emphasises the motif. Amongst the most representative models of this series, it is worth noting a brooch composed of a central element in black onyx, decorated on the sides with two small symmetrical bouquets of flowers executed in brilliants, surrounded by a filament in black enamel and enhanced by a touch of red coral. A barrette representing five myosotis in round brilliants, again edged with black, and finished at the ends with stylised leaves linked by a small loop in onyx, is equally remarkable. There were also brooches of which the model was very close to that of tie-pins. They were mounted on platinum or white gold, composed of two separable elements in onyx, and decorated with inlaid geometrical motifs in white gold, platinum, pearls and diamonds.

The masterpiece in the Art Deco style from the house of Boucheron is the famous *devant de corsage,* specially conceived and produced for the *Exposition des Arts décoratifs* of 1925. This brilliantly polychromatic piece of jewellery, mounted on palladised gold, was composed of a flat mosaic of geometrical elements, surrounded by a narrow edging of diamonds, in scalloped lapis lazuli, onyx and jade, with turquoises and coral.

In the same style, there is also a necklace, composed of five rows of *cannetilles,* alternately in coral and onyx, decorated with four motifs in onyx chips, edged

1. *Brooch in onyx, brilliants, black enamel and coral, mounted on platinum. Boucheron (1925).*

2. *Brooch in brilliants, black enamel and coral, mounted on platinum. Boucheron (1925).*

3. *Brooch in brilliants and black enamel, mounted on platinum. Boucheron (1925).*

4. *Brooch in brilliants, onyx and black enamel, mounted on platinum. Boucheron (1925).*

with diamonds, and including, in the centre, a large coral. The necklace is completed by a pendant consisting of an onyx, coral and diamond drop.

Very characteristic of this period around 1925 is a bracelet consisting of rectangular motifs in coloured semi-precious stones, with an engraved floral design. Each motif is surrounded by small brilliants.

*Watch-brooch in yellow gold, enamel and diamonds. Boucheron (1925).
Daniela Balzaretti Collection (Bergamo).*

*Rectangular brooch in gold,
silver, lapis lazuli and
quartz. Ring in gold,
sapphires, diamonds and
green hardstone.
Boucheron (1925).
Photo: Sotheby's.*

Cigarette box in diamonds, onyx and jade, mounted on platinum. Boucheron. Photo: Sotheby's.

Rectangular cigarette case in black lacquered gold. The lid consists of a jade plaque set off by baguette cut diamonds and grey agate. Boucheron (1928) Boucheron Archives.

So-called 'Orage' (Storm) brooch
in brilliants and black enamel,
mounted on platinum.
Boucheron (1925).

Bracelet consisting of jade discs alternating with onyx plaques decorated with floral motifs in brilliants. Boucheron (1925)

Bracelet of brilliants and onyx mounted on platinum. Boucheron (1925).

Bracelet consisting of onyx links alternating with hardstones. Boucheron (1925).

Brooch in diamonds, onyx and black
enamel, mounted on platinum.
Boucheron (1925).

In general, rings were set in platinum, and the principal stones were coloured and precious or semi-precious (usually cabochon cut), surrounded with small diamonds, encircled in turn by a filature of black enamel. Essentially earrings were long pendants, sometimes finishing in pearl drops.

The influence of the Orient on Boucheron is revealed by a whole series of brooches representing highly coloured samurais. The palette is provided by paste, lacquers and ivory, surrounded by a geometrical frame in platinum and brilliants.

The Boucheron brooch exhibited in 1925 under the name *Orage* (Storm) is a characteristic example of figurative jewellery. A series of stripes (the lightning) in brilliants, flash against a background streaked with black lacquer (the rain), perfectly rendering the impression of lightning in a stormy sky.

One also finds a wide variety of articulated bracelets, composed of flat links of square or rectangular shape, alternating with motifs in onyx or semi-precious stones, prism-shaped or cabochon cut: large or small bracelets, mounted on platinum, and composed of motifs decorated with brilliants to represent stylised roses, joined, for example, by rectangular links.

From 1926, long necklaces began to appear, with rectangular links set with diamonds, and finishing in a pendant. These were very fashionable in 1928-9. The pendant became more and more important, and was often hexagonal in form.

Rectangular brooches in platinum with geometrical designs were also in vogue. Baguette cut brilliants traced broken lines creating empty spaces (openwork). The brooch thus gained in transparency and lightness. Small bouquet-brooches, mounted on platinum, also used baguette cut diamonds in conjunction with brilliants. There was an explosion of engraved coloured

Series of pendant earrings in onyx drops, jade, cornaline and brilliants. Boucheron (1925).

Necklace of coral, onyx and diamonds, ending in a pendant consisting of a drop in coral, onyx and diamonds.

Platinum, enamel, onyx and brilliants ring. Boucheron (1925).

stones, suggesting the chromatic harmonies of flower arrangements.

Boxes, beauty-cases and cigarette-cases were highly sought after in the Twenties. Boucheron created a number of articles which fully expressed the Art Deco style. In this vast repertoire, in which the jeweller gave unbridled rein to the development of his fantasy, geometrical designs dominated. A few pieces of exceptional beauty stand out. For example, a cigarette-case in black enamelled gold, produced in 1929, whose lid is made of a plaque of jade embellished with baguette cut diamonds and grey agate. A rectangular beauty-case, enamelled in red and decorated with two circular plaques in dark green nephrite with carved flowers in open-work. Another cigarette-case, extremely elegant in its deceptive simplicity, which takes the form of a strict black onyx rectangle, decorated in the centre with a lozenge of carved imperial jade, the hinges and catch in platinum, set with small diamonds.

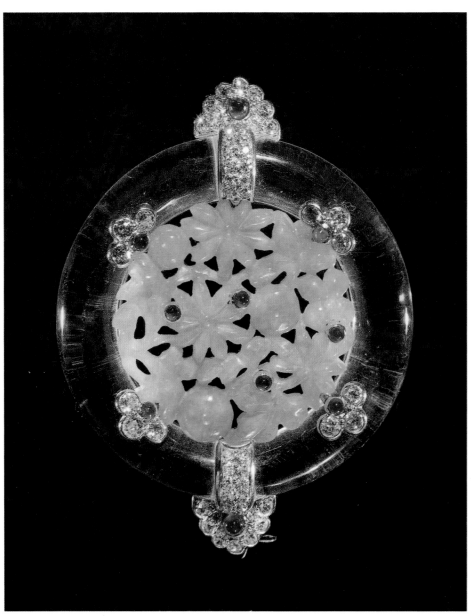

Brooch composed of a ring in rock crystal, embellished with a jade plaque, diamonds and rubies, mounted on platinum. Cartier. Daniela Balzaretti Collection (Bergamo).

CARTIER

The Art Deco jewels produced in Cartier's workshops always kept faith with a certain tradition, from which all excess was excluded. The euphoria of the Roaring Twenties had no effect at all on this impassive respect for the past.

It was in 1847 that Louis-François Cartier, founder of the dynasty, opened his first jeweller's shop in Paris. In 1853 he set up in the rue Neuve-des-Petits-Champs, and then, in 1859, he opened a branch on the boulevard des Italiens.

The beauty and refinement of his creations very quickly brought him a prestigious clientele. Apart from anything else, he became the favourite jeweller of the Princess Mathilde, the daughter of King Jérome and cousin of Napoleon III. He became official purveyor of jewellery to the Empress Eugénie.

The Franco-Prussian war encouraged the prudent Louis-François to open a branch in London.

A year later, he retired from business in order to devote himself to the study of Oriental languages. He called on his son Alfred to be his successor.

In 1878 the Paris International Exhibition confirmed the supremacy of France in all of the decorative arts. The Americans were henceforth to be the best clients of metropolitan France.

Alfred had four children, Louis, Pierre, Jacques and Suzanne. All of them received a complete artistic education.

In 1898, Alfred took his eldest son, Louis, into partnership. This coincided with the firm moving to 13 rue de la Paix, an address which was certainly well chosen, next to the celebrated Ritz Hotel, and close to the great fashion designer of English origin, Worth, who had invented the crinoline. The two families became joined by marriage. Louis married Worth's grand-daughter, and his sister, Suzanne, married his son Jacques. The first fifteen years of the century witnessed the triumph of Cartier. Royal appointments became too numerous to count.

The Prince of Wales, the future Edward VII, became an *habitué* of the firm. He went as far ordering twenty-seven diadems for his Coronation in 1902. But the Cartier style was not exclusively reserved for the crowned heads of Europe. It was the predilection of maharajas, Oriental princes, and those recent descendants of Midas, the American millionaires whose names have become part of history, Vanderbilt, Morgan, Gould, Astor...

This phenomenal success, this supremacy unprecedented in the history of jewellery, derived not only from the creation of dazzling parures for princely clients, but also from the production of astonishing precious objects, always perfectly made, thanks to the many technical innovations suggested by Louis Cartier, the inventive genius of the family, who always knew how to balance technical needs with aesthetic demands.

At the turn of the century, he introduced platinum into high-class jewellery in a peremptory and definitive way. The use of this metal allowed the infrastructure of the article of jewellery to become at once lighter and stronger.

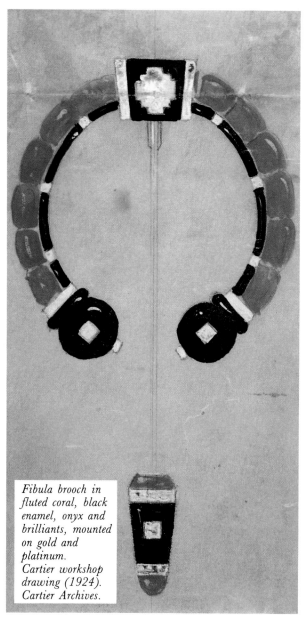

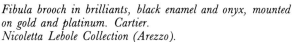

Fibula brooch in fluted coral, black enamel, onyx and brilliants, mounted on gold and platinum. Cartier workshop drawing (1924). Cartier Archives.

Fibula brooch in brilliants, black enamel and onyx, mounted on gold and platinum. Cartier. Nicoletta Lebole Collection (Arezzo).

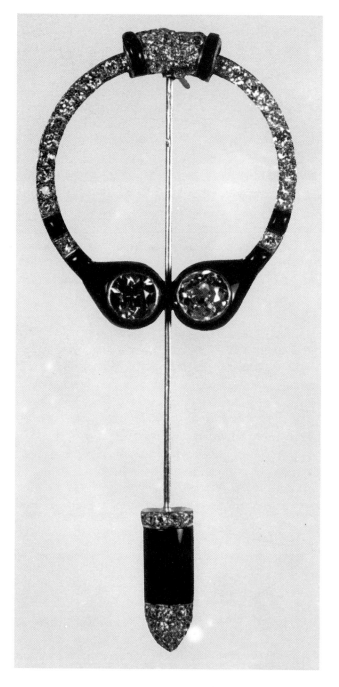

Amongst examples of this excellent blend of the practical and the aesthetic are their extraordinary clocks and *pendulettes,* in which precious materials and perfection of form and execution rival technical bravura.

Their first wristwatch, created in 1904 for the Brazilian aeronautical pioneer, Santos Dumont, also illustrates the revolutionary nature of this aesthetic directed towards the functional. This wristwatch, specially commissioned from Louis Cartier by the aviator, allowed him to check the time without letting go of the aeroplane's controls.

Although attentive to the technological progress of his time, Louis Cartier did not allow this to make him neglect decorative innovations. Fascinated by the choreography and sets of Diaghilev's Ballets russes, he took up some of

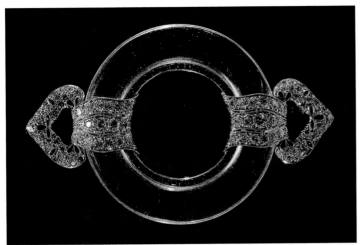

Brooch composed of a ring in rock crystal, diamonds and onyx, mounted on platinum.
Cartier. Daniela Balzaretti Collection (Bergamo).

Brooch in onyx, jade and diamonds, mounted on platinum. Cartier. Nicoletta Lebole Collection (Arezzo).

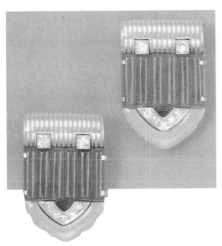

Clips in gold, enamel and jade. Cartier. Photo: Sotheby's.

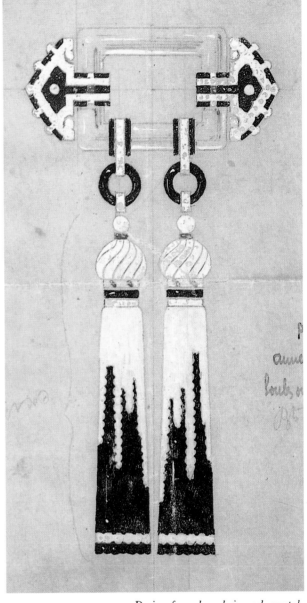

Design for a brooch in rock crystal, onyx and brilliants mounted on platinum. Cartier (1924). Cartier Archives.

their themes. and developed them in terms of highly coloured jewellery. Then cubism offered a revelation of the beauty and harmony of geometrical design. He exploited this new vein in luxury objects specially conceived for the 1925 Exhibition.

Various branches were set up abroad — London in 1901 and New York in 1908, under the direction of the brothers, Louis and Jacques. The international reputation of Cartier's was confirmed in 1910 with the establishment of two new branches, one in May, in Moscow (was this a direct assault on the illustrious Fabergé?), the other in December, in the Persian Gulf.

In the 1920s there was a new expansion of production, with the setting up of the 'S' department, the forerunner of today's boutique. This department was run by Jeanne Toussaint. An alter ego of Louis Cartier, she was to become, in 1925, jointly responsible for high-class jewellery.

Shoulder brooch consisting of a crystal link pavé set with brilliants and pendant of emeralds, onyx, pearls and brilliants; setting in platinum. Cartier (1924). Cartier Archives.

Certificate of M. Cartier, member of the selection committee for the International Exhibition of Decorative Arts, Paris 1925.

Left. Brooch consisting of two discs of shaded jade and black enamel with dragons; mounted on gold and platinum. Cartier (1924). Cartier Archives.

Right. Pawl brooch consisting of two ornamental palms in brilliants, black enamel mounted on platinum. Cartier (1924). Cartier Archives.

For a second time, the business was put in jeopardy by war. The activities of the 'S' department were given up provisionally. Jeanne Toussaint took on sole responsibility for the Cartier 'institution' in the absence of Louis, who had left France for the United States, where he died in New York in 1942.

The Cartier archives, from 1905 to the present day, consist of life-sized photographs of the firm's complete production. This makes it possible to follow, step by step, the stylistic development of their Art Deco creations, the first hints of which appeared in about 1910, and to identify the significant stages in that development.

With Cartier, the first period was marked by a change in the style of the designs, but more importantly by a change in the association of colours. The traditional palette was subjected to the impact of the Ballets russes, and, as a result underwent a transformation.

Brooch pavé set with brilliants and Greek motifs in onyx, mounted on platinum. Cartier (1923). Cartier Archives.

Belt buckles, consisting of a crystal link and, at the ends, palms of onyx and brilliants mounted on platinum. Cartier (1924). Cartier Archives.

Belt buckle in jade, onyx and brilliants, mounted on platinum. Cartier (1923). Cartier Archives.

'S' shaped brooch in coral, onyx and brilliants decorated with an emerald, mounted on platinum. Cartier (1923). Cartier Archives.

Belt buckle consisting of a ring of onyx and brilliants, coral and pearls in Arab motifs: mounted on platinum. Cartier Archives (1923).

Brooch composed of two 'D' shaped motifs in brilliants, onyx and emeralds on a platinum mounting. Cartier (1924). Cartier Archives.

Brooches consisting of an onyx ring and palm motifs in brilliants. Mounted on platinum. Cartier Archives (1923).

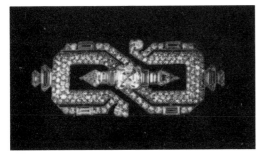

'S' shaped brooch in brilliants mounted on platinum. Cartier (1929). Cartier Archives.

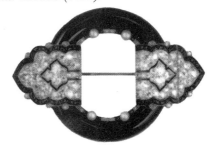

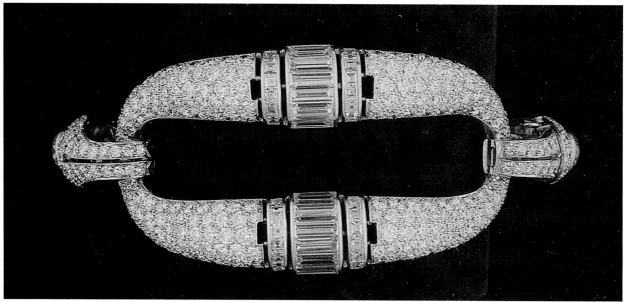

Bracelet in baguette cut brilliants, mounted on platinum. Cartier. Photo: Sotheby's.

Brooch in enamel and diamonds, mounted on platinum. Cartier. Nicoletta Lebole Collection (Arezzo).

New harmonies of intense colours appeared, strongly contrasted — unusual mixtures of red and black, blue and green, blue and violet.

Enamelled planed surfaces were paired with coral and onyx. Sapphires, emeralds and rubies were married with jades and amethysts, creating an original palette.

With Cartier, however, the revolution in jewellery which was developing in the period immediately preceding the First World War, was never pushed to the extreme — that is to exuberant geometrical design. These new ideas were to burgeon again in the aftermath of the war, and were to bloom fully, in a vast range of decorative motifs, on the occasion of the celebrated Exhibition of Decorative Arts of 1925. Cartier did not show his jewellery at the Grand Palais, with the other jewellers, but at the Pavillon de l'élégance, with the fashion designers. There he exhibited one hundred and fifty pieces produced between 1922 and 1925.

According to the newspapers of the time Cartier showed, amongst many other objects: 'A wide, flat bracelet, on which square diamonds alternated with pink coral. Two large squares of brilliants surround the clasp... A hexagonally cut emerald, framed by a circle in onyx, inlaid with diamonds, coral and brilliants.'

But Cartier's were also producing a more severe style of jewellery, to harmonise with the combinations of black and white which were fashionable in dress. Thus jabot-pins with ratchet-fasteners or double bayonet joints were numerous.

Brooch composed of an onyx ring with diamond motifs at the sides, mounted on platinum. Cartier.

Brooch in rock crystal, diamonds and enamel, mounted on platinum. Cartier. Photo: Sotheby's.

The jabot-pins of 1922-3 were finished at the ends with small triangles of diamonds or, in the more decorative versions, at one end an onyx disc with a diamond surround and, on the other, a decoration in coral and sapphires.

1923 is the date of the famous brooch in the form of a closed umbrella, with grooves, constructed in onyx, brilliants, pearls and and coral. It is also the date of a remarkable series of arrow brooches in platinum, again decorated with brilliants, or partly covered in brilliants and black enamel.

The fibula brooches of 1922 consist of an onyx link decorated with brilliants. Of all articles of jewellery, it is the brooch which, at this period, lent itself to

1. *Brooch in the shape of a triumphal arch with brilliants and onyx, mounted on platinum. Cartier, between 1928 and 1930. Photo: Sotheby's.*

2.3. *Brooches in the shape of a temple and a pagoda, consisting of brilliants on a platinum mounting. Cartier (1927).*
Cartier Archives.

Pendant earrings composed of emerald pearls, brilliants and fine pearls, mounted on platinum.
Cartier (1924).

Left. Basket of flowers brooch in brilliants, emeralds, rubies and sapphires, mounted on platinum. Cartier (1929). Cartier Archives.

Right. Owl brooch in emeralds, rose, black enamel, mounted on platinum. Cartier (1929). Cartier Archives.

84

the largest number of new ideas. One often finds pendant brooches, circular brooches, made of a link in rock crystal or onyx, decorated with symmetrical lateral motifs (arrow heads in diamonds, etc.). The possible combinations were infinite. Sometimes the link was square or hexagonal in shape, in this case it was referred to as a buckle brooch, sometimes this was replaced by an 'S' shape, but it was always decorated with diamonds and discreet filaments in black lacquer.

Between 1923 to 1925 was, as we have already pointed out, the period of the great vogue for tassels, inspired by their equivalent in upholstery. With Cartier, this decorative motif was expoloited in various ways.

Another motif characteristic of the firm was the picot, which consisted of pavé set diamonds decorated with black onyx points. This could can be set in a brooch or a pendant, or even used as a linking motif in a necklace, or as a decoration for combs.

The combination of brilliants and onyx led Louis Cartier to create the thin strap bracelet in which small plaques of onyx stand out from pavé set diamonds to create the impression of spots. Thus was launched the famous series of so-called 'panther' bracelets, which corresponded to the reverse of the creative development which occurred in 1948. From the first specimens of abstract panthers came the inspiration, in about 1948, for a famous series of naturalistic panthers, which we shall discuss later.

The so-called *devant de corsage* (stomacher) brooches are particularly representative of Cartier's production in the years 1923-5. These were large brooches of geometrical design in precious stones, with cascades of *chenilles* of brilliants set in platinum. At the same period Cartier was also producing brooches composed of a semi-circle in coral decorated with baguette cut diamonds, an emerald cabochon and two large drop cut diamonds.

Between 1923 and 1925 Oriental art came into Cartier's repertoire. Abstract motifs borrowed from Islamic art (stars and geometrical themes suggested by decorative motifs deriving from carpets or Oriental miniatures) were the first sources of inspiration for geometrical ornamentation. Cartier's *chinoiseries* were amongst the most sophisticated objects created by the firm at this period. For

Necklace of emeralds,
sapphires and turquoises,
mounted on gold.
Cartier (1929).
Cartier Archives.

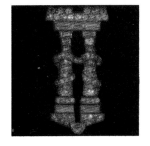

their orientally inspired creations, they often used original objects imported from the East or bought from antique dealers — pieces in jade, carved ivory — which could be marvellously integrated with lacquers and enamels, thanks to the tendency towards 'cross-breeding' which characterised Art Deco.

The themes most frequently exploited were fantastic beasts and Chinese dragons, which became used more and more as decorations on pins, bracelets and brooches and, a little later, on boxes and cases. The fabulous bestiary of

Right. Clip brooches (one in the shape of a stylised temple) in brilliants mounted on platinum. Cartier (1927). Cartier Archives.

85

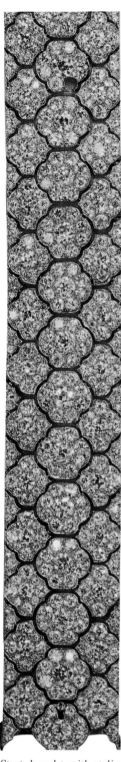

Strap bracelet with stylised floral motifs in diamonds, mounted on platinum. Cartier Photo: Sotheby's.

Toilet case in gold and black enamel decorated with a vase of flowers, in coral, sapphires, emeralds and diamonds. Cartier. Photo: Sotheby's.

Oriental art was brought into force, and reproduced with the bright and glittering colours of fine gemstones, emeralds, rubies, sapphires, coral, etc. The well-known open bangles in enamelled gold known as *Chimeres* (Chimerae) were decorated at each end with the head of a fabulous creature, embellished with cabochon-cut sapphires and cabochons of engraved emerald. The Chinese sign for long life (*shou*), a round medallion with horizontal arms, was also taken up as a decorative motif. And brooches were produced in the form of pagodas and small Buddhas.

The necklaces dating from 1925, with engraved emerald cabochons alternating with small Oriental pearls, are undeniably fascinating. These necklaces ended in a hexagonal engraved emerald pendant, finishing in turn with round, cabochon-cut emeralds and pearls. The clasp and the links were of platinum set with tiny brilliants. In about 1925, a hexagonal emerald was mounted in this way on a sautoir of Oriental pearls, ending in a tassel.

At about the same time Egyptian art made a tumultuous entry into Cartier jewellery. Trapezoid Egyptian temples, edged top and bottom with onyx baguettes, and sometimes covered with precious stones, were mounted as brooches. Representations of sphinx on a pedestal in hard gemstone, of the god Horus in the form of a falcon with spread wings, of the goddess Isis, and even of scarabs, were used to decorate brooches.

Pendants were in the shape of lotuses. Hieroglyphs became much appreciated as decorative elements, particularly for cases. One example, dating from 1924, hanging from a black silk cord, presents flat surfaces in mother-of-pearl, beautifully decorated with hieroglyphs. The pediment of a temple in coral and gold is supported by slender columns, also in coral. In the centre is a lapis lazuli stele, representing a figure in turquoise-blue porcelain, finishing in a lotus-flower of coral and onyx.

Toilet case in gold composed of a slab of lapis lazuli decorated with a vase of flowers in jade, rubies, coral and diamonds. Cartier. Photo: Sotheby's.

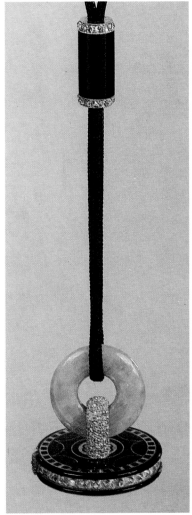

Pendant watch in black enamelled gold and diamonds, link in jade, toggle in black enamelled platinum and diamonds. Cartier circa 1925

But the principal masterpiece amongst Cartier's Egyptian creations is a box in the form of a sarcophagus, dating from 1925. Its lid is of engraved Persian ivory of the 18th century. The base is in finely chiselled gold. Two of the sides are enamelled, with lotus flower and tree motifs in gold, whereas the other two represent, on one side, the Sphinx of Guiseh and, on the other, the face of the Pharoah Tutenkhamen, engraved on a cabochon-cut emerald surrounded by sapphires.

Business reasons led Cartier's to become interested in Indian art. During the 1920s, maharajahs and Indian dignitaries began to frequent 13 rue de la Paix and, perhaps even more so, the London branch, to which they regularly took antique pieces of traditional jewellery for resetting according to the taste of the day. In this way, Louis Cartier became familiar with the typically Indian decorative motifs and jewellery techniques which influenced him considerably. A typical example of this Indian influence is the plume, a traditional turban decoration, which became the fashionable aigret of the period.

The many trips which Louis Cartier made to India in order to acquire merchandise influenced the creation of necklaces in coloured precious stones, cabochon-cut, especially emeralds, in the production of triumphal arches in coloured stones, and in brooches in the shape of palms.

In a sense the influence worked in both directions, since Cartier began to obtain fabulous royal commissions. For example, the crown produced for the Maharajah of Kapurtala in 1926, dominated in the centre by an extraordinary emerald of 177 carats, or the complete set of jewellery created for the Maharajah of Patiala.

The more frankly European jewellery of 1926 was marked by the appearance of the first clips, usually in the shape of cones. These were still to be very much in vogue in the 1930s.

At the same period — and indeed, until 1928 — 'fruit basket' polychromatic brooches were being produced, as well as strap bracelets with garlands of fruit and flowers, luxuriously inlaid with emeralds, rubies and engraved sapphires.

At the end of the 1920s the magnificent series of brooches in the shape of temples, triumphal arches and pagodas, the structural motifs emphasised by baguette-cut brilliants, enjoyed an enormous vogue.

Other highly successful articles produced by Cartier's at that time were boxes and cases (card-cases, powder compacts, cigarette-cases, toilette-cases and vanity-cases).

Among the many decorative themes taken up, the oriental retained pride of place. A whole series of precious objects were decorated in black lacquer (burgau), inlaid with coloured mother-of-pearl representing Chinese

1

2

3

4

characters in garden scenes. Gold boxes were also decorated with engraved mother-of-pearl in different colours showing Japanese pastoral scenes. Besides these objects, a number of boxes with an enamelled background had geometrical floral motifs clearly deriving from Indian art.

The production of clocks and carriage clocks deserves a chapter to itself. Their formal luxuriance and the technical feats which they implied have never been equalled. Their manufacture was entrusted to a workshop directed by Maurice Coüet (1885-1963), who had inherited the tradition of the great Breguet through his grandfather. From 1911 onwards he worked exclusively for Cartier.

In 1913, Louis Cartier created his first mystery clock, directly inspired by the masterpieces of nineteenth century clock-making. The mystery of the functioning of this extraordinary object was based on the principle of a fascinating optical illusion. The hands seem to float in empty space and to be turned by the void. They do not move as in an ordinary clock, for each is fixed to a glass disc and it is the discs, set in a worm gear, which turn.

As the technology developed (Coüet passed from a double lateral axis to a single axis), the aesthetics of Cartier clockmaking went through many revolutions. Thus, there were clocks in the form of fantastic beasts and in the shape of temple gates, the famous portico clocks. At the beginning these various objects (including the models sold in America) all came from Cartier's Parisian workshop. In 1919 and 1920, to satisfy increasing export demand, Cartier set up an international firm, the 'European Clock and Watch Company' which poured onto the market, for almost two decades, an impressive number of 'recent creations'.

1. Strap bracelet patterned with geometrical lines in diamonds, onyx and emeralds, mounted on platinum. Cartier (1922). Cartier Archives.

2. Bracelet composed of two straps in brilliants and onyx linked by two onyx rings, mounted on platinum. Cartier (1922). Cartier Archives.

3. Bracelet composed of an openwork strap in brilliants, coral and onyx, mounted on platinum. Cartier (1922). Cartier Archives.

4. Bracelet composed of interspersed motifs in brilliants and coral, with an onyx border, mounted on platinum. Cartier (1922). Cartier Archives.

1. Gold and black enamelled vanity case,
monogrammed and decorated with diamonds.
Cartier. Photo: Sotheby's.

2. So-called 'mystery' clock in black
enamel, decorated with coral, rock
crystal and diamonds. Cartier (1928).

3. Powder compact in gold, black and blue enamel
and diamonds. Anonymous. Photo: Sotheby's.

CHAUMET

Two centuries of the history of jewellery are associated with the Chaumet dynasty, founded in 1780 by the jeweller Etienne Nitot, supplier of jewellery to Bonaparte, to whom we owe not only the diamond decorated sword 'Le Régent' worn by Napoleon on the day of his Coronation, but also the so-called 'Charlemagne' crown, and the tiara worked by Augustin that the Emperor offered as a gift to Pope Pius VII.

On his death Etienne Nitot was succeeded by his son. He created the jewellery of Marie-Louise, including the set which she wore on her wedding day. Fossin, a fashionable jeweller under the Restoration, took over from the younger Nitot. Theophile Gautier and Alfred de Musset both quote his name. Fossin went into partnership with Morel. The City of Paris ordered from them the sword it wanted to offer to the Count of Paris. Then came a new, ambitious generation. Prosper Morel went to prospect Russia and won as clients the Tsar and his court. This is the point at which appeared the name of Joseph Chaumet, son-in-law to Prosper Morel and expert in gemmology.

The history of the firm, very eventful in the nineteenth century, was less exciting in the first quarter of the twentieth century. Chaumet actively took part in the big international exhibitions. The style of this prolific jeweller bears the stamp of the important creative currents of the period.

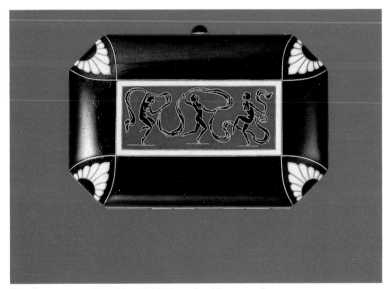

Powder compact in gold and black and white enamel.
Ghiso.
Photo: Sotheby's.

Toilet case in gold and black enamel, decorated with stylised floral motifs in coral, lapis lazuli and diamonds. Chaumet (1925).

THE MELLERIOS, KNOWN AS THE MELLERS

Clip composed of brilliants and emeralds, mounted on platinum. Mellerio dits Meller. Mellerio dits Meller Archives.

It is not often that one encounters a dynasty of jewellers going back to the sixteenth century and still active today. This is, however, the case of the Mellerio family, known as the Mellers, who are justly proud of their history.

The Mellerio ancestors, established in the Val Vigezzo in Italy (Lombardy) were cutting native Alpine crystals and stones at a very early date. They also did filigree work in gold and silver, making buttons for robes and belt-buckles. The members of the family who came and set themselves up in Paris after the battle of Melegnano in 1515 became expert in jewellery and the goldsmith's craft through contact with Parisian artisans. In particular, they learnt the new techniques of chasing and enamelling. But they had a difficult life, prey to the jealousy of their local competitors, who did not look kindly on these newcomers. At the instigation of these Paris competitors, the corporations and tax officials ferociously persecuted the intruders, until they had no other option but to solicit the protection of Marie de Médicis.

The Florentine birth of the Regent worked in their favour and grace was bestowed on them. A royal decree bestowed on the 'natives of the country of Lombardy' the freedom to ply their trade, that is: 'to carry and sell cut crystal, metalwork and other small goods' in Paris and the rest of the kingdom.

In 1635, Louis XIII confirmed and reinforced the protection offered to the Lombards, 'in consideration of services rendered'. The Mellerios were then suppliers to the King, the Queen, the Queen Mother and the important members of the court.

To distinguish them from their compatriots of the same name, Marie de Médicis called them the 'Mellers'. From that time on their trade name has been 'Mellerio dits Meller'. Anne of Austria, and later Louis XIV, renewed their privilege.

Until 1750, they had no fixed commercial premises. At that date they set up shop in the Lombard quarter, and then in the rue Vivienne. At the time of the Revolution, the family returned to its native land. In 1786 Jean-Baptiste Mellerio returned to the rue Vivienne, where he opened a shop called 'A la Couronne de fer' ('The Iron Crown'). As well as the custom of Versailles, he acquired that of the Tuileries.

Under the Restoration, the firm set up what were to be its definitive premises in the rue de la Paix.

For the Mellerios, the beginning of the nineteenth century coincided with a period of prosperity which was to be suddenly interrupted by the 1848 Revolution. The insurrection and the economic crisis forced them to close down. Nevertheless, the Mellerios refused to admit defeat. In fact they were to establish a business in Madrid, where they became suppliers to Queen Isabella II and Eugène de Montijo. They also opened a branch in Baden-Baden.

Today, François Mellerio, successor to his father Emile and his uncle Hubert, presides over the destiny of the company, at 16 rue de la Paix.

It is regrettable that such a long tradition should not be documented by

So-called 'panier' brooch, decorated with brilliants, rubies, emeralds and sapphires, mounted on platinum. Mellerio dits Meller (1925). Mellerio dits Meller Archives.

substantial archives. The Art Deco productions of the Mellerios correspond to the principal trends of the period in jewellery. Representative of the objects produced in 1925 is a brooch representing a basket, mounted on platinum and decorated on the sides with clusters of emeralds, rubies and sapphires, cabochon-cut and engraved, surrounded by brilliants and rod-shaped diamonds.

Another brooch of brilliants set in platinum reflects the Egyptian influence in its motif (a stylised falcon with spread wings), structured around a large oval sapphire. The brooch is completed by a chenilles fringe of brilliants.

A pendant brooch in platinum, decorated with a rectangular citrine of extraordinary cut, dates from 1920. It is surrounded by a double row of brilliants of octagonal design, embellished with eight rectangular cut aquamarines.

Brooch in brilliants with large sapphire in the centre, mounted on platinum. Mellerio dits Meller. Mellerio dits Meller Archives.

Pendant brooch with brilliants, aquamarines, and, in the centre, a large citrine: mounted on platinum. Mellerio dits Meller. Mellerio dits Meller Archives.

93

NOURY - MAUBOUSSIN

According to an official document drawn up by the Mauboussin jewellery firm in 1925, its history goes back to about 1827, '...when in the narrow rue Greneta, at No 24, there existed already a jewellery manufactory', which acquired daily an increasing importance. Its expansion allowed the firm to diversify into the direct purchasing of raw materials at the source of production, cutting of stones, and all the stages in the production of an article of jewellery.

In about 1920, the firm arrived at an important turning point. 'In 1923,' stipulates the document referred to above, 'M. Mauboussin, who had been with the firm since 1877, having begun by working with his uncle, M.B. Noury, then was made a partner, and finally, in 1903, sole proprietor, fulfilled a long-awaited dream. He bought two buildings forming a single block between the rue Saint-Augustin, de Choiseul and the rue Monsigny.'

The shop was organised in the following way: 1 rue de Choiseul contained the buying department, and No 3 of the same street housed the sales and display rooms. Finally, by adding a storey to the two buildings, it was possible to create the space necessary for a model workshop, 'a triumph of the light and hygiene indispensible to a luxury craft'.

At the same time, the firm opened branches in New York, Buenos Aires and Rio de Janeiro, and showed at all the great international exhibitions: Rio de Janeiro, *hors concours*; French Exhibition in New York, 1924; Milan Exhibitions of 1923 and 1924; Colonial Exhibition in Strasbourg, 1924. Finally, its participation in the 1925 Paris Exhibition of Decorative Arts was rewarded with a *Grand Prix*. At this exhibition the firm displayed pieces in which the purest of modern styles was allied with those distinctive features of French art, richness, taste and elegance.

From this point onwards, the firm was set up in the place Vendôme.

Which jewellery by Mauboussin reflects most faithfully the style of the 1920s? The fashion for coloured stones which spread in about 1925, and was successfully maintained until 1928 was especially suited to the form of inventive genius particular to the firm: 'Current fashion gives us a favourable fortune of colour. It loves the polychramatic effects of flowers and fruit, and introduces them wherever it can, even in the jewels which adorn feminine grace.' These words were to be read in the publicity brochures devoted to a series of articles of jewellery in coloured stones produced by the rue de Choiseul workshops.

The celebrated pendant *'Au rubis merveilleux'* framed in a platinum setting with geometrical motifs in baguette-cut diamonds in no way contradicts this slogan. This piece, ending in two drops of rubies, brilliants and onyx, hangs from a black cord by a half ring in onyx.

An oval brooch, heavy as a belt buckle, decorated with coloured flowers, glittering with reflected light, is another example, as is a platinum comb, flowered with sapphires, flashing with brilliants, the indispensable complement to the cropped haircut.

Mauboussin shop window displays.

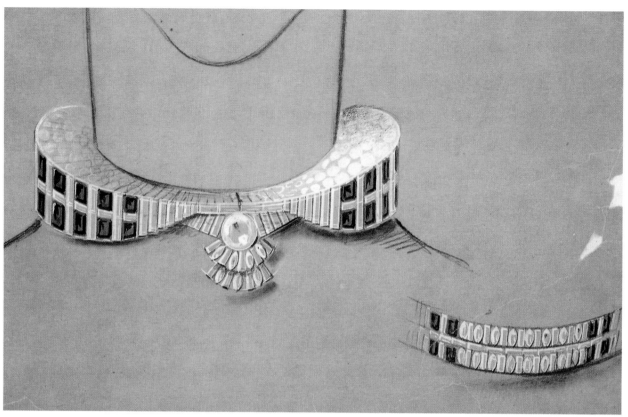

Design for a necklace to be produced in platinum, diamonds and emeralds. Mauboussin.

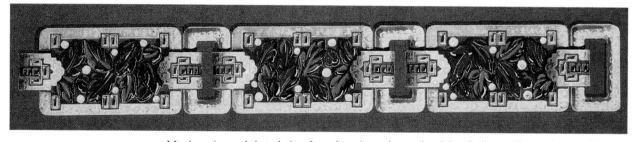

Mauboussin workshop design for a bracelet to be produced in platinum, diamonds, sapphires, rubies and engraved emeralds. Mauboussin Archives.

One particular bracelet emphasises the felicitous association of emeralds, sapphires and rubies. A succession of rectangular links, scattered with diamonds, joins motifs which display a central composition consisting of small stylised leaves in engraved precious stones of three colours.

This predilection for colour on the part of Mauboussin appeared in a striking way in the many exhibitions — each devoted to a different coloured stone — which they organised. In 1928, for example, Mauboussin displayed in their showrooms a collection of contemporary jewellery and illustrious emeralds. Famous stones were shown: an emerald, known as Napoleon's emerald, of 24 carats 38, which had been given by Bonaparte in 1800 to Josephine de Beauharnais, who was about to be crowned Empress; the three magnificent pear-shaped emeralds, set in a ring representing a clover-leaf, which was given by Napoleon III to the Empress on the occasion of the birth of the Imperial Prince; the emerald set in a ring, known as the *Queen of Naples's emerald,* which was also a classified piece. This private exhibition was so impressive, and created such a stir, that the organiser felt obliged to follow it up quickly.

A new exhibition opened on 4th June 1930. This time the theme was the ruby, a glittering stone, emblem of enthusiasm and strength.

In the *L'Illustration* of the same day there appeared the following comment: 'A strong sense of unity emerges from this exhibition devoted to the ruby...' And, further on in the same article: 'Indeed, nothing is livelier nor more sociable than the ruby. It lends itself to infinite colour combinations, giving very different effects, depending on whether it is associated with the deep blue of the sapphire or wed to the unfathomable liquid depths of the diamond.'

Of the modern pieces shown at this exhibition, some are described in the article which appeared in *L'Illustration*: 'Opulent rings set with rubies of a perfect colour, a number of them in that fiery and indefinable tint known as *sang de pigeon,* which is often a feature of fine Oriental rubies. Some are exceptionally large. It may be that the poetry of memory will be linked to the incarnadine droplets of the smaller rings, which are like wild flowers beside hothouse roses. The pendant earrings were designed to set off bob-cut hair, in the midst of which combs in pale tortoiseshell flecked with rubies lend a precious note. Again, sparkling dots of rubies glitter on tiny oval or rectangular watches, each of a different design, in this incomparable variety of knick-knacks, of trifles, born of the jeweller's ingenuity, and which have now become necessary to contemporary elegance, ready at a moment's notice to take up everything which flatters its love for what is new and original.'

Mauboussin preached a certain independance for jewellery in relation to the conditioning imposed by women's fashion: 'Against the dry formulae of the cubists, the cold stiffness which clashes with the softness and fluidity of women's evening dress, Mauboussin sets the seductive quality of gentle curves, a nuanced feminity in the piece of jewellery, a harmony of lines which perhaps links two opposing poles and two differing concepts, in the sense that it does not at all repudiate realism, and yet, without returning to romanticism, it scrupulously avoids denying it.'

Amongst the articles of coloured jewellery by Mauboussin, we should draw attention to the pendant-brooches in the shape of an octagonal ring, mounted on platinum, decorated with mother-of-pearl and scattered with diamonds. The pendant ends in a coloured precious stone in the form of a drop or an engraved cabochon.

Another pendant-brooch has a châtelaine (formerly a pendant chain) decorated with rows of brilliants alternating with rows of coloured precious stones. A rectangular pendant, decorated with a stylised flower and leaf motif in multicoloured precious stones, completes the piece.

Pendant in diamonds mounted on platinum with onyx and black enamel: in the centre a large ruby surrounded by small brilliants. Mauboussin (circa 1925).

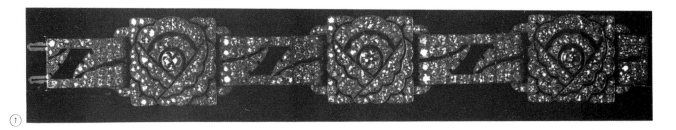

①

②

③

④

1. Bracelet mounted on platinum, composed of articulated openwork plaques pavé-set with diamonds. Mauboussin (circa 1925).

2.3. Bracelets composed of articulated plaques in platinum with geometrical flower designs in brilliants, coloured stones and enamel. Mauboussin (circa 1925).

4. Bracelet mounted on platinum, composed of three mother-of-pearl plaques embellished with floral motifs in diamonds and black enamel. Mauboussin (circa 1925).

A kind of pentagonal pendant represents a vase of flowers, again of geometrical form in coloured stones, surrounded by closely-set brilliants.

With Mauboussin, the tassel is also used as motif for a pendant-brooch: the Oriental cluster of pearls, decorated with brilliants and onyx, is hung from a chain composed of flat, circular links in alternating black (enamel) and white (diamonds).

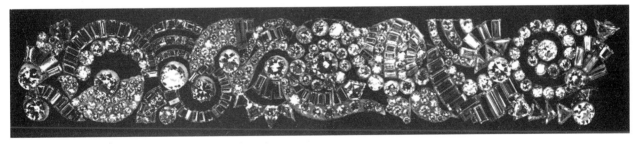

Studies for bracelets to be produced in platinum and diamonds. Mauboussin (1931).

Another series of brooches is composed of oval and rectangular motifs, flat in form, decorated with stylised foliage in brilliants, rubies and onyx.

Finally a particular group of brooches consists of studded brilliants on which appear geometrical motifs in the form of branches bearing roses or other flowers, generally created in onyx, jade and coloured precious stones. Some have in the centre a large cabochon-cut precious stone (Nos 84666, 83324, 84260, 84962).

The various shapes and forms of decoration used for brooches have their faithful replica in the motifs used for bracelets. Some take the form of a succession of motifs in mother-of-pearl, surrounded with brilliants and decorated with stylised polychromatic flowers. These motifs are joined by rectangular links scattered with brilliants. Others are made up of two or three fretted motifs, decorated with geometrical flowers in brilliants, coloured stones, and enamels.

*Above. Series of wrist-watches mounted on platinum and diamonds. In the centre,
a pendant watch mounted on platinum, diamonds and pearls.
Mauboussin Archives (1925).*

*Above and opposite: Series of pendant brooches and pendants in platinum, diamonds, enamel,
onyx and coloured stones. Created by Mauboussin circa 1925.*

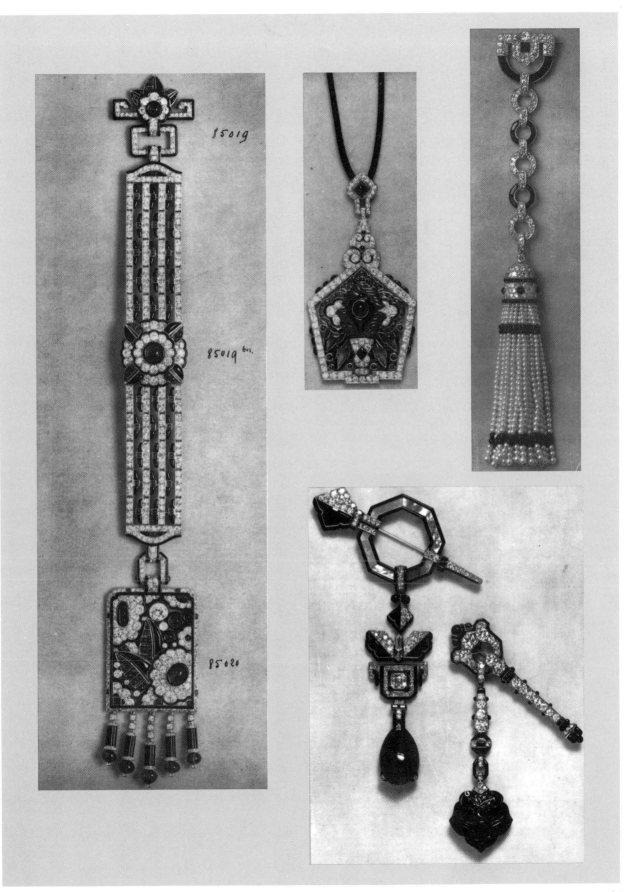

85019

85019 bis.

85020

Above and opposite page: Series of brooches in diamonds, onyx, enamel, jade, rubies, emeralds, sapphires, mounted on platinum. Created by Mauboussin between 1925 and 1929.

84250

Mauboussin workshop in the 1920s.

Above and opposite page: Series of brooches produced by Mauboussin between 1925 and 1930.

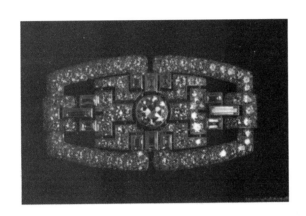

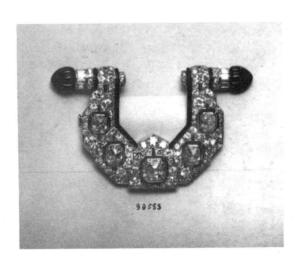

Series of boxes and vanity cases produced by Mauboussin in the 1920s.

In the 1920s Mauboussin produced a series of large necklaces, including heavy chains in brilliants alternating with coloured precious stones of large dimension: these chains were almost always embellished by a pendant echoing the decorative motifs of the chain.

It is worth mentioning here the famous 'Fountain' diadem, studded with baguettes, created by Mauboussin in 1925.

The masterly qualities of the rue de Choiseul workshop are also reflected in a remarkable collection of useful items such as boxes and cigarette-cases, of which it might be interesting to describe a few examples:

A vanity case in black-enamelled gold, composed of three geometrical motifs (hinges and clasp) in platinum and brilliants, unites simplicity and refined elegance (No 87000). The same motifs are to be found in a more embellished version of the same model, to which has been added a decoration of medallions in carved jade. (No 87001).

A cigarette-case made in lacquered gold, decorated with a medallion in

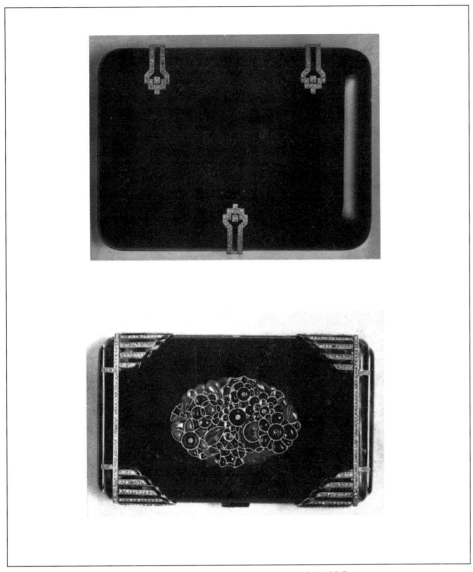

Series of boxes and vanity cases produced by Mauboussin in the 1920s.

polychrome enamel representing stylised flowers, is particularly successful. In addition lines of small brilliants adorn the corners and edges (No 2278). The lid of a magnificent box is entirely covered with a carpet of highly coloured flowers engraved in precious and semi-precious stones.

The mark of purest Art Deco style is to be found in two other boxes: the first in black lacquer decorated with six Iribe roses (M.1); the lid of the second, in mother-of-pearl figures a typically 1925 fountain, with sprays of water in brilliants.

Mauboussin used a host of other subjects for decoration of boxes and cases. A delicate enamelled landscape, probably representing an Austrian church, adorns the lid of a cigarette case (No 85567), whereas a box in lacquered gold, which reveals an undeniable Persian influence, is decorated with hunting scenes (B 2795). There are also a whole series of square, rectangular or octagonal toilette-cases from which are hung, by magnificent polychrome enamelled chains, jewelled lipstick cases.

Series of boxes and vanity cases produced by Mauboussin in the 1920s.

Series of vanity cases produced by Mauboussin in the 1920s.

Necklace mounted on platinum, in brilliants with a sapphire in the centre of the pendant. Mauboussin (circa *1929*).

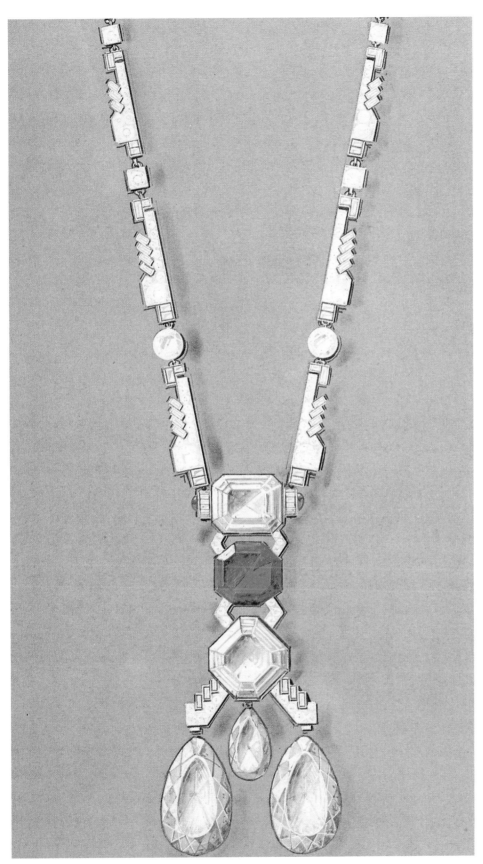

Design for a necklace to be produced in platinum, diamonds and emeralds.
Mauboussin (circa *1930*).

VAN CLEEF AND ARPELS

Van Cleef et Arpels, a firm born of the amalgamation of two diamond families, also produced articles of jewellery characteristic of the general trend. In 1906, the three Arpels brothers, Charles, Julien and Louis, went into partnership with Alfred Van Cleef, who had just married their sister Kiki. They set up their shop in the place Vendôme.

The official chronicle offered by the firm is rather meagre in details. It is worth noting, however, that it began to expand in 1924-25 with the opening of a shop in Cannes. The situation of this shop was as strategic as could be desired, on the Croisette, not far from Poiret's. The opening of branches throughout the world contributed to the rise of the firm, whose efforts were crowned by the award of *Grands Prix* at the exhibitions of the period. It was at the Exhibition of Decorative Arts of 1925 that they first won a prize for 'marvellous roses, diamonds and rubies interlaced with emerald leaves, delicately mounted on a bracelet'.

They also invented exclusive items, for example the evening bag christened *'minaudière'* (simperer) — the name was registered as a trade-mark by Van Cleef et Arpels — and discovered new techniques, such as the mystery, or invisible, setting which will be discussed in the chapter dealing with the 1930s.

During the 1920s, the firm's creative potential developed in many directions. Their Egyptian pieces — and more particularly their series of brooches and bracelets — were characterised by a highly refined level of execution. The bracelets were flexible. They took the form of bands studded with brilliants mounted on platinum, of small motifs in sapphires, rubies, emeralds and onyx calibrés, bringing lively touches of colour into scenes of Egyptian life, a man bowing to the Pharoah, for example. The ornamentation was inspired by the usual repertoire of motifs deriving from Egyptian religious symbolism: composite deities, cosmic bodies, principally the sun, animals, particularly snakes, falcons, vultures (symbol of the ka or the soul) ibises, baboons, and in addition, hieroglyphs interpreted in a more or less whimsical way.

The production of motifs executed in the fashionable colours, black, white and red, was also particularly prolific. For example a jabot pin mounted on platinum and composed of two symmetrical motifs in the shape of elongated lozenges. Around a small lozenge in very bright coral, a double border of onyx alternates with lines of brilliants. Or a rectangular barrette brooch with rounded ends, mounted on platinum, with a decoration consisting of three triangles of engraved coral, surrounded by a double row of brilliants standing out against a shiny background in onyx. And a bracelet of rigorously geometrical design is composed of rectangular motifs in coral alternating with segments set with brilliants, linked by hinges in onyx.

White, red and black are the component elements of the harmony of a pendant made of diamonds, onyx and rubies, decorated with intertwined snakes and lotus flowers inspired by Egyptian decorative motifs.

Towards the end of the 1920s Van Cleef et Arpels conceived a noteworthy

Cigarette case in gold and black enamel, decorated in the centre with a pagoda in diamonds.
Van Cleef et Arpels (1925). Photo: Sotheby's.

series of heavy bracelets in which geometrical motifs in platinum, set with
brilliants and baguette-cut diamonds are alternated with a showy decoration
of rubies.

A magnificent selection of boxes and cases for all kinds of purpose (cards,
cigarettes, powder, etc.) is also characteristic of the work of Van Cleef et Arpels
between 1925 and 1928. A considerable number of pieces were inspired by
Oriental art: for example, the series of boxes whose lids decorated with inlaid
mother-of-pearl suggest a Chinese landscape with a temple or a pagoda with
gilded outlines and the classical trebase.

A rectangular card-case in gold, produced in about 1928 reflects the Persian
influence. It is of pink and soft blue enamels with a symmetrical broken line
in the form of pyramid-shaped steps separating the colours, and is embellished
with sapphires and diamonds.

A cigarette-case, designed in 1928, in gold and polychromatic translucent
enamel, is inspired by Renaissance motifs, which are taken up on the inside
of the lid. The most magnificent of these cases is undoubtedly a toilet-case in
mauve jade embellished with three stylised roses in rubies and brilliants, with
emerald leaves.

Besides these highly sophisticated models, there also existed a whole series
of pieces which were more simply decorated, though not lacking in charm and
elegance. This is undeniably true of the models lacquered in black or black and
red, with simple side decorations of geometrical motifs in small brilliants.

Brooches in diamonds, rubies and emeralds, mounted on platinum.
Van Cleef et Arpels Archives (1925).

Brooch in diamonds, emeralds, onyx and enamel, mounted on platinum. Signed: Lacloche, Paris. Private Collection.

Brooch decorated with three triangles of engraved coral, onyx and diamonds, mounted in platinum. Van Cleef et Arpels Archives (1925).

Bracelet in coral, onyx and brilliants. Van Cleef et Arpels Archives (1925).

Bracelet influenced by the Egypt of the Pharoahs in calibré-cut diamonds, sapphires, rubies, onyx, mounted on platinum. Van Cleef et Arpels Archives (1925).

Pendant brooch in diamonds, onyx and enamel, mounted on platinum. Van Cleef et Arpels Archives.

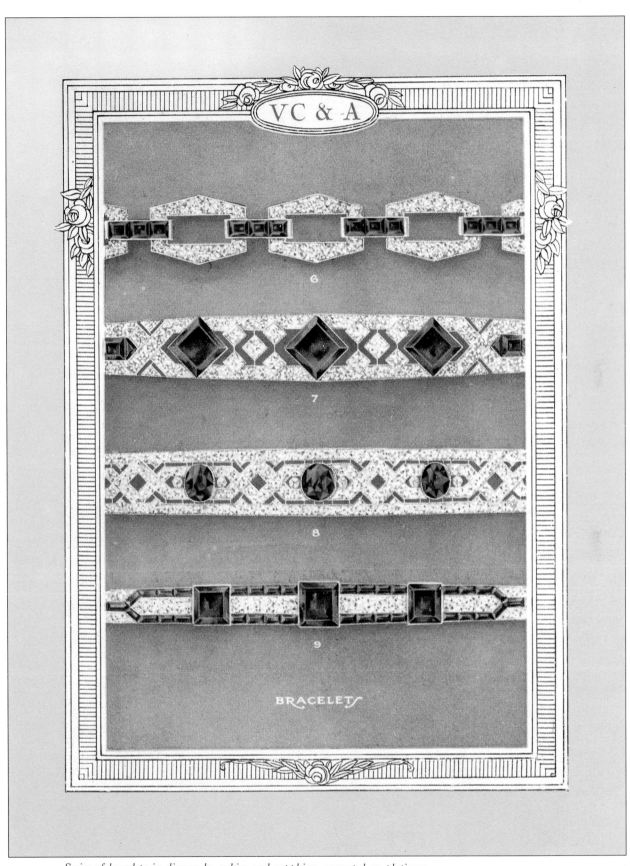

Series of bracelets in diamonds, rubies and sapphires, mounted on platinum.
Van Cleef et Arpels Archives.

Designs for bracelets in baguette-cut brilliants and rubies, mounted on platinum.
Van Cleef et Arpels Archives.

Toilet case in gold, black and blue enamel and diamonds, decorated with mother-of-pearl marquetry representing a Chinese scene. Van Cleef et Arpels Archives (1925).

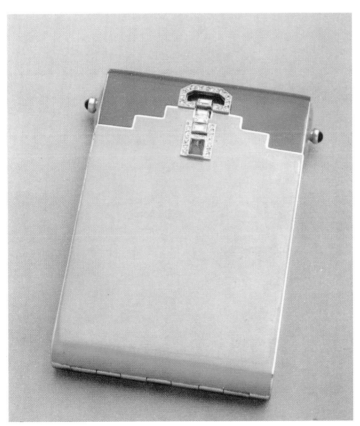

Card case in gold, pink and blue enamel, diamonds and sapphires. Van Cleef et Arpels Archives (1928).

Cigarette case in gold and translucent multi-coloured enamels. Van Cleef et Arpels Archives (1928).

121

Cigarette case in gold and red and black enamel, representing a Chinese-style landscape. Lacloche (1925). Photo: Sotheby's.

Toilet case in gold and mauve jade, decorated with stylised flowers in diamonds, rubies and emeralds: edged with black and green enamel. Van Cleef et Arpels Archives (1925).

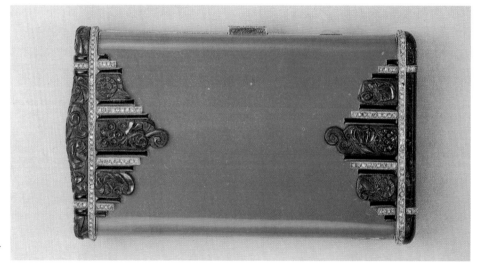

Toilet case in gold and red enamel, decorated with floral motifs in lapis lazuli and diamonds. Van Cleef et Arpels. Photo: Sotheby's.

122

OTHER JEWELLERS

Beside these great firms, still active in the Paris market, there were others, well-known in their time, but now disappeared.

Such is the case of Dusausoy (founded in 1840), Lacloche Frères (which closed its doors at the beginning of the sixties), and Janesich (which disappeared at the beginning of the last war). André Aucoc (an established jewellery and silver firm), where Lalique served his apprenticeship, is another. Amongst the other jewellers, famous half a century ago, who played their part in forming the 1925 aesthetics, were: Bensimon; Jean Desmares; Le Roy; Robert Linzeler; Marchak; Ostertag; Marc; Worms; Henry Kahn; Velley and Herz-Belperron.

Finally, we should mention René Boivin, a firm founded in 1892 and still active today. René Boivin, married to Jeanne, sister of the dress-designer Paul Poiret, worked for ten years with the famous jewellery designer Suzanne Belperron.

Although it is in France that Art Deco jewellery attained its peak of splendour, it is also true to say that other European countries played their part in creating this style of jewellery. Alongside the cream of French jewellery, the 1925 International Exhibition in Paris showed a wide panorama of contemporary foreign jewellery.

Austria was represented by a series of pieces, consisting largely of brooches and pendants marked by rigorous geometrical design and contrasting colours, in the style of the Wiener Werkstätte. These were principally designed by the architect, Joseph Hoffmann.

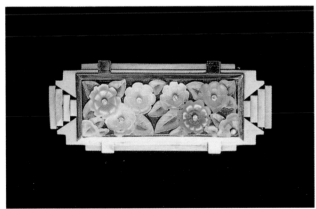

Brooch in two colours of gold. In the centre engraved floral motifs in hardstones and diamonds (1925). Claudio Zannettin Collection (Cortina).

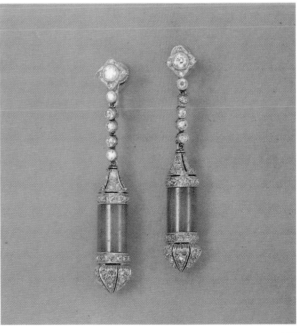

Right:
Pendant earrings in jade and diamonds, mounted on platinum. France (1925). Photo: Sotheby's.

Pendant brooch in onyx, coral and diamonds. France.
Claudio Zannettin Collection (Cortina).

Brooch comprising a ring in rock crystal, decorated on the
sides with diamonds, and mounted on platinum. France.
Photo: Sotheby's

Pendant watch in diamonds, emeralds and pearls, mounted on
platinum.
Adler Collection (1925).

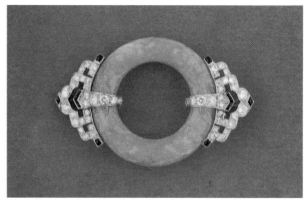

Brooch consisting of a jade ring decorated on the sides with
motifs in diamonds and onyx, mounted on platinum.
Adler Collection (Geneva).

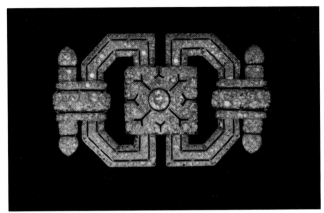

Diamond brooch, mounted on platinum. France.
Photo: Sotheby's.

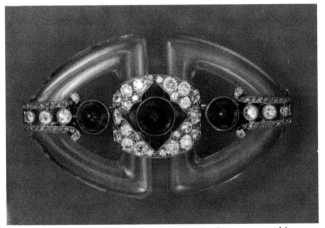

Brooch in rock crystal, diamonds and cabochon-cut.sapphires,
mounted on platinum. Photo: Sotheby's.

Right.
Pendant brooch mounted on platinum with emeralds.
Cusi di via Clerici Archives (Milan).

Belgium won a prize for the creation of an anchor-shaped pendant in lapis lazuli and brilliants, bearing the stamp of Wolfers et Coosemans. According to the monograph on Philippe Wolfers by his son Marcel, he tried in 1920 to impose a new direction on jewellery. From then on, it was to be marked out like a diagram, bare, functional in form, so as to allow the essential parts to be produced industrially, although the advent of industrial design was still a long way away. In 1912, he was working innovatively, and showing the first sketches of what were to become the gold-work, porcelain, glasses and crystals of the *Pavillon d'honneur de la Belgique* at the Universal Exhibition of Decorative Arts in Paris in 1925.

Denmark exhibited pieces of jewellery in chased silver and gold, chains decorated with flowers, none of which gave any hint of the imminent arrival of the Scandinavian modernist movement. The work of the great Danish jeweller, Georg Jensen (1866-1935) should not be passed over.

Great Britain was represented by the firm Wright and Hodge with necklaces still imbued with the neo-Gothic style of the nineteenth century.

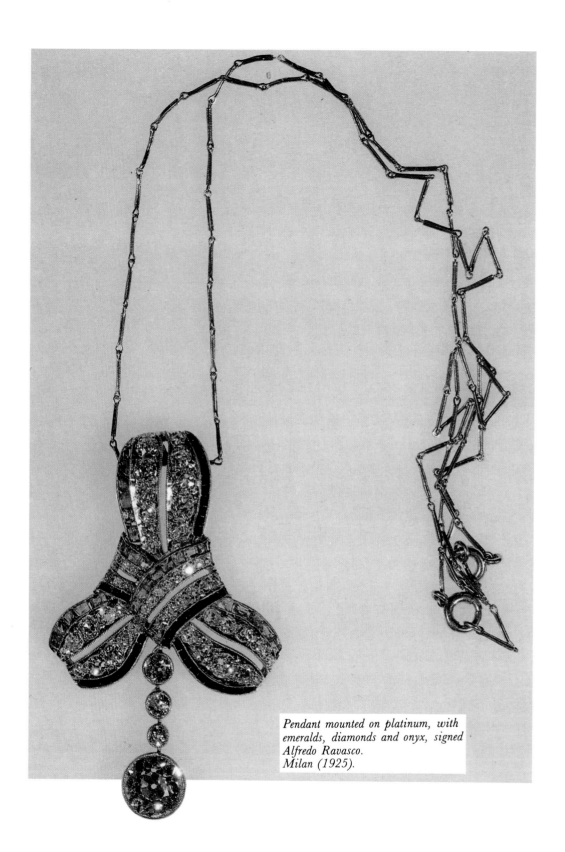

*Pendant mounted on platinum, with emeralds, diamonds and onyx, signed Alfredo Ravasco.
Milan (1925).*

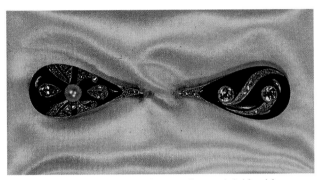

Jabot pin consisting of two plaques of onyx inlaid with diamonds and a single pearl, mounted on platinum. Private Collection.

Brooch in brilliants, coral and onyx, mounted on platinum. Franco Bernardini Collection (Milan).

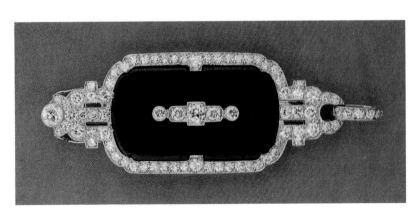

1. Bracelet in diamonds, rubies, calibré-cut sapphires, mounted on platinum. Carlo Eleuteri Collection (Rome).

2. Brooch in diamonds and calibré and cabochon-cut emeralds, mounted on platinum. Carlo Eleuteri Collection (Rome).

3. Pair of clips in rock crystal and diamonds, mounted on platinum. Carlo Eleuteri Collection (Rome).

Pendant mounted on white and yellow gold in onyx and brilliants. Adler Collection (Geneva).

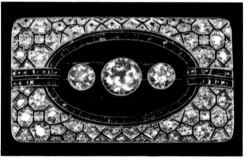

*Series of diamond
brooches mounted on
platinum.
Labiner Collection.
Munich.*

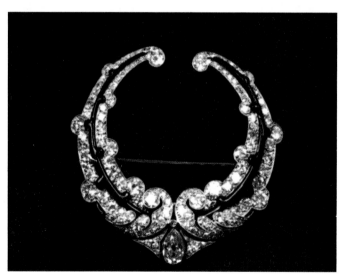

Italy was there with jewellery pointing to the influence of the 'Liberty' style and attachment to regional traditions. Already in 1923, an important exhibition held at the Villa Reale in Monza had recognised the merit of the Milanese jeweller, Alfredo Ravasco (1873-1958), whose creations were already a precocious form of Art Deco.

Born in Genoa, the son of a goldsmith, he studied 'arts' at the Brera in Milan. By 1906 he was exhibiting. It was in the 1920s that his creative spirit brough him recognition. He produced jewellery, flat and geometrical pendants and bracelets, but also knick-knacks, boxes and vases in malachite, onyx, jade, lapis lazuli, crystal, coral, etc.

His preferred subjects were animals (snakes, peacocks, octopuses, etc.), flowers and vegetables. He was Director of the School for Cutting and

Pendant earrings in diamonds mounted on platinum. France. Photo: Sotheby's.

Pendant earrings in diamonds and onyx, mounted on platinum. Photo: Sotheby's.

Pendant earrings in diamonds and sapphires, mounted on platinum. Photo: Sotheby's.

Pendant earrings in pearls and diamonds, mounted on platinum. Photo: Sotheby's.

Engraving Coral at Torre del Greco, and also took part in the 1925 Paris Exhibition.

The Swiss contribution was disappointing as far as jewellery was concerned. Indeed, Switzerland only exhibited enamelled pieces, having as their subject Alpine landscapes. On the other hand, their selection of watches and, above all, wrist-watches, was dazzling.

One of the countries notable by its absence from the Exhibition was Germany. Nevertheless, at this period, their jewellery industry was

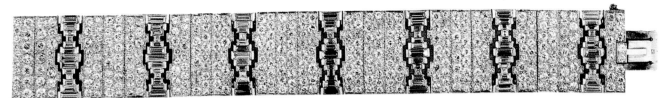

Flexible bracelet in baguette-cut brilliants, mounted on platinum. France. Photo: Sotheby's.

Bracelet in diamonds and emeralds, mounted on platinum. Adler Collection (Geneva).

*Brooch in platinum, diamonds, onyx
and rubies: in the centre a large
emerald.
Adler Collection (Geneva).*

*Wrist-watch with hidden face, in diamonds and onyx mounted on platinum.
Photo: Sotheby's.*

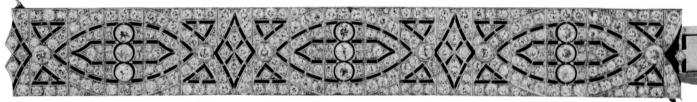

Flexible bracelet in diamonds mounted on platinum. France. Photo: Sotheby's.

Diamond bracelet with stylised motifs in onyx, mounted on platinum. France. Photo: Sotheby's.

*Bracelet in the Oriental style with articulated plaques in lapis lazuli decorated with black
and red enamel, alternating with circular motifs in diamonds, jade and sapphires: mounted on
platinum. France (1925).*

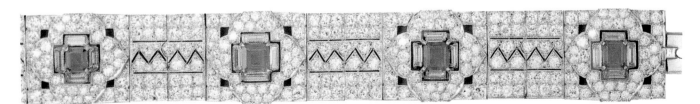

Bracelet in baguette-cut brilliants and emeralds, mounted on platinum. France. Photo: Sotheby's.

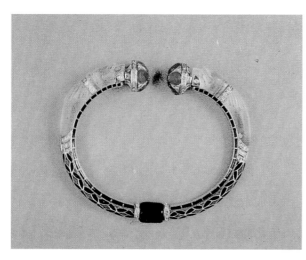

*Bracelet in rock crystal, black
and green enamel, diamonds
and cabochon-cut rubies.
Photo: Sotheby's.*

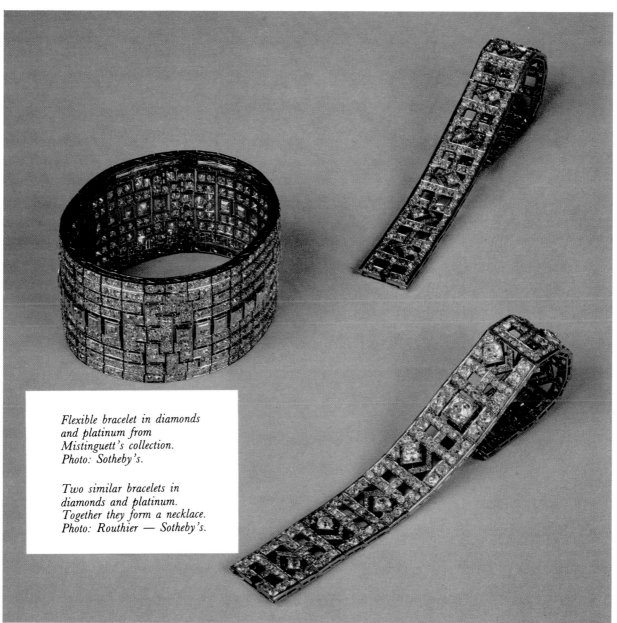

*Flexible bracelet in diamonds
and platinum from
Mistinguett's collection.
Photo: Sotheby's.*

*Two similar bracelets in
diamonds and platinum.
Together they form a necklace.
Photo: Routhier — Sotheby's.*

Diamond bracelet decorated with fountain motifs in calibré-cut sapphires. France.

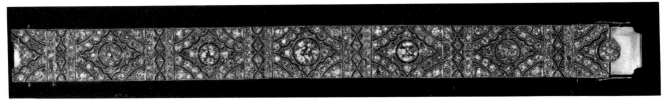

Diamond bracelet mounted on platinum. France. Photo: Sotheby's.

Articulated bracelet mounted on platinum with diamonds, jade and rock crystal.
Photo: Sotheby's.

Bracelet with cabochon-cut moonstones and diamonds, mounted on white gold. Photo: Sotheby's.

Bracelet in diamonds and lapis lazuli. Photo: Sotheby's.

flourishing, both in Pforzheim and Hanau. However, in the former of these two cities, jewellery was rather inclined towards the mass production of articles whose structure in base metal was plated with precious metal (rolling technique). Hanau, on the other hand, was producing items of jewellery in valuable materials, and in a style which reflected the influence of cubism and the rational innovations of the Bauhaus. While discussing German jewellery of this period, we should draw attention to three rings designed in 1925 by the German painter Karl Schmidt-Rottluf. In the book by A. Ward, *et al,* entitled *The Ring from Antiquity to the Twentieth Century,* they are mentioned as being strongly influenced by African art. The first ring, in the shape of a buckle, is in metal storied with triangular engravings of a primitive and irregular design. The second, in the form of a large oval platform, is crowned with an opal fixed by four claws in silver. The last of the three is in the shape of a mushroom, with a nephrite cap, held by claws of relatively crude workmanship.

We should also draw attention to the great vogue for amber in the production of necklaces, brooches and bracelets. This organic material (like ivory and jet) was suited to the geometrical style, and mounted on gold and silver.

The type of amber containing insects was particularly sought after in the Germany of the 1920s.

Chapter V

Jewellery of the 1930s
White Jewellery

The 1930s were marked by the vogue for white jewellery, which achieved an undeniable triumph at the Exhibition at the Palais Galliera in Paris in 1929.

In *L'Orfèvrerie, la Joaillerie* (The Craft of the Goldsmith and Jewellery), published in 1942, Georges Fouquet wrote: 'If the theme of the 1925 Exhibition had been "colour", that of the Galliera Exhibition proved to be "white". With few exceptions, jewellery was composed solely of diamonds. But a new harmony was revealed, by the use of a judicious mixture of baguette-cut and round-cut brilliants. Through the felicitous use of these different cuts, of these different ways of playing with precious stones, it was possible to obtain varied, one could almost say coloured, effects.'

The models were structurally geometrical, usually in platinum or grey gold. They were sumptuously covered with pavé set diamonds laid out in symmetrical lines, separated by very delicate divisions, always in precious white metal. Nevertheless, the designs were less minutely carried out than in the case of the white jewellery of the 1920s.

In the 1930s, bracelets in platinum and brilliants were all the rage. They were usually strap bracelets, characterised by a strictly geometrical design on an openwork framework in platinum, mostly articulated and set with brilliants of varying sizes and cuts.

Different geometrical designs offered infinite combinations and a wide range of decorative themes. There were strap bracelets decorated with parallel rectilinear rows of brilliants against which stood out larger brilliants.

Other interesting designs featured busy, criss-crossed lines, punctuated by triangular or trapezoid motifs.

Some flexible bracelets were composed of rectangular motifs with a foliated openwork decoration surrounded by diamonds (if baguette-cut they might be disposed in a fan-shape). These motifs were joined by rectangular, hexagonal or octagonal links. The whole would be set with brilliant-cut diamonds. Usually there was a larger diamond in the centre of each rectangular motif.

As time went on, it was possible to discern a softening of the strictly geometrical style of decoration, which became progressively invaded by curves, garlands, loops and spirals.

To avoid falling into the monotony of the 'completely white', jewellers sometimes introduced a touch of colour: an emerald, a ruby or a sapphire.

During this period in which white jewellery held sway, the same motifs would naturally reappear in bracelets and necklaces, the brooch in a given set of jewellery being simply a repetition of the motif of the bracelet.

Brooches usually consisted of rectangular, hexagonal or oval plaques, with a base (in platinum or grey gold) pavé set with brilliants.

Obviously, alongside the classical pieces, there were also extraordinary and unusual models. In the jewellery produced by Cartier between 1929 and 1930, it is worth drawing attention to an S-shaped brooch mounted on platinum and pavé set with brilliants, and a clip-brooch in platinum and brilliants, in the form of a cone-shaped capital.

Page from a catalogue showing models of bracelets in diamonds mounted on platinum. Mauboussin. Mauboussin Archives.

Of the same year is the square clip-brooch mounted on platinum, framed with baguette diamonds with, in the centre, a large round brilliant, and the shoulder brooch mounted on platinum, with a mobile rosette motif, composed of three superimposed plaques, pavé set with brilliants, in the centre of an openwork motif set with brilliants of different size and cut. The sides consist of two articulated leaves, pavé set with round and baguette-cut brilliants. Each end finishes with a pear-shaped brilliant.

The Cartier workshops also created the triangular clip-brooch of 1930, mounted on platinum, decorated with a Greek motif in baguette-cut brilliants, with a large round brilliant in the centre.

A clip-brooch of 1930, mounted on platinum, in the shape of a convex rectangle, was pavé set with round brilliants. The bottom part consisted of two shorter segments — one in round brilliants, the other in baguette-cut brilliants.

Amongst the Cartier creations very fashionable at the beginning of the 1930s, was the clip-brooch in the form of a vertical half-disc, in baguette-cut brilliants with a mobile ring pavé set with round brilliants, and a barrette in platinum and brilliants bearing a trapezoid motif also in brilliants, decorated with a fringe of pearls alternating with lines of brilliants.

Amongst the models created by Mauboussin of the same period, there survives a whole series of flexible pendant brooches, in platinum and brilliants, of different sizes. One is composed of a D-shaped motif, pavé set with diamonds. From it hangs a rectangular pendant, consisting of a central chain

Page from a catalogue showing different models of brooches in platinum, diamonds, pearls and sapphires. Mauboussin. Mauboussin Archives.

with rectangular links, flanked on both sides by three articulated rows (caterpillars) of baguette-cut brilliants.

Another brooch by the same jeweller is a platinum circle, pavé set with diamonds, from which hangs a tear-drop motif in round and baguette-cut brilliants.

Equally characteristic of this series is a pendant brooch composed of a platinum barrette pavé set with round brilliants alternating with baguette-cut brilliants. Above the barrette is a composition of alternating baguette-cut and round brilliants of different sizes.

A brooch by Boucheron representing a stylised bow, the loops of which consist entirely of baguette-cut diamonds, dates from 1932.

Then, within these decorative motifs, there was a gradual emergence of curves and scrolls, softening and rounding the corners of what had previously been rigorously angular. Similarly a hint of colour tempered the dominance of the diamond. For this purpose a single stone was always taken, usually an emerald, a ruby or a sapphire.

Another distinctive feature of the 1930s was the proliferation of clips. Clips could be worn singly or in pairs. Joined together they formed a brooch. This leads us to the subject of multi-purpose jewellery, of which, in the 1930s, there was a considerable repertoire. Necklaces could be worn as diadems, bracelets could become necklaces, clips could be made into a brooch, and so on. The most interesting example was that of clips. Placed side by side they formed an

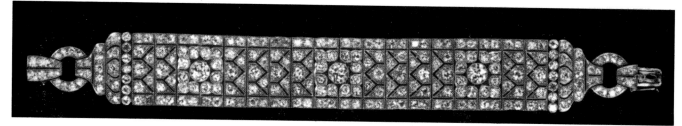

Diamond and platinum bracelet. Photo: Sotheby's.

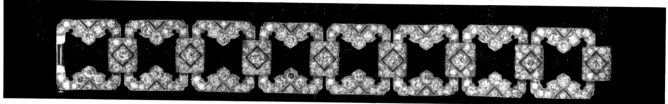

Platinum and diamond bracelet. Photo: Sotheby's.

Bracelet consisting of articulated motifs in diamonds, mounted on platinum. Photo: Sotheby's.

Articulated bracelet in diamonds and platinum. Photo: Sotheby's.

Articulated bracelet in diamonds, consisting of three rectangular sections joined by square links in diamonds: mounted on platinum. Photo: Sotheby's.

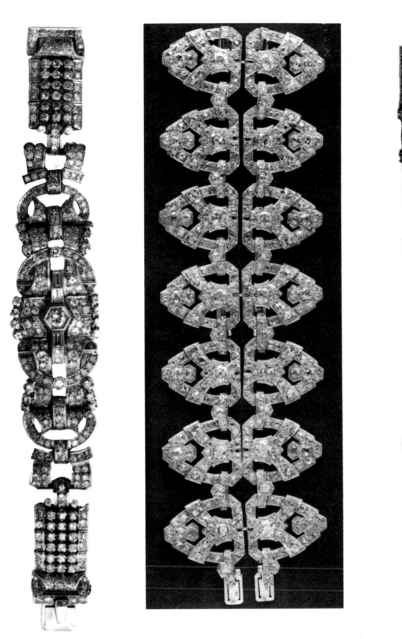

Left and right: Platinum and diamond bracelet. Photo: Sotheby's.

Centre: Bracelet with geometrical motifs set with diamonds mounted on platinum. Mellerio dits Meller. Mellerio dits Meller Archives.

imposing brooch. Applied to a bangle, they served as its principal decoration, while hung from the centre of a necklace they played the role of pendant.

In the context of multi-purpose jewellery, we should mention a necklace, created in 1929 by Cartier, which could also be worn as a diadem. The necklace serving these two purposes was a platinum choker, consisting of fifteen rectangular motifs set with round brilliants.

In 1931, Cartier created two flexible barrettes in platinum composed of a series of claw brooches or clip-brooches, set with round and baguette-cut brilliants.

137

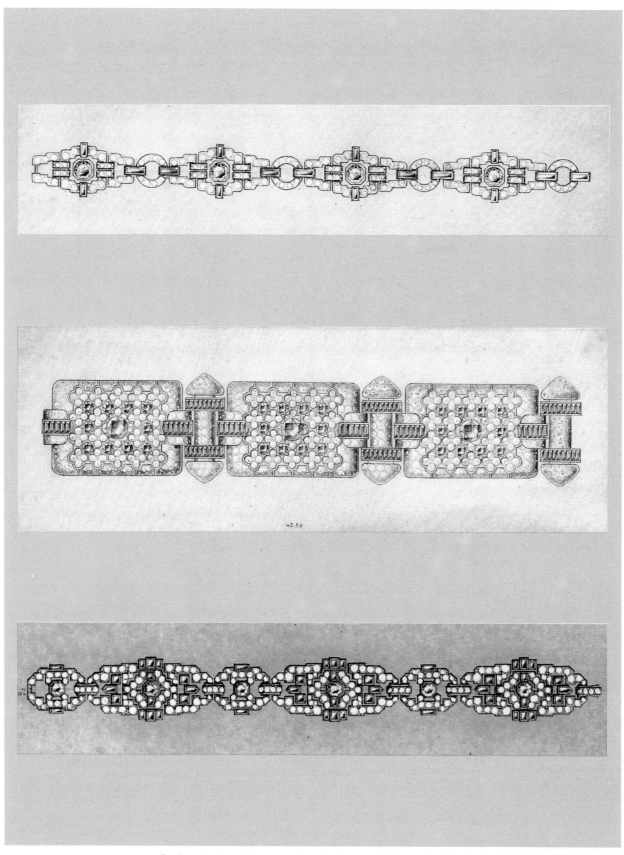

Designs for bracelets mounted on platinum and decorated with diamonds. Circa *1932-34.*
Cusi di via Clerici Archives (Milan).

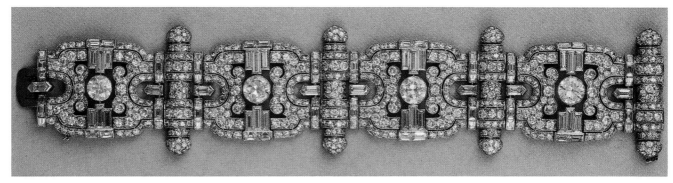

Bracelet in diamonds mounted on platinum. Photo: Sotheby's.

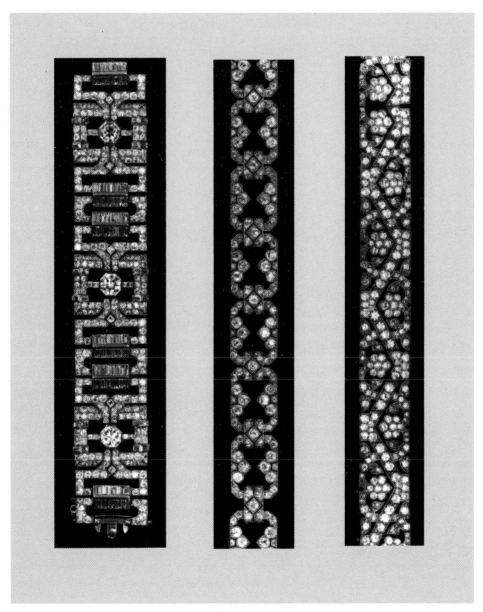

Left: Bracelet in round and baguette-cut brilliants mounted on platinum. Photo: Sotheby's.

Centre: Bracelet in diamonds mounted on platinum. Photo: Routhier-Sotheby's.

Right: Articulated bracelet with links in diamonds, mounted on platinum.

1. *Bracelet consisting of three articulated segments decorated with diamonds and mounted on platinum. Photo: Sotheby's.*

2. *Diamond bracelet mounted on platinum. France. Photo: Sotheby's.*

3. *Bracelet in platinum and brilliants. Photo: Sotheby's.*

4. *Brooch in platinum and brilliants. Photo: Sotheby's.*

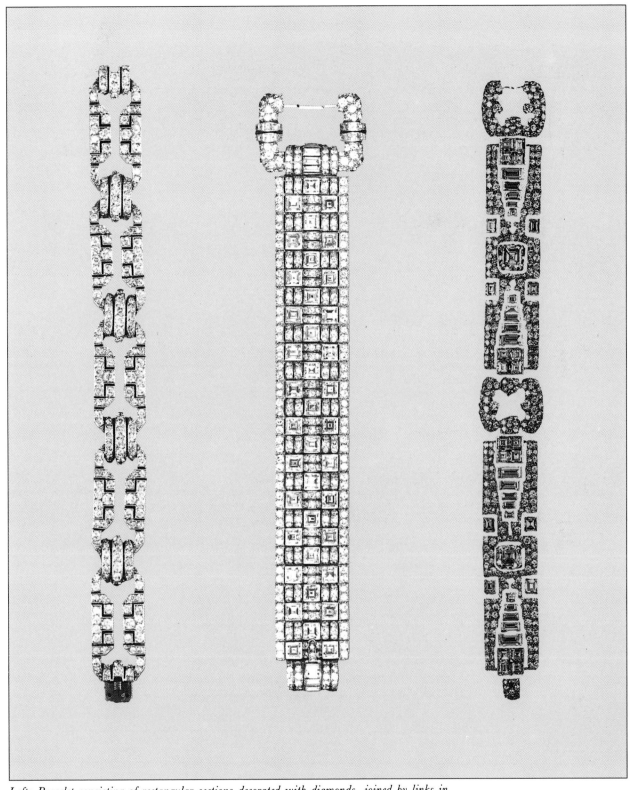

Left: Bracelet consisting of rectangular sections decorated with diamonds, joined by links in diamonds, mounted on platinum. Photo: Sotheby's.

Centre: Bracelet in diamonds mounted on platinum. Photo: Sotheby's.

Right: Strap bracelet decorated with round and baguette-cut brilliants, mounted on platinum. Cartier (1929). Cartier Archives.

Brooch in round and baguette-cut brilliants mounted on platinum. Cartier (1930). Photo: Sotheby's.

Diamond and platinum clip. Cartier (1930). Photo: Finarte.

Six clips of unequal size, each representing the same flower in diamonds, with a ruby in the centre, were worn during the day as false buttons on a black dress or a light tailored costume, and in the evening were distributed between two bands of platinum to embellish a bracelet.

In the 1930s the necklace was an important element of feminine adornment. Necklaces usually took the form of chains in precious metal of moderate length (gone were the days of the pearl sautoirs), decorated in the centre with elaborate pendants, one of the last vestiges of the inheritance of the 1920s.

Chains with rectangular, square or round links were always set with brilliants of different sizes. Pendants were either pavé set with diamonds or a large gemstone surrounded by smaller brilliants or chenilles.

A necklace created by Mauboussin in 1929 is the perfect illustration of this. It consists of a platinum chain with irregular links set with brilliants. The central pendant is composed of a large coloured cabochon-cut stone, surrounded by a geometrical motif in brilliants, completed by a flexible fringe of baguette-cut diamonds.

Brooch in round and baguette-cut brilliants mounted on platinum. Janesich. Photo: Sotheby's.

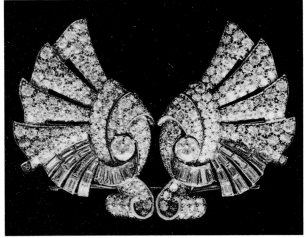

*Pair of clips in round and baguette-cut brilliants mounted on platinum.
Photo: Sotheby's.*

*Brooch in the shape of a rose, mounted on platinum, decorated with diamonds, emeralds, rubies and onyx.
Van Cleef et Arpels (about 1930).*

The series of large necklaces created by Boucheron between 1930 and 1931 is equally characteristic. These are mounted on platinum with large round brilliants and thin pencil lines of onyx.

Like bracelets and brooches, necklaces followed two rules, that of absolute whiteness or that of whiteness set off by a single colour introduced by a precious stone. This was equally true of chain necklaces and pendants.

It should be noted here that during this decade the London branch of Cartier was more innovative than the parent company in the field of high fashion necklaces.

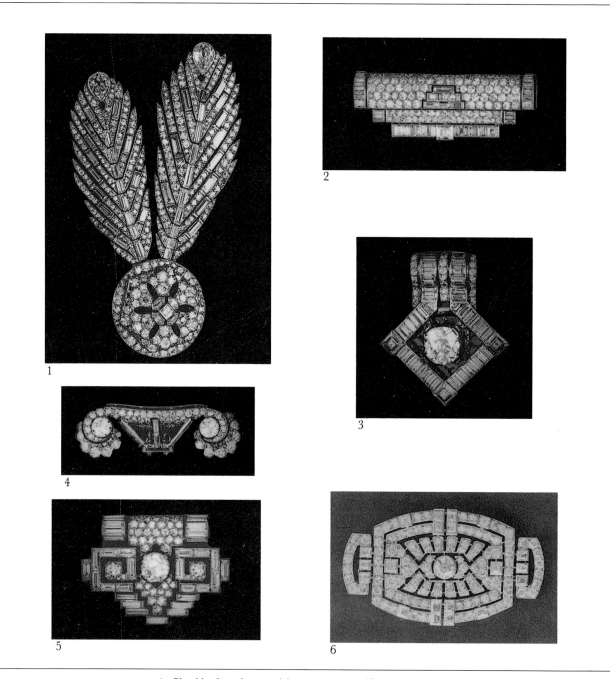

1. Shoulder brooch comprising a rosette motif and two leaves in brilliants, mounted on platinum. Cartier (1929). Cartier Archives.

2. Brooch in round and baguette-cut brilliants, mounted on platinum. Cartier (1930). Cartier Archives.

3. Clip brooch in round and baguette-cut diamonds, mounted on platinum. Cartier (1929). Cartier Archives.

4. Clip brooch in brilliants and platinum. Cartier. Cartier Archives.

5. Clip brooch in round and baguette-cut brilliants, mounted on platinum. Cartier (1929). Cartier Archives.

6. Brooch in diamonds and platinum. Mellerio dits Meller. Mellerio dits Meller Archives.

Brooch in brilliants mounted on platinum.
Mellerio dits Meller.
Mellerio dits Meller Archives.

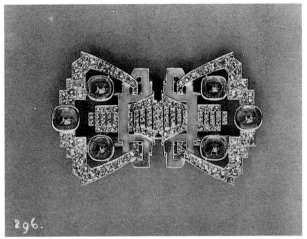

Pair of clips in diamonds, enamel and cabochon-cut
sapphires, mounted on platinum. Mellerio dits Meller.
Mellerio dits Meller Archives.

Pair of clips in diamonds and platinum.
Photo: Sotheby's.

Rectangular brooch in platinum and brilliants.
Photo: Sotheby's.

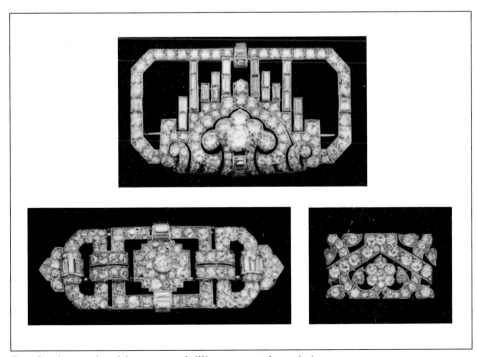

Brooches in round and baguette-cut brilliants mounted on platinum.

145

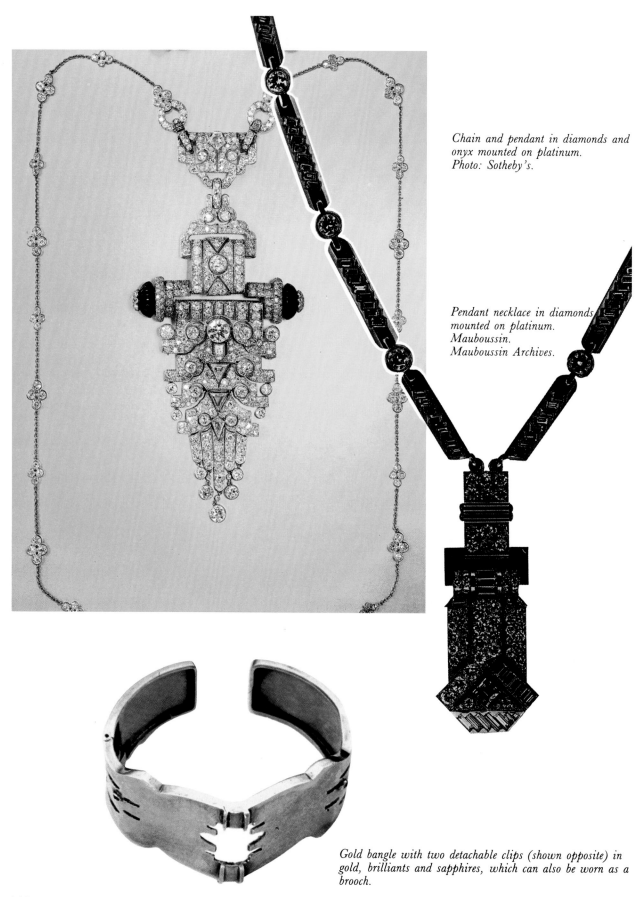

Chain and pendant in diamonds and
onyx mounted on platinum.
Photo: Sotheby's.

Pendant necklace in diamonds
mounted on platinum.
Mauboussin.
Mauboussin Archives.

Gold bangle with two detachable clips (shown opposite) in
gold, brilliants and sapphires, which can also be worn as a
brooch.

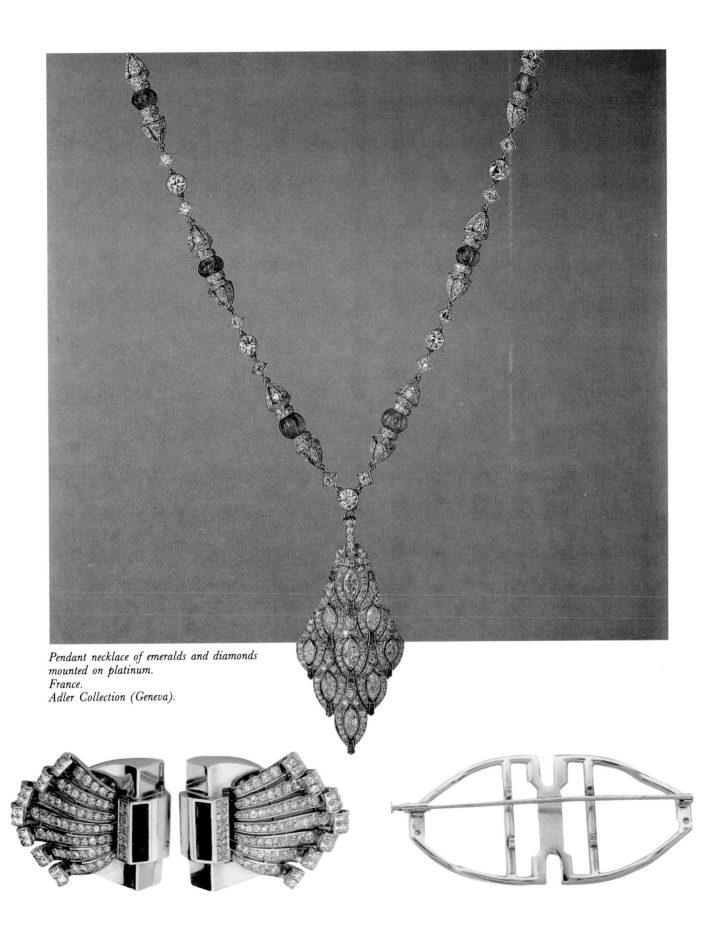

*Pendant necklace of emeralds and diamonds
mounted on platinum.
France.
Adler Collection (Geneva).*

Sautoir in diamonds and platinum embellished with a detachable pendant.
Two brooches in diamonds and platinum.
Mauboussin.
Mauboussin Archives.

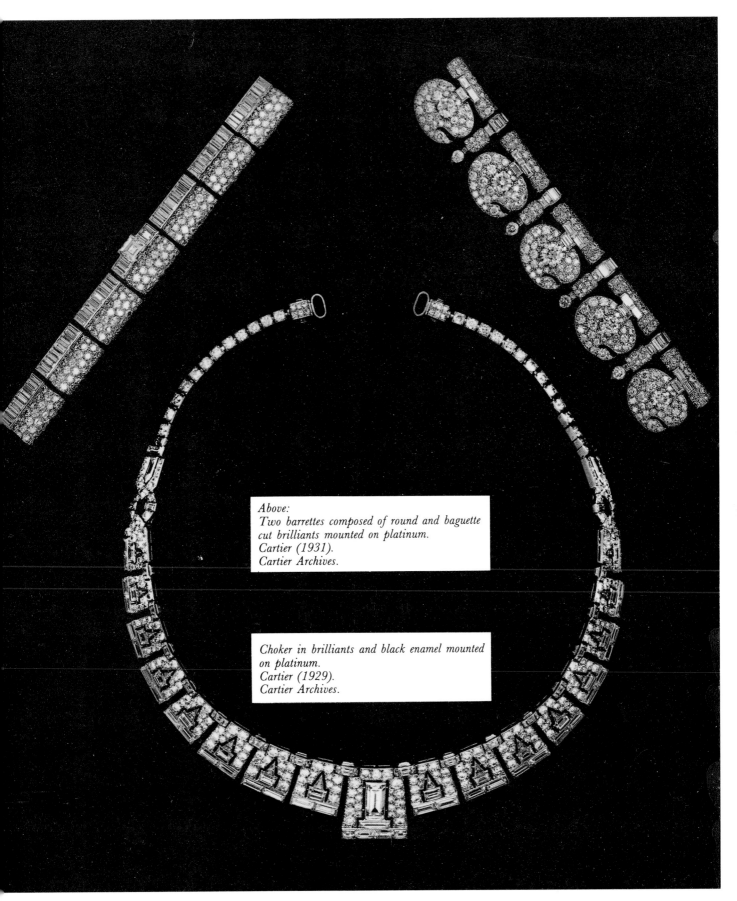

Above:
Two barrettes composed of round and baguette cut brilliants mounted on platinum.
Cartier (1931).
Cartier Archives.

Choker in brilliants and black enamel mounted on platinum.
Cartier (1929).
Cartier Archives.

Design for a demi-parure mounted on platinum with brilliants and rubies. (1933).
Cusi di via Clerici Archives (Milan).

Design for a necklace mounted on platinum with brilliants and a sapphire.
Cusi di via Clerici Archives (Milan).

Rounded diamond and platinum ring.
Van Cleef et Arpels.
Photo: Sotheby's.

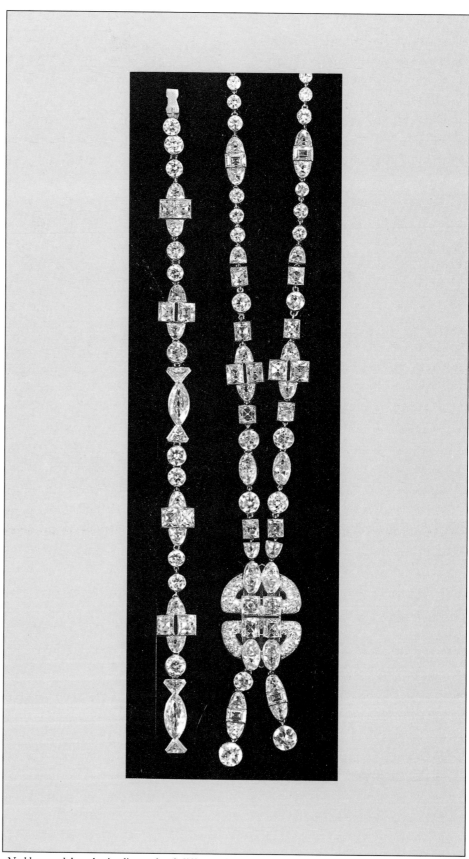

Necklace and bracelet in diamonds of different sizes, mounted on platinum. Van Cleef et Arpels.
Photo: Sotheby's

Platinum and diamond brooch. Cartier, London (1930). Photo: Sotheby's.

Platinum and diamond necklace, which can be divided into two bracelets. Photo: Sotheby's.

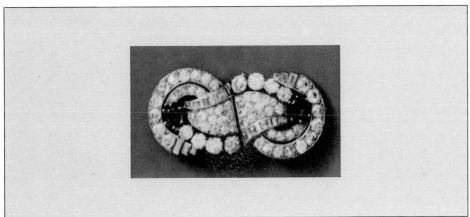

Clip in diamonds, rubies and emeralds, mounted on platinum. Photo: Sotheby's.

POLYCHROMATIC JEWELLERY

Although white jewellery is emblematic of the 1930s, it is nevertheless true to say that jewellers, still influenced by the tendencies of the preceding decade, continued to produce a considerable amount of polychromatic jewellery. Apart from the continuity of a certain tradition, other factors seem also to have contributed to the development of polychromatic jewellery. A particular case was the 1931 Colonial Exhibition in Paris, which offered a complete cultural panorama of the various French colonies, from African art to Indo-Chinese art. This initiative doubtless awakened an interest in the French public for exotic art, and had a certain influence on fashion and even taste. It should also be noted that during the same period the development of communications was bringing together the different continents — Europeans were starting to travel far abroad, discovering *in situ* the origins of their fascination with, for example, the art and culture of mysterious India.

Pendant necklace in diamonds, onyx and emeralds, mounted on platinum. Cartier. Photo: Sotheby's.

154

Pair of earrings of carved emeralds, diamonds and pearls. Cartier.

Necklace in graduated ribbed cabochon-cut emeralds, alternating with small discs in diamonds. Cartier.

On the other hand, the Maharajahs were beginning to acquire the habit of making long stays in the European capitals, and this, as we have already seen, also played a part in influencing the art of jewellery.

The great jewellers who maintained close relations with their Indian clientele created articles of jewellery in the Indian style, rich in marvellous coloured gemstones, usually cabochon-cut, sometimes engraved.

Necklace in emerald,
brilliants and black enamel,
with clusters of rubies and
onyx, mounted on platinum.
Cartier (1929).
Cartier Archives.

Pendant necklace in diamonds and
emeralds, mounted on platinum.
Mauboussin. Mauboussin Archives.

156

Hindu-style necklace consisting of motifs in gold and brilliants, pampilles, emeralds and rubies, engraved leaves, brilliants and fine pearls. Engraved emerald pendeloque on silken cord. Cartier (1936). Cartier Archives

In his recent book on Cartier, Hans Nadelhoffer refers to the very large number of articles of jewellery created specially for the Indian market. In 1930 Cartier was producing pieces in engraved emeralds for the Aga Khan. In 1931, he created for the Maharajah of Navanagar a diamond necklace composed round the famous Queen of Holland diamond. In 1935, the Maharajah of Patna entrusted to Cartier an Indian necklace in emeralds and rubies for modernisation. In 1937, Cartier created for the Maharajah of Navanagar a

Emerald, diamond, sapphire and ruby floral bracelet.
Van Cleef et Arpels. Photo: Christie's.

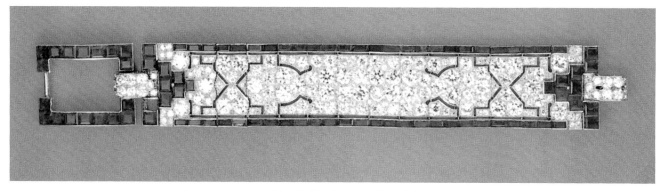

Diamond and sapphire flexible bracelet. Signed Cartier.
Photo: Christie's.

Emerald and diamond clip brooch with a
carved emerald leaf in the centre.
Cartier. Photo: Christie's.

Diamond and emerald brooch pendant with two cabochon emerald drops
suspended from a kite-shaped diamond.
Photo: Christie's.

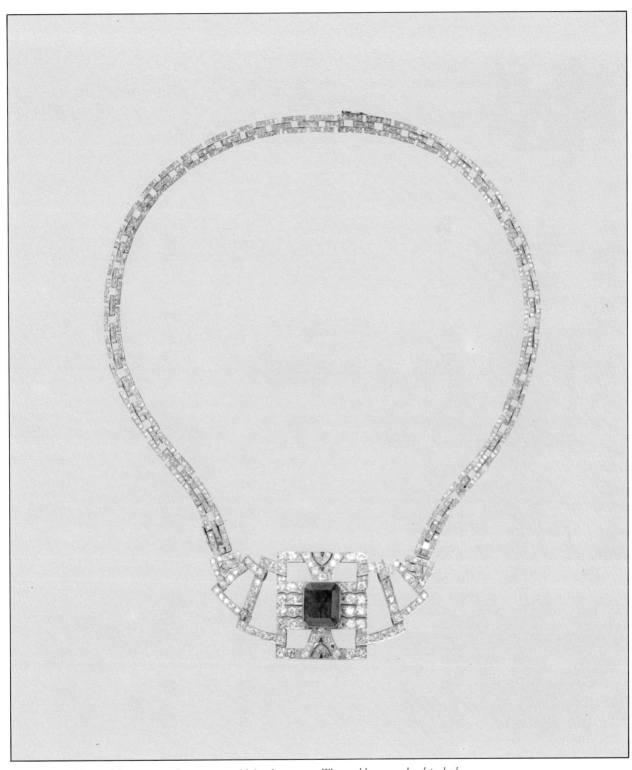

*Diamond necklace with a rectangular cut emerald in the centre. The necklace can be detached
for wear as two bracelets.
Photo: Christie's.*

Pendant necklace in diamonds and rubies mounted on platinum. Mauboussin. Mauboussin Archives.

Diamond necklace embellished with a large platinum-mounted coloured stone. Mauboussin Archives.

sarpech (turban ornament) with the famous Tiger's Eye diamond.

It is certain that these royal commissions exerted a general influence on the jewellery produced at this period. An example is the diadem produced by the Cartier London workshop in 1930, which took the form of a bandeau decorated with a fringe of cabochon-cut emeralds, adorned in the middle by a lyre-shaped motif, containing as centre-piece an imposing engraved emerald. This piece rivalled Indian jewellery in its magnificence, its originality and the choice of large stones in different colours.

Necklace decorated with brilliants of varying cut and rubies, mounted on platinum. The central motif is detachable. Cartier (1936). Cartier Archives.

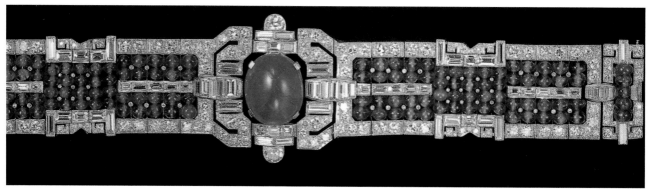

Diamond and ruby bracelet with a cabochon-cut ruby in the centre, mounted on platinum. France. Photo: Sotheby's.

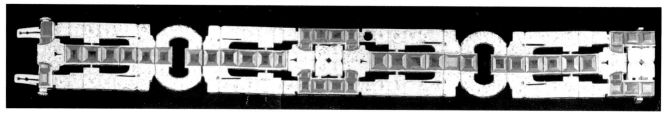

Bracelet in diamonds and square cut rubies mounted on platinum. Photo: Sotheby's.

Bracelet of diamonds and emerald drops, mounted on platinum. Photo: Sotheby's.

Opposite page:

1. Articulated bracelet in sapphires and diamonds mounted on platinum. Cartier, London (1935). Photo: Sotheby's.

2. Flexible bracelet in diamonds and sapphires mounted on platinum. Photo: Sotheby's.

3. Articulated bracelet composed of rectangular plaques decorated with diamonds joined by links of sapphires: mounted on platinum. France (1930). Photo: Sotheby's.

4. Flexible bracelet in diamonds and calibré-cut sapphires mounted on platinum. France (1928). Photo: Sotheby's.

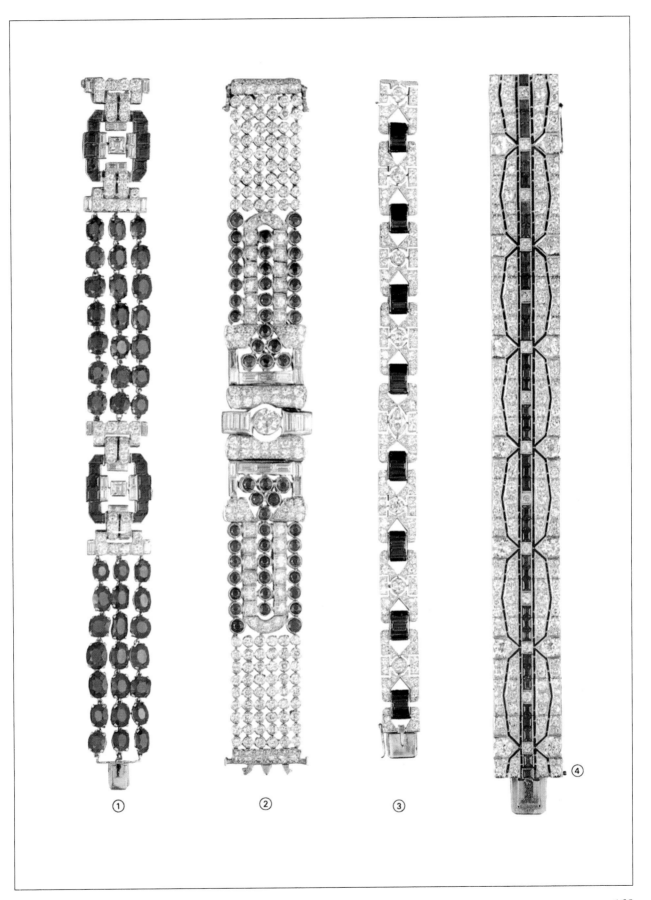

①   ②   ③   ④

Left: Multicoloured bracelet representing a garland of fruit and flowers in rubies, emeralds, engraved sapphires and diamonds. Cartier (1929). Photo: Sotheby's.

Centre: Bracelet in round and baguette-cut brilliants with engraved cabochon-cut rubies mounted on platinum. Cartier.

Right: Ruby, diamond and platinum bracelet. Drayson (London). Photo: Sotheby's.

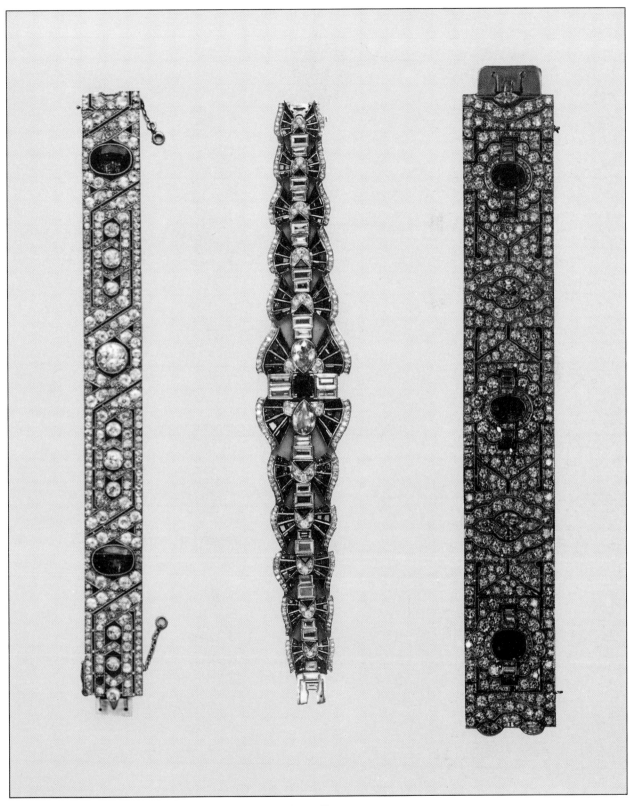

Left: Bracelet of diamonds and emeralds mounted on platinum. France.
Photo: Routhier — Sotheby's.

Centre: Bracelet in platinum, diamonds and rubies. Photo: Sotheby's.

Right: Platinum, diamond and sapphire bracelet. Photo: Sotheby's.

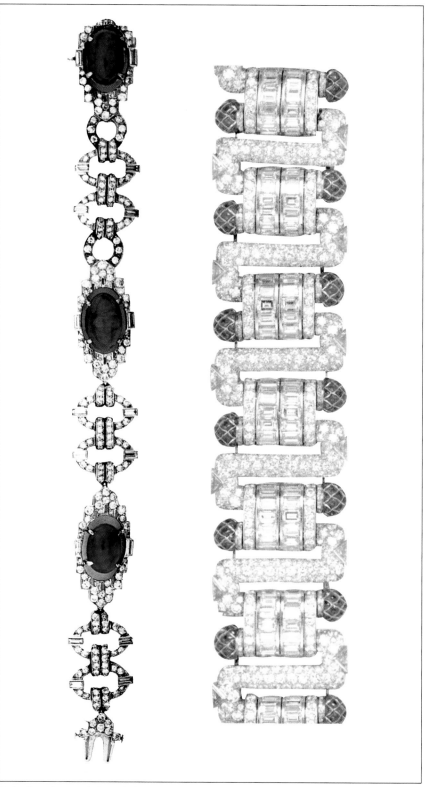

Left: Bracelet consisting of three plaques of diamonds and sapphires joined by links in diamonds, mounted on platinum. Janesich. Photo: Routhier-Sotheby's.

Centre: Articulated bracelet consisting of three plaques with cabochon-cut rubies and diamond links, mounted on platinum. Private Collection.

Right: Bracelet of rubies and brilliants mounted on platinum. France. Photo: Sotheby's.

Left: Diamond bracelet mounted on platinum. Cartier. Photo: Sotheby's.

Centre: Bracelet consisting of round and baguette-cut brilliants and cabochons of emeralds mounted on platinum. Cartier (1936). Cartier Archives.

Right: Articulated bracelet in platinum and diamonds with a cabochon-cut sapphire in the centre. Signed: Gattle. Photo: Sotheby's.

Alongside the fashion for Indian styles, there continued the production of multicoloured pieces of jewellery composed of small leaves and berries represented by engraved cabochon-cut rubies, emeralds and sapphires, the first examples of which went back as far as the beginning of the 1920s. In this style was a series of bracelets by Cartier, mounted on a platinum and diamond branch, decorated with leaves set with engraved cabochon-cut rubies and emeralds, and berries in onyx. There also exists a necklace with clusters of berries in emeralds, balls of sapphires and emeralds, engraved sapphires and leaves set with engraved cabochon-cut rubies, to which are joined thirteen briolette sapphires.

A double clip which the wife of the American musician Cole Porter commissioned from Cartier in 1935, was set with engraved sapphires, rubies and emeralds, surrounded by brilliant and baguette-cut diamonds.

In 1936, Cartier created earrings composed of engraved emeralds with a motif of diamonds in the form of a calyx, beneath an emerald ball and a flower in diamonds.

During the 1930s, most Parisian jewellers revealed the same taste for polychromatic pieces as in the 1920s.

Mellerio's produced a very fine interpretation with ravishing panier brooches mounted on platinum, in brilliants and cabochons of engraved emeralds, rubies and sapphires. The same is true of Mauboussin's, who continued to produce polychromatic models similar to those which had made their name in 1920.

Nevertheless, the opulence of this jewellery decorated with large precious stones seems to be in complete contradiction to the rather morose economic climate of the 1930s (aftermath of the Wall Street crash). Some saw these jewels as a safe, easily transportable, investment.

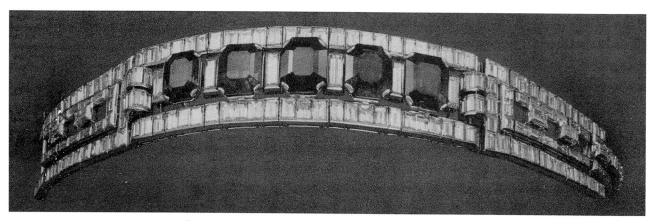

Diamond and sapphire bracelet mounted on platinum. Cartier. Photo: Sotheby's.

The stylistic development of jewellery thus took on a new direction, for these precise reasons, in terms of heavier forms, and more massive structures. Volutes, floral elements, foliated motifs and garlands, motifs borrowed directly from the Louis XVI style, made their appearance. In short, the new style of jewellery was completely different — while maintaining its roots in Art Deco, it began to be inspired by traditional schemas.

Pair of clips in diamonds and rubies, mounted on platinum.
Private Collection.

Pair of clips forming a brooch in diamonds and sapphires mounted on platinum. France.
Photo: Sotheby's.

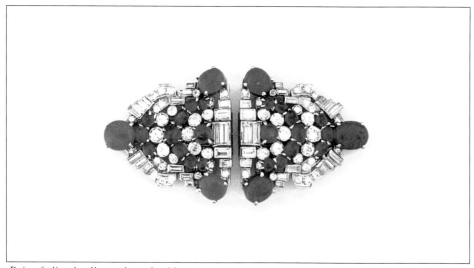

*Pair of clips in diamonds and rubies
mounted on platinum.
Private Collection.*

*Brooch in diamonds, engraved cabochon-
cut emeralds and rubies and baroque
pearls mounted on platinum.
Claudio Zannettin Collection (Cortina).*

*Pair of clips forming a brooch, in
diamonds and aquamarines mounted on
platinum. Cartier (1935).
Daniela Balzaretti Collection (Bergamo).*

170

Design for a diadem in platinum and diamonds.
Cusi di via Clerici Archives (Milan).

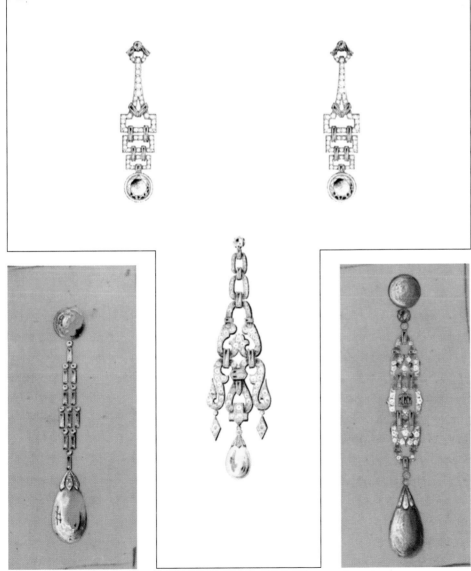

Designs for pendant earrings mounted on platinum with brilliants and pearls.
Cusi di via Clerici Archives (Milan).

Costume Jewellery

If high fashion jewellery of the 1920s and '30s reflected, in its magnificence and its novelty of conception, the ostentation of an exceptional epoch, the same is also true of the costume jewellery of the period. The latter reflected the evolution of taste and the various intellectual currents of the time, but was also the product of a popular art aimed at the widest possible diffusion. By virtue of this, it retained the essence of the most distinctive characteristics of the various styles of jewellery, while amplifying them as far as permitted. Thus the general aesthetic of Art Deco was even more clearly defined in costume jewellery.

The range of costume jewellery was extremely wide. It included products inspired by the artist-jewellers. These pieces were both simple and sophisticated with multiple geometrical forms, alternating polished metal surfaces and polychromatic synthetic materials. The strict designs of the jewellers, in black and white, rock crystal and onyx, were here translated into plastics. Exoticism was by no means deterred by the precariousness of the means available, and all the motifs appearing elsewhere, Egyptian and Chinese, for example, were also to be found in the art of costume jewellery.

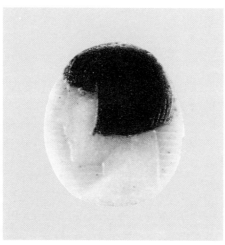

Plaque in glass paste by Amalric Walter representing the profile of a woman's head with bob cut. Circa 1925.
Photo: Sotheby's.

Plaque in glass paste by Amalric Walter with two carved fish. Circa 1925.
Photo: Sotheby's.

Pendant in glass paste by Gabriel Argy-Rousseau with a ladybird design in red, mauve and green on a neutral background. Circa 1925.
Photo: Sotheby's.

The white jewellery which was at the height of fashion towards 1929 was no longer the exclusive prerogative of high class jewellery. It also proliferated in imitations. Costume jewellery replicated all the most daring innovations in jewellery design using non-precious materials. Thus, where before there had been lacquer, now there was paint. Instead of, for example, jade or onyx, bakelite or galalith were to be found, and multicoloured gemstones were replaced by imitation pearls.

172

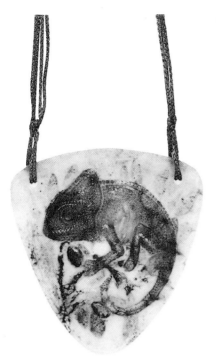

'Chameleon' pendant in glass paste by Amalric Walter after a model by Henri Bergé. Circa 1920. *Photo: Sotheby's.*

Pendant in grey-blue tinted opalised glass. Lalique (circa 1925). Photo: Sotheby's.

Pendant in glass paste by Amalric Walter with a motif of a brown bird perched on a branch (circa 1920). Photo: Sotheby's.

Pair of drop-shaped earrings in glass paste by Gabriel Argy-Rousseau, Mauve and red pattern on a neutral background. Photo: Sotheby's.

Pendant in glass paste by Gabriel Argy-Rousseau with a low relief pattern of a black and white flower on a neutral background decorated with mauve chevrons. Circa 1925. *Photo: Sotheby's.*

Pendant of celluloid and paste with black silk tassel.
Signed: Auguste Bonaz (circa 1925).
Umberto Accenti Collection (Milan).

Pendant in enamelled metal and marcasite. Private Collection.

Left: Sautoir in galalith and imitation pearls with tassel
pendant. Circa 1925. Private Collection.

Right: Sautoir in crystal and imitation pearls with tassel
pendant.
Circa *1925. Private Collection.*

The great vogue for bracelets opened up an enormous field of experimentation. Designs, in the form of solid bangles, varying in size and amount of decoration, usually in plastic, resin, bakelite or celluloid, were mass-produced. There also existed articulated bracelets, composed of motifs decorated with designs in relief or metallic inlays, linked to each other by an elastic cord.

The vast range of costume jewellery also included necklaces, either solid or articulated, pendants in synthetic materials hung from chains, brooches, clips, brooch-buckles, belt-buckles, and of course, rings.

Pendant in silver, moulded glass and enamel. Lalique (circa 1925). Umberto Accenti Collection (Milan).

But it is worth pointing out that the term 'costume jewellery' applies not only to cheap mass-produced articles in humble materials, but also to all the products of a delirious imagination, usually one-off creations, signed by well-known manufacturers like Bonaz, Bablet, Bastard, Barboteaux, Miault, Greidenberg, Truffier and many others.

These pieces were made in silver, marcassite, ivory, amber, tortoiseshell, cloisonné enamel, mother-of-pearl and wood. A number of articles of jewellery in glass come into this category, for example the models in moulded glass produced by the master glassmaker Lalique (1860-1945) between 1920 and 1940. At this period his necklaces of colourless or slightly coloured glass representing leaves, fruit, insects, birds and flowers (a dahlia model had an unprecedented success) were very fashionable. This was also true of his glass pendants, necklaces and bracelets composed of elements in opalescent glass with naturalistic or abstract motifs, threaded on to a silken cord or an elasticated strip.

It should however be noted that none of these fragile adornments can be compared to the sumptuous and expensive jewellery produced by Lalique before the First World War.

Gabriel Argy-Rousseau (1885-1953), an engineer and master glassmaker, produced a fine collection towards 1925: pendants and medallions in translucent glass paste with a moulded base, in low relief, all hung from silken cords. Alongside these are to be found brooches and earrings, again in glass paste, in the form of drops with a design in mauve and pinkish-red (incarnadine) for example, on a colourless background.

Amalric Walter, trained at the Sèvres School of Ceramics, and the founder of a glass paste workshop at Daum's, also produced pendants and brooches in this medium. His predilection was for insect and flower motifs.

Between 1925 and 1930, the goldsmith Jean Puiforcat adapted the abstractive elements of modernism to the creation of inexpensive articles of jewellery of purely decorative function. It is more or less in these terms that *Vogue* discussed the costume jewellery which he exhibited at the 1925 International Exhibition: 'And even the false jewellery is of an exceptional quality, using suitable materials to obtain its effects and rediscover its true function, that of an essentially ephemeral form of ornament.'

It is clear that the success and development of costume jewellery after the Exhibition is due to a large extent to the international extension of the American economic crisis of 1929. Obviously this phenomenon was linked to the contemporary boom in synthetic materials.

Plastics, synthetic resins (perspex, for example) offered an inexhaustible range of potential surrogates for natural raw materials of animal origin, like ivory, tortoiseshell, amber and horn, particularly favoured by the Art Deco style.

The invention of these synthetic products goes back as far as the middle of the last century — this is worth noting, since they are thought to be very

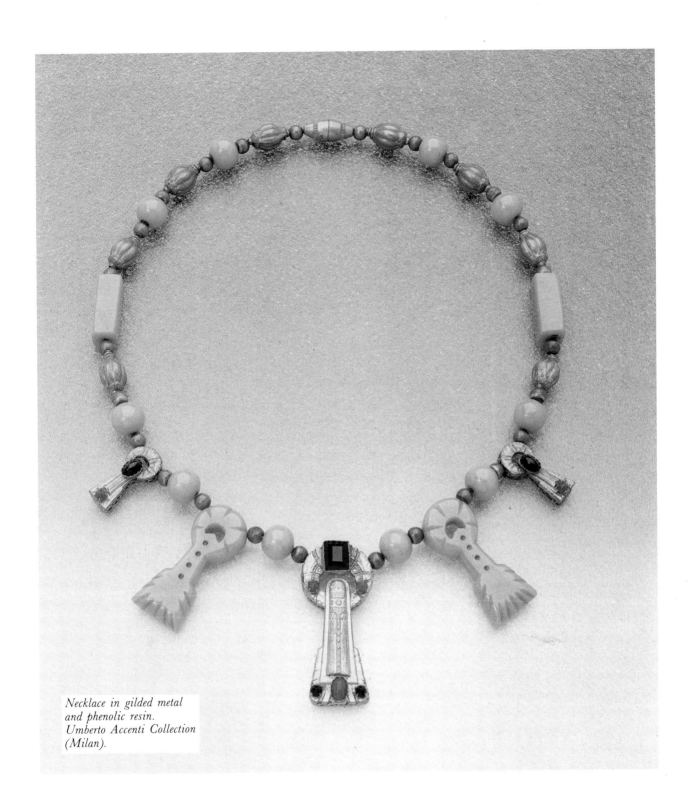

*Necklace in gilded metal
and phenolic resin.
Umberto Accenti Collection
(Milan).*

recent. Indeed, 1862 was the year in which parkesine was born. This was a semi-synthetic resin resembling ivory and horn, invented in England by Alexander Parkes. In 1869, John Hyatt in the United States took out a patent on celluloid, a semi-synthetic material deriving from cellulose, which offered interesting applications. In sheet form, it could be printed on, and thus used for all kinds of covering. The range of colourings which could be obtained was infinitely variable. Celluloid can be used to imitate tortoiseshell, ivory and, with the addition of metallic pigments, mother-of-pearl.

In Germany in 1899, thanks to A Spitteler and W. Krische, galalith or milkstone (from the Greek *gala* or milk) was created. This is a substance deriving from casein to which formaldehyde has been added. A few years later, a similar substance called erinoid was put on the market in England. It was only in 1907 that Leo Backeland developed the first purely synthetic resin, to which he gave the name bakelite.

Originally the colouring of this material was limited to dark tones, usually brown and black. But in 1920 chemical research allowed the range of colours of bakelite to be extended.

Art Deco, thirsty for innovation, was able to derive the greatest benefit from all these new materials which could evidently be shaped at will.

Clearly, costume jewellery represented the field of application *par excellence* for these materials, which lent themselves to the most daring experiments and produced the most remarkable results. It became possible to make such successful imitation jewels that it was sometimes difficult to tell them from the real thing.

The fashion for costume jewellery, at this time in full swing, met with the unqualified approval of the great fashion houses, who began to create jewellery specifically adapted to their new collections.

Amongst the innumerable articles of costume jewellery bearing the Chanel signature, it is worth recalling a series inspired by the natural world and reproduced in the April 1938 issue of *Vogue*. It consists of a necklace made up of tassels and oak leaves in transparent enamel, a necklace composed of pansies in graduated colours of enamel with green leaves, and a brooch composed of multicoloured *pampilles*.

Not even the house of Cartier scorned the use of plastics. At that time it was usually acrylic materials, particularly widely used for the clasps of evening bags, but around 1930 there was even a woman's watch created in bakelite.

In 1926, Worth launched a necklace made of crystal pearls spaced out on a silk cord. Vionnet's preference was for black and white, crystal and synthetic material. Among other pieces, Paquin presented an evening comb topped by an orchid in blue and white imitation stones.

Elsa Schiaparelli, who was keenly interested in costume jewellery, presented eccentric, innovative designs, marked by the non-conformist aesthetic which generally characterises her work. Schiapparelli often drew inspiration from her illustrious artist friends for her creations.

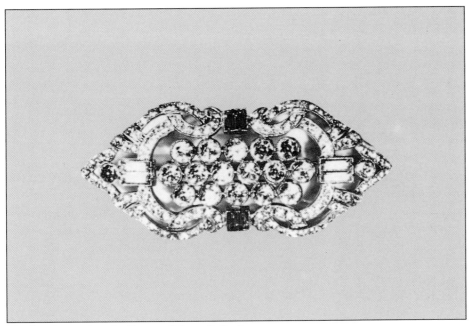

Metal and paste brooch. France. Private Collection.

Silver and coral brooch. Italy (circa 1930). Private Collection.

The whole range of this work was to be seen at the *Hommage à Schiapparelli* organised in Paris in 1984. Amongst other pieces was a plastic brooch of 1936, probably designed by Christian Bérard, representing three horses pulling a Roman chariot. There was also a starfish shaped brooch in gilded yellow plastic designed in 1937 by Salvador Dali. And, by the same artist, of the same date, a brooch in gold-plated plastic featuring a siren.

Jean Cocteau was the creator of a brooch in the shape of an eye, dating from 1937. It consisted of a lacquered cord as the eyelid, with a false moonstone as the iris, and a drop-shaped pearl as a tear.

Bracelet in silver and glass paste simulating lapis lazuli. France. Private Collection.

179

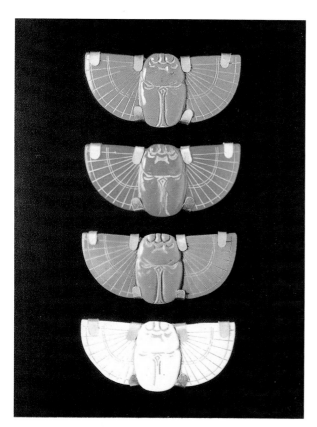

Series of galalith 'scarab' brooches. France (circa 1925).
Umberto Accenti Collection (Milan).

Series of celluloid 'cicada' brooches.
France (circa 1925).
Umberto Accenti Collection (Milan).

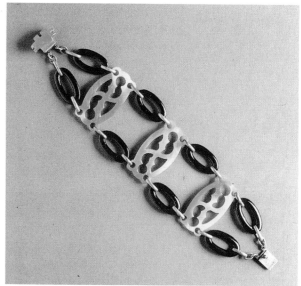

Galalith bracelet. France (circa 1925).
Umberto Accenti Collection (Milan).

Earring pendants in galalith. France (circa 1925).
Umberto Accenti Collection (Milan).

Bracelet, brooch and ring in silver, marcasite and lapis lazuli,
Signed: Theodor Fahrner.
Private Collection.

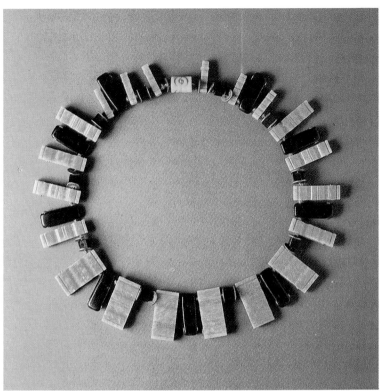

Galalith necklace. England (circa 1925). Umberto Accenti Collection (Milan).

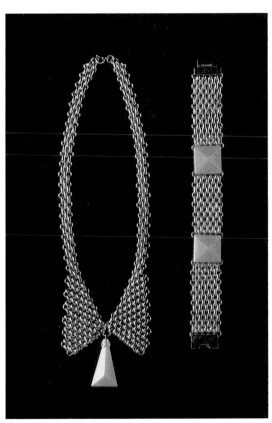

Necklace and bracelet in metal and galalith.
France (circa 1930).
Umberto Accenti Collection. (Milan).

Necklace in metal and galalith. Private Collection.

In the iconographical repertoire of jewellery signed by the famous dress-designer were included many themes inspired by nature. Flora inspired, for example, a 1937 brooch, made of glass and plastic, in the shape of a carnation, and another, of the same year, in the form of a bluebell with *pampilles* hung in the centre, embellished by two leaves in copper. The *demi-parure* of 1937-39 representing bunches of grapes in white metal with pearls and lavender and green paste, is of the same inspiration.

Also, in the same vein are a clip composed of a branch of eglantine in enamel and pearls, photographed for *Vogue* in 1938, and another clip consisting of three orchids in enamel.

This natural imagery was completed by animals and insects — the plastic bracelet in the form of a fish, for example, created in 1936, in all likelihood after a design by Christian Bérard, or the brooch of 1937, representing a large fly in gilded metal, paste, diamond and topaz.

Schiaparelli's costume jewellery now has its place in the museums. One can see, in the Brooklyn Museum, an extraordinary insect necklace created in 1930, consisting of a transparent vinyl collarette, specked with a number of insects in coloured metal.

It is impossible to discuss the subject of designer costume jewellery without mentioning Jean Sclumberger, a figure of the first rank in this field, who worked in Paris at the end of the 1930s. Schlumberger and Schiaparelli worked closely together from 1937 to 1939 and produced countless astonishing creations.

In 1937-38 the famous roller-skate brooches were produced. Also, a large brooch in the shape of a sun and its rays, and a series of flexible bracelets and the very well-known gilded brooches in the shape of angelets, nicknamed 'Petits Amours' (Little Loves), which were pinned to the lapel of tailored costumes.

Speaking of the articles of jewellery created for Schiaparelli, Jean Schlumberger recalled, in an interview published in the catalogue for the 1984 Paris exhibition, that, in 1938, there had been 'for the Circus collection, curious specimens like the buttons in the form of a clown's head and the large ostrich brooches,.. and for the pagan collection, vegetable jewels, bracelets dotted with enamelled carrots...'

Vogue, referring in 1938 to this jewellery inspired by vegetables, made the following comment: 'Long live vegetarianism, and if you don't want to fail to keep up your raw vegetable diet, wear carrots, cauliflowers, leeks, tomatoes, aubergines... as bracelets or buttons.' And Schlumberger added: 'Not forgetting such singular creations as earrings in the shape of ears' (and the necklace of swans' necks)...

The latter, deriving from a very high degree of fantasy, were brilliant precursors of Schlumberger's imaginative American work, when he set himself up in New York in the 1940s.

CHAPTER VI
THE SECOND GENERATION OF 1930 s JEWELLERY

From 1935 comes a turning point in the evolution of jewellery. Two principal changes stand out. One of these influenced white jewellery of the end of the 1920s and the beginning of the 1930s. The other, more revolutionary, was the reappearance of yellow gold, which began to appear in the jewellery produced at the end of the 1930s.

Let us, however, begin with the first of these developments. White jewellery changed in volume. The flat structures of the 1920s gave way to curved forms with rounded edges (gone the days of sharp edges). Jewellery from now on was to be highly constructed, made out of juxtaposed volumes of impressive structure, solid, indeed often rigid.

In the review *Art Vivant* of November 1936 this was expressed in the following terms: 'Nevertheless, bracelets, brooches and clips, whether by Boucheron or Cartier, those masters of modern jewellery, those masters of style no longer content with flat jewellery with large pavés of stones, create an infinite variety of bracelets, brooches, clips and rings, whose relief is heightened by the felicitous disposition of space.'

This increase in three-dimensional volume is particularly noticeable in clips, which, although retaining a rigorously geometrical design, also reveal a certain plasticity. Their curved surfaces, embellished by projecting volutes or loops and multiple folds in the metal, allow this result to be achieved.

The evolution towards a three-dimensional quality in the jewellery of the 1930s is to be found not only in the category of white jewellery, but also in polychromatic jewllery. This tendency is evident in bracelets, brooches and clips. The dominant feature is the facet, emphasised by abstract or naturalist motifs in relief, or by alternating the colours of the stones. A good example is

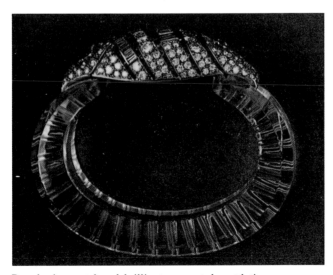

Bracelet in crystal and brilliants, mounted on platinum.
Cartier (1934).
Cartier Archives.

1. Bracelet composed of round and baguette-cut brilliants mounted on platinum. Photo: Sotheby's.

2. Ring with a marquise-cut diamond in the centre, mounted on platinum. Photo: Sotheby's.

3. Brooch in round and baguette-cut brilliants mounted on platinum. Photo: Sotheby's.

the unusual necklace by Van Cleef et Arpels of 1937, of considerable volume, although lightly structured. It is a choker, recalling the stiff collarettes in pleated lace of the Renaissance. The necklace consists of a platinum trellis embellished with two lines of baguette-cut diamonds, from which is suspended a fringe of round diamond *pendeloques:* in the centre of this fringe is a large pear-shaped diamond.

A Mauboussin necklace (see page 96) unquestionably belongs to the same family. Set in its entirety with round brilliants and baguette-cut diamonds, it

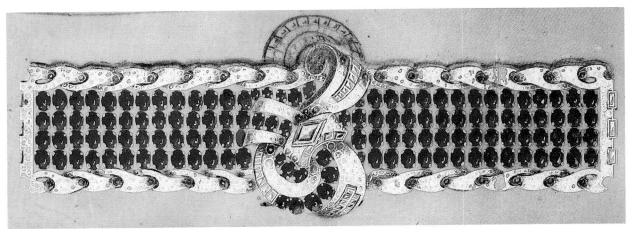

Design for bracelet in platinum, sapphires and brilliants. Cusi di via Clerici Archives (Milan).

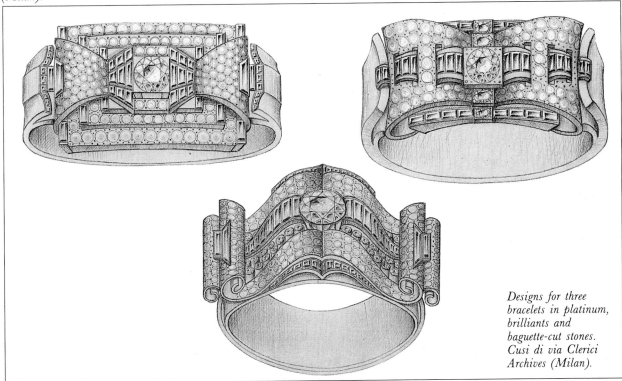

Designs for three bracelets in platinum, brilliants and baguette-cut stones. Cusi di via Clerici Archives (Milan).

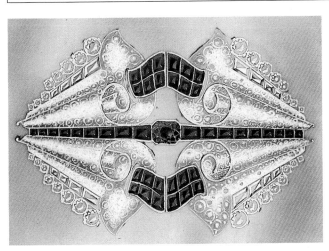

Design for brooch in platinum, sapphires and brilliants. Cusi di via Clerici Archives (Milan).

185

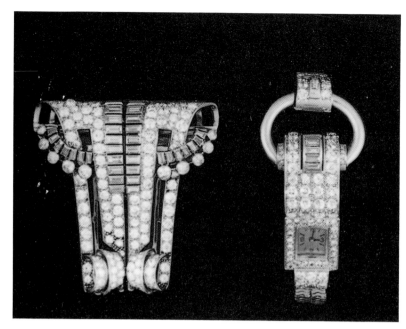

Wrist-watch in platinum and diamonds and clip brooch in white gold and diamonds. France (1930). Photo: Sotheby's.

Bracelet and clip in diamonds and sapphires mounted on platinum. Cartier (1937). Photo: Sotheby's.

Necklace and bracelet mounted on platinum with brilliants. Signed: Gazdar. France. Photo: Sotheby's.

186

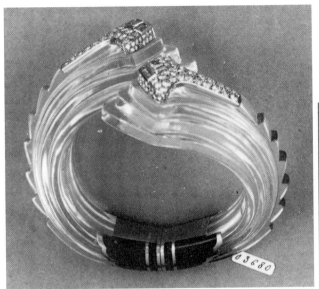

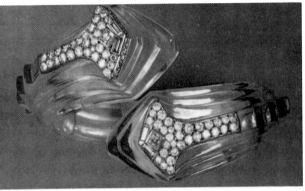

Bracelet in cut crystal with appliquéd round baguette-cut brilliants, mounted in platinum. Cartier (1935). Cartier Archives.

Bracelet in crystal with appliquéd brilliants on platinum mount. Cartier (1935). Cartier Archives.

Crystal bangle with sides pavé set with round brilliants, mounted on platinum. Cartier (1934). Cartier Archives.

Left: Bracelet composed of round and baguette-cut diamonds and cabochon-cut emeralds, mounted on white gold and platinum. Boucheron. Photo: Sotheby's.

is made even more precious by a double line of emeralds.

But solidity and plasticity were, of course, not the only characteristic features of this generation of jewellery. In many cases imagination — aided by the masterly technique of the jeweller — was given full rein. Thus there appeared flexible mountings which seemed to be trying to rival the softness of the textiles used by the dress-designers.

The review *Femina* for May 1935 bears witness to this: 'By the perfection of their technique jewellers have managed to make metal and precious stones take on the soft appearance of textiles, or else impose on them the rigid, massive look of wood or stone hewn from the living rock. In either case, their success is astonishing. The art of jewellery with flexible mountings seems almost to be

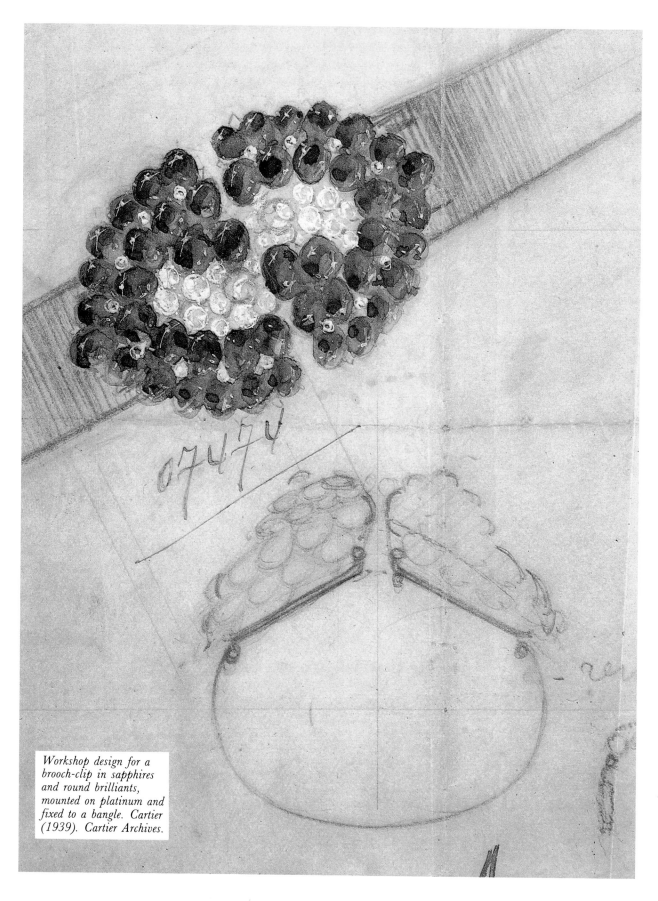

Workshop design for a brooch-clip in sapphires and round brilliants, mounted on platinum and fixed to a bangle. Cartier (1939). Cartier Archives.

Bangle in platinum and sapphires. Nicoletta Lebole Collection (Arezzo).

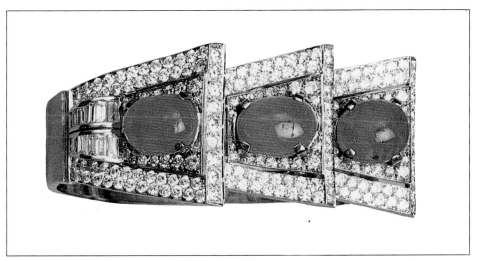

Bangle in platinum, diamonds and emeralds. Lacloche. Nicoletta Lebole Collection (Arezzo).

trying to rival that of the dressmaker ruffling a panel of material or that of the florist crumpling an artificial flower.'

Thus, a particular bracelet by Cartier looks like a ribbon wrapped round the wrist, tied with a 'ruffled' bow consisting of two loops passing one through the other and held by a hook in lapis lazuli. A diamond brooch, also by Cartier, a triumph of lightness and flexibility, is in the form of a rose. Only the heart is fixed. The petals seem malleable, capable of taking on the form and direction that one might wish to give them.

In the heavy style, on the other hand, there is a large bracelet in black enamel which gives an impression of weight and solidity. It is decorated with a small round watch in relief.

Also in the May 1935 issue of *Femina* we find the following comment: 'The huge ensemble which Herz has produced for one of his clients is composed of a large brooch, a ring, two clips and a bracelet in agate and amethysts. Of a simple, clear line, 'tailored cut' as one might say, these stones are assembled with a marvellous decorative sense. To be admired is the shape of the bracelet whose double band of agate, cut in a single piece, is held by a motif in metal and amethyst. The contrast between the two stones provides a fine colour effect, which will allow these jewels to be worn equally well with an evening dress and with afternoon wear. These examples show that bracelets seem to be playing an important role in contemporary fashion. They are placed in full view over the glove.'

The vogue for the clip continued. Cartier had a new idea, that of the large clip reminiscent of a clothes peg. It could be used as a fastening for a glove. Translated into the medium of precious stones, it was a large item of jewellery to be worn on a drape or a low neckline.

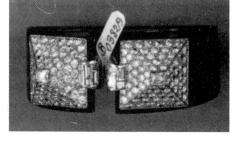

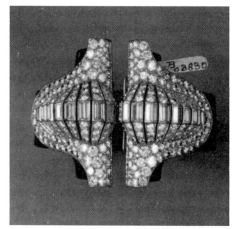

Series of bracelets with detachable clip-brooches in black lacquer and diamonds, mounted on platinum. Cartier (1935). Cartier Archives.

*Necklace in sapphires
and brilliants mounted
on platinum.
Cartier (1939).
Cartier Archives.*

*Necklace consisting of three rows of coral and pearl drops with clusters of pearls, onyx, coral,
emeralds and brilliants: mounted on platinum. Cartier (1938). Cartier Archives.*

Brooch in sapphires and brilliants, the sapphires mounted using the 'invisible' setting technique.
Van Cleef et Arpels.
Photo: Sotheby's.

Quite apart from the changes in style we have been discussing, the multi-purpose article of jewellery continued to be very fashionable. This explains the profusion of jewels in platinum and diamonds or platinum and coloured precious stones, rich in decorative motifs which could be interchanged at will, and thus adaptable to all circumstances. In a flash, a fine diamond brooch could be changed into two identical clips. A bracelet embellished by two clips could be worn in its most precious form, or stripped of its decorative motifs, which could then be used as peg brooches.

In November 1934, *Vogue* told its readers: 'This variety of use, this play of different combinations and the renewal which they give rise to, offer an added attraction to the intrinsic beauty of this modern jewellery.'

The same review cited various specimens of multi-purpose jewellery, some of which were truly unusual: 'The clip formula has in no way exhausted its resources. Cartier has seen how to develop it in an extremely ingenious way: a long flexible strip of diamonds mounted on clips, the manner of their disposition allowing them to be worn in different places, in a straight line or in a curve. At will, this extremely novel article of jewellery can be used as a bracelet encircling the bottom of the sleeve or as a shoulder ornament.'

Elegance and refinement were here coupled with an indisputable practical element. This was also the case with another creation by the same jeweller. Small spirals of stones mounted on clips and intended to be placed in the hair. One or two were enough to retain natural curls, or a whole row could be set along a centre parting, or placed in a semi-circle round the head, in the manner of a tiara.

The bracelet is manifestly the article of jewellery most suited to modification. We have only to think of the numerous specimens produced by Cartier in 1935 and 1936. These models were always presented in the form of bangles with detachable motifs lending themselves to infinite combinations. An example is a bracelet in black lacquer on grey gold, embellished by two detachable clips in the form of pyramids, mounted on platinum and pavé set with brilliants, or there is another specimen, again in black lacquer on grey gold, decorated with two claw-brooches, this time in the form of shields, set with brilliants. Finally, a flexible bracelet in black lacquer on gold, decorated with a detachable triangular claw-brooch set all over with brilliants.

Multi-purpose jewellery was very widely diffused. Indeed, in 1935, *Vogue* reproduced a whole series of multi-purpose bracelets which, although mass-produced, were not very different from the pieces indicated above.

These bracelets took the form of bangles, decorated with various types of clip. One consists of superimposed squares of platinum, topped with a pavé of baguette-cut diamonds with an oval diamond in the centre. Another consists of two volutes in relief, liberally set with diamonds.

Again by Cartier, and of the same period, is a bracelet mounted on platinum, composed of a pavé set band of round brilliants and baguette-cut brilliants, decorated in the centre with a removable plaque enriched with thirteen claw-set cabochon emeralds.

An article in the June 1939 issue of *Femina* confirmed the success of multi-purpose jewellery, the fashion for which was far from ephemeral: 'A diamond bracelet by Mellerio can become in turn a *devant de corsage* or an epaulette with the principal motif on the shoulder. The epaulette in turn, worn the other way round, can serve to hold together the low neckline of a formal evening dress.'

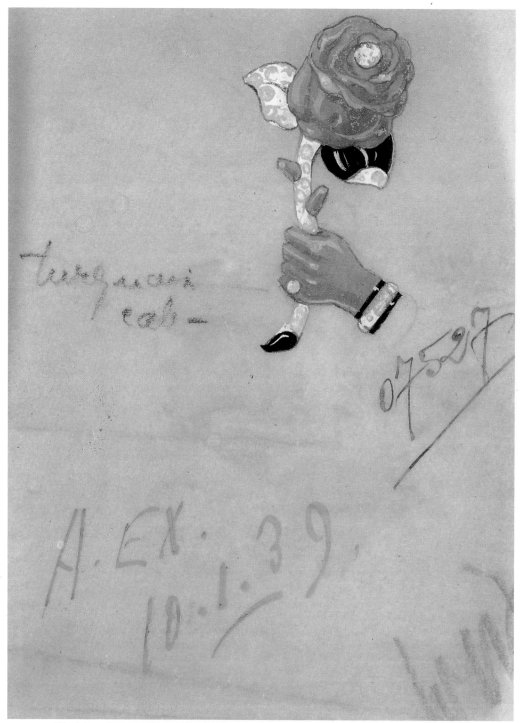

Workshop drawing: brooch in the shape of a hand holding a rose, in pink coral, black enamel, brilliants and turquoises. Cartier (1939). Cartier Archives.

Clearly, it was not only the bracelet, but also the necklace, which could be the basis for dual purpose jewellery.

This was the case with the choker created by Cartier in 1936. Three lines of round brilliants and baguette-cut brilliants were set off by a detachable central motif in very high relief, set with rubies and brilliants which, if necessary, could become a magnificent brooch. The same was true of the

Workshop drawing: brooch in the shape of a ladybird in coral, black lacquer and brilliants. Cartier (1935). Cartier Archives.

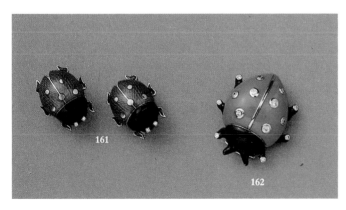

161. *Pair of enamel ladybird earclips, with diamond-set eyes. Cartier. Photo: Christie's.*

162. *Coral and diamond ladybird clip brooch with black enamel head and legs. Cartier. Photo: Christie's.*

Brooch in the shape of a camelia in white enamel on gold, with a ladybird in coral and brilliants. Cartier (1935). Cartier Archives.

necklace produced by Cartier in 1939, mounted on platinum and decorated with oval sapphires and baguette cut-brilliants. This necklace was embellished with two detachable motifs in the form of clusters of sapphires which could, if necessary, be used as claw brooches.

Still of the same period were to be found articles of jewellery clearly inspired by naturalist themes.

'The fetish in vogue is the Cartier ladybird', proclaimed *Femina* in June 1935. 'The new and unexpected article of jewellery taking off this spring is a

'Black slave' clip-brooch in black lacquer on silver, gold, turquoises and pearls. Cartier (1936). Cartier Archives.

peg brooch rather than a clip. It can be worn anywhere, on the hat or the glove or the bodice.'

The body of this charming piece of jewellery was in pink coral and black enamel. Its spots were small diamonds which, although embellishing it, did not make it too costly a fantasy.

The same naturalistic tendency was to be found in the peg brooch in the shape of a camelia produced by Cartier in about 1937. This was made of white enamel on gold, with a square brilliant in the centre: on the side a detachable peg brooch in the form of a ladybird in coral, pink brilliants and black lacquer.

There were also brooches in the form of a blackamoor's head (created by Cartier in 1936-37), with the face in black lacquer, topped by a cream lacquer turban, set with turquoise cabochons or a selection of coloured stones.

In December 1937, *Femina* made the following announcement: 'The "1938 fetish" will be the Sioux Indian's head, following on the 1937 black boy.' The February issue of *Le Jardin des Modes* added its support: 'Negroes, still very fashionable a few months ago, are being replaced by Red Indians. Their feathered head-dresses are very decorative.' Another decorative feature from Cartier dates from 1937-38. It consists of a brooch representing a hand holding a rose. There were to be innumerable replicas of these creations.

Another piece dating from around 1938 is a peg brooch mounted on grey gold, representing an ivory rose, whose black lacquer leaves have veins of yellow gold. The stem is of calibré-cut coral, and dew-drops are made up of five bouton pearls. The small ladybird is in coral and black lacquer.

For Christmas 1938 Cartier launched a series of gold and enamel brooches representing playing cards and the following summer saw the triumph of his Snow-White bracelet, which consisted of a chain from which hung pendants representing the characters in the story.

The June 1938 issue of *Femina* notes that: 'Walt Disney has given Cartier the exclusive rights to the characters of Snow White.'

In February 1938, *Vogue* described a clip by Van Cleef et Arpels in the following terms: 'A splendour in the realm of jewellery: in the shape of a chrysanthemum entirely in rubies, highlighted by baguette-cut diamonds in a mystery setting.'

The same magazine noted, in February 1939: 'Three clips, each suggesting a rose made of rubies in a mystery setting, finished by leaves in diamonds.'

In about 1935 Van Cleef et Arpels developed the ingenious technique known as mystery, or invisible, setting. This constituted a small revolution in the setting of precious stones. Until then the stone had either been enclosed within the narrow circle of the mounting, or had been held in place by claws.

This new technique reversed the cause of the problem. The edge of the stone was hollowed out and the metal thread of the mounting fitted into it. Half the thickness of the metal thread slotted into one stone, and the other half into the adjacent stone. The metal was thus invisible on the surface of the piece, but the stones were nevertheless solidly fixed. The secret of the mystery setting was

Brooch in coral and pearls, mounted on grey gold. Cartier (1938).
Cartier Archives.

revealed by looking at the reverse of the piece, a latticework of gold, as astonishing as the article of jewellery itself, a perfect receptacle in which each stone — however tiny — fitted into its appointed place. Using this exclusive process, the execution of which implied many hours of highly skilled labour, Van Cleef et Arpels created band bracelets, brooches and clips, usually in the form of flowers.

Another innovation also bore the Van Cleef et Arpels signature. This was the famous *minaudière*, going back to about 1930, which is the subject of an amusing anecdote.

An excellent client of Van Cleef et Arpels, Florence Gould, the wife of Frank J. Gould, an American railway magnate, had the questionable habit, when she went out in the evening, of stuffing her keys, her make-up kit and all kinds of other things, into a metal box of fifty Lucky Strikes.

Louis Arpels found this habit unwise and, to say the least, inelegant, and this led him to look for a solution. A few months later, he presented his version of a metal hand-bag: an evening pouch in precious materials, gold, lacquer and precious stones, with various compartments reserved for all the things which were indispensible for an evening out (powder, comb, lipstick, small change, cigarettes, etc.).

But what name could be found for this *vade-mecum*? Esther Van Cleef, Louis's sister, nicknamed 'Kiki', used to make play of simpering while she was making-up. This inspired her brother, who decided to make her god-mother to his evening bag, which he baptised *'minaudière'* (simperer). Today, this trade name is still exclusive to the house of Van Cleef et Arpels.

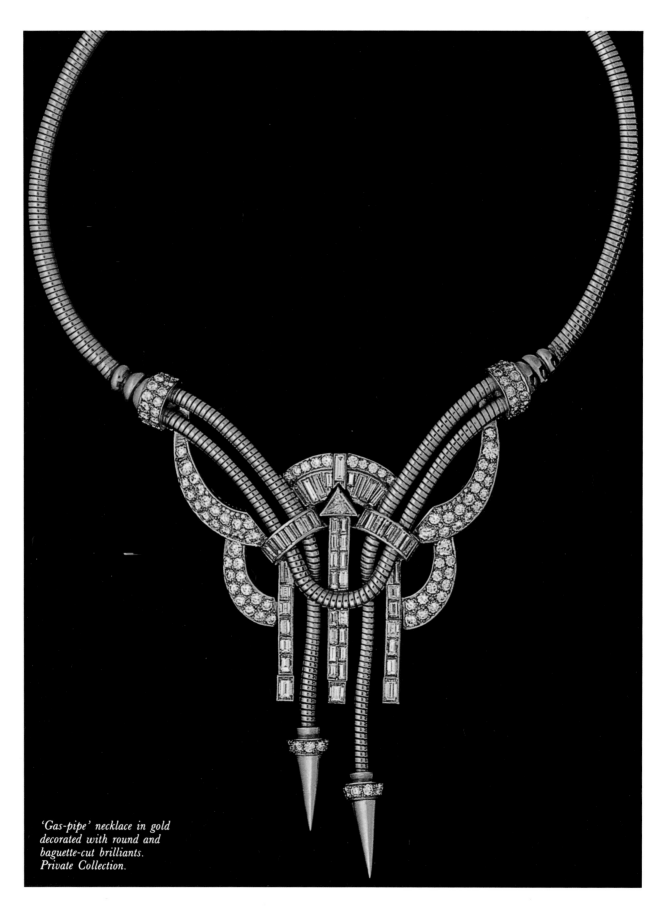

'Gas-pipe' necklace in gold
decorated with round and
baguette-cut brilliants.
Private Collection.

CHAPTER VII

GOLD JEWELLERY OF THE 1930 S

In June 1937, the review *Femina* annnounced: 'Cartier is bringing gold jewellery back into favour. This summer we shall see it used for day-wear as well as for evening-wear'. 1937 thus seems to have been the official date for the re-introduction of gold jewellery into circulation.

In fact, the archives of firms consulted by us tend to prove that timid attempts had been made from 1935 onwards to bring the yellow metal back into favour. Clearly, in the course of the three previous decades, gold had never been completely abandoned. The production of classic bracelets in the form of chains had been steady but this kind of jewellery was of course not fashionable.

There must have been reasons for this resurgence and it is well known that economic factors always preside over the destiny, not to say the vicissitudes of taste and fashion. The 1929 Wall Street crisis was very deeply felt in the Europe of the early 1930s. In France, the crisis was a prolonged one, and the formation of the Popular Front, in 1936, was one of its consequences. The following year marked the first devaluation of the French franc.

Jewellers sought to ease the problems inevitably encountered in a luxury market by diversifying their production, using a precious metal less expensive than platinum and increasing the creation of utilitarian pieces accessible to a wide audience. Such changes did not occur unannounced. They happened progressively and, as it turned out, became manifest between 1935 and 1940.

It is possible to identify three periods in this fashion for gold jewellery, so well suited to the pre-war years affected by the crisis. The first stretches from 1935 to the beginning of the Second World War. The second coincides with the duration of the War and the third begins with the period of post-war reconstruction and extends to the beginning of the 1950s.

Each of these phases is characterised by slight modifications in the structure of the article of jewellery and the types of alloys used, in which gold is a significant component. Rather than adopting the term 'first transitional period' or 'Lambeth Walk' to identify the first phase, we prefer to stick to the following formula: *Gold jewellery of the 1930s*. More precise, but equally

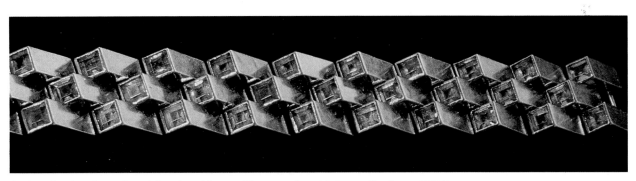

Section of a 'moving staircase' bracelet with emeralds mounted on platinum. Boucheron (1935).

Advertisement for Cartier jewellery published in the June 1937 issue of the magazine 'Femina'.

Voici le bijou d'or.

Cartier remet en honneur le bijou d'or que nous verrons cet été aussi bien le jour que le soir. C'est ainsi qu'il vient de créer cet ensemble : collier, bague, bracelet, qui constitue une parure d'incomparable élégance. Une grappe de raisin forme le motif original de ce beau modèle destiné à marquer une étape dans la mode française : "Exposition 1937".

Femina Juin 1937

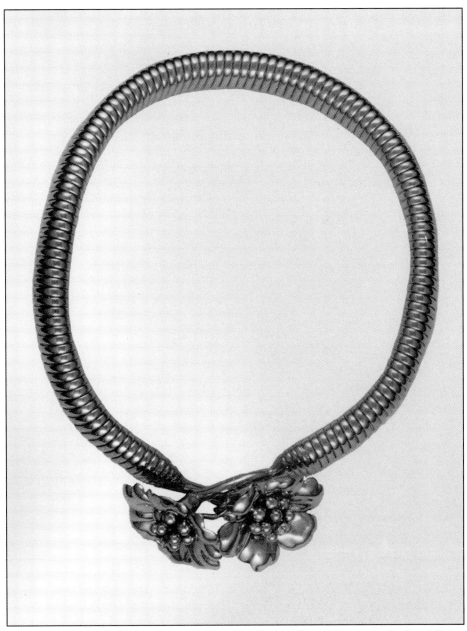

'Gas-pipe' necklace in gold with a flower at each end, in gold and diamonds. Cartier (1937). Cartier Archives.

questionable, is the expression to be found in an article in *Le Figaro* of May 1984, in which Sylviane Humair talks of the 'Lambeth Walk' style, 'that syncopated jazz tune which, for historians, symbolises Europe dancing on top of the Nazi volcano'.

It seemed preferable to us to retain the formula *gold jewellery of the 1930s*, because it is essentially a question of the first phase of a style which was to assert itself, as we shall see, both in Europe and the United States, in the middle of the following decade, in the form of the gold jewellery of the 1940s.

According to approximate statistics deriving from a survey carried out amongst a number of jewellers active half a century ago, it seems that gold jewellery accounted for about a third (and at the most, 50%) of the overall

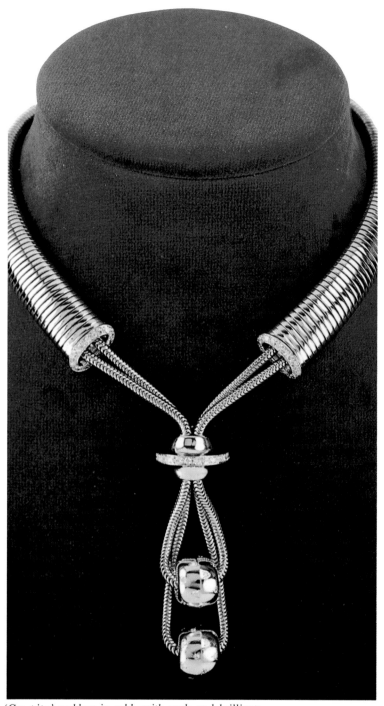

'Gas-pipe' necklace in gold, with cords and brilliants.
Van Cleef et Arpels (1937).

production of jewellery, which naturally included jewellery in platinum and precious stones of the same period.

Production of this first period was characterised by the use of gold in conjunction with the liberal employment of precious stones (sometimes of large dimensions), and then by the frequent combination of gold and platinum. Often the geometrical forms characteristic of Art Deco were to be found, but expressed three dimensionally. We have already remarked on the preponderance in gold jewellery for brooches and bracelets, forms which superseded other articles of jewellery and accessories.

This renewed fashion for gold drew enthusiastic support, not only from the great high fashion jewellers, but also from the less well-known. The prototype pieces we shall draw on here, as precursors of the 1940s style, will necessarily be restricted to those bearing the hallmark of the most famous designers.

Shown here is the famous 'moving staircase' bracelet by Boucheron — a flexible piece composed of three rows of motifs linked like the teeth of a gearing mechanism, finished with precious stones (sapphires, diamonds, rubies).

Another important piece in the series created by Boucheron between 1936 and 1938 was undoubtedly a bangle in yellow gold, enriched at the front by a bridging motif composed of two plaques decorated with a pavé of square sapphires surrounded by round brilliants.

In 1936 Boucheron created another gold bangle of similar form. The decoration, previously pavé set brilliants, here consisted of two lines of sapphires.

Cartier created, around 1934-35, a design in the form of a flexible tube, called the *serpent* (snake) or *tuyau a gaz* (gas-pipe). This was one of the leading innovations in jewellery production of the 1940s, and was particularly suited to bracelets or to wrist-watches of a sporty kind.

It was not surprising to see this flexible tube used later as a necklace by all the jewellers. It was often decorated with detachable clips, usually representing flowers or bouquets of flowers, set with coloured precious stones.

Yellow gold bracelet, with sapphires and brilliants. Boucheron (1936-38).

Above: 'Gas-pipe' necklace enhanced by five detachable clips in gold and topaz. Cartier (1937). Cartier Archives.

Below: Double 'gas-pipe' necklace enhanced by five clip-brooches in emeralds edged with diamonds. Cartier (1937). Cartier Archives.

'Gas-pipe' necklace in gold with clusters of gold balls in the centre. Cartier (1936).
Cartier Archives.

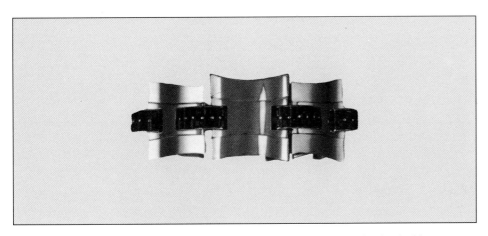

Gold link bracelet pavé set with calibré-cut sapphires. Cartier (1936). Cartier Archives.

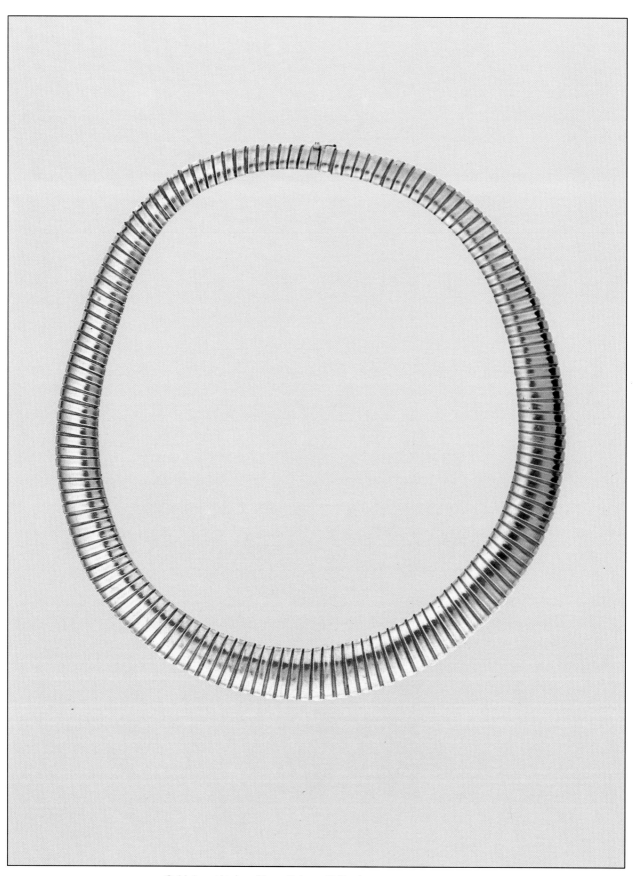

Gold 'gas-pipe' necklace. Private Collection.

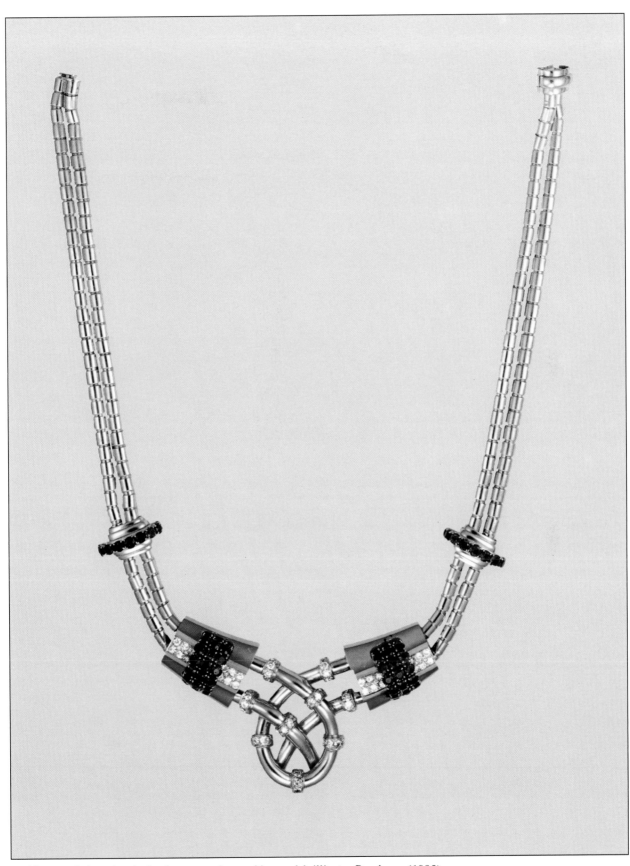

Necklace consisting of articulated segments in sapphires and brilliants. Boucheron (1935).
Boucheron Archives.

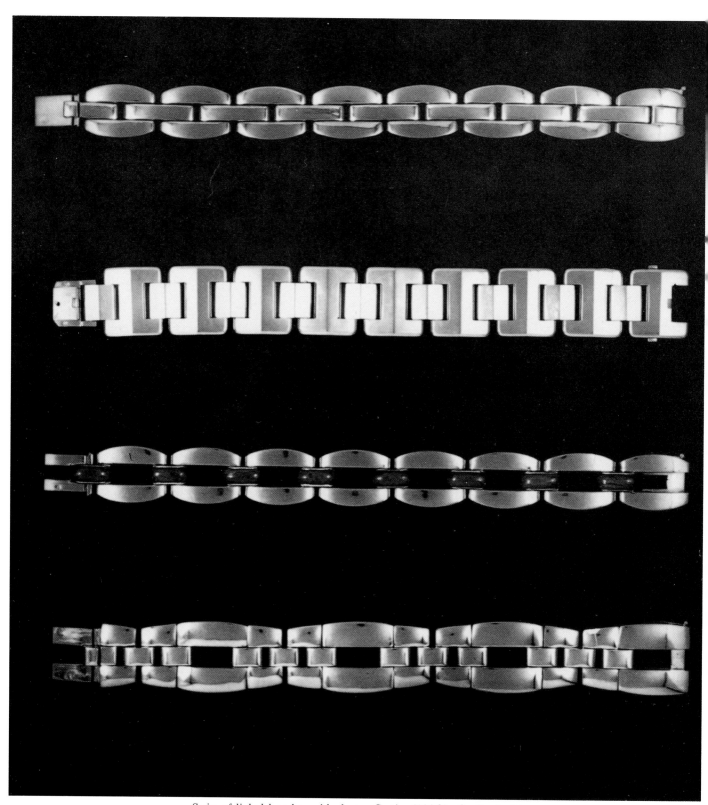

Series of linked bracelets with clasps. Cartier (1930). Cartier Archives.

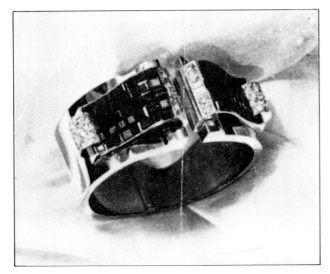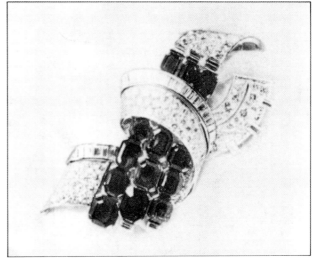

Drawings advertising Cartier and Mauboussin jewellery published in the June 1937 issue of the magazine 'L'Officiel de la Couture'.

Another necklace, *à boules d'or* (golden balls), was a notable creation of Cartier around 1937.

Amongst the gold bracelets by Cartier, designed in 1936, was one composed of twelve cones in alternating red and yellow gold, also a bracelet with spring motifs in burnished gold, linked to each other by hinges in gold pavé set with calibré-cut sapphires, and the very original model, composed of two crossed bands, one in gold, the other in black enamelled gold, which could be moved close to or away from each other, thanks to the play of a mobile decorative element embellished with a cabochon-cut sapphire.

A Cartier design, composed of six or seven motifs in gold, articulated and of rectangular shape, dates from 1938. Each of the motifs was decorated in the centre with two parallel lines of calibré-cut sapphires.

The *queue de rat* (rat's tail or Brazilian link) appeared at about the same time (around 1937-38). This was a long flexible structure, composed of a series of links of rectangular section. This way of working in gold was to be used for the creation of necklaces, bracelets and wrist-watches until 1950.

The quintessential item of this style of production at Van Cleef et Arpels was the bracelet known as *Ludo* or *à nid d'abeille* (honeycomb), created around 1934. This design continued to be produced and imitated until the end of the 1940s. It was a flat band bracelet, composed of small articulated hexagons in gold (joined in a structure resembling that of a honeycomb), each decorated in the centre with a small star set precious stone (usually a ruby or a brilliant). The clasp of this bracelet was a kind of buckle, usually rectangular, pavé set with square brilliants, rubies or sapphires. It is worth noting that the *Ludo* bracelet was often accompanied by matching clips, picking up the buckle motif, and richly decorated with precious stones.

Another variant of the *Ludo* design was a bracelet known as the *ceinture* (strap and buckle) or *jarretière* (garter). This was composed of an articulated band made up of small interwoven rectangular plates of burnished gold in a chequerboard pattern with a large clasp also set with many precious stones.

'Safety-pin' brooch in gold, crowned with a round cabochon in lapis lazuli. Cartier (1937). Cartier Archives.

Triangular clip in yellow gold, round and baguette-cut brilliants.
Mellerio dits Meller.

Clip in red gold and synthetic rubies.
France.

Clip in yellow gold, brilliants and rubies.
Mellerio dits Meller.

There were also bracelets by Cartier dating from 1936, in burnished yellow gold with a detachable clip brooch in the shape of a trapezium decorated with three rows of topazes, in tones varying from pale yellow to Sienna. And there is a bracelet by Mauboussin, dating from 1937, consisting of a gold bangle embellished by clip brooches in the shape of large buckles covered with several lines of round brilliants and pavé set square coloured stones.

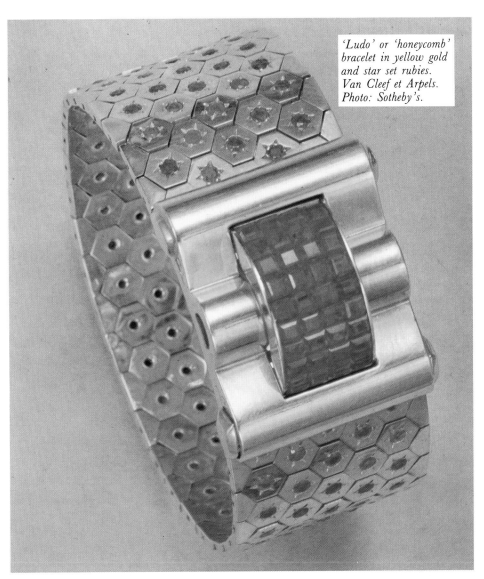

*Brooch in gold, diamonds and
cabochon-cut rubies.
Private Collection.*

Clip-brooch in the form of a
palm tree in gold, sapphires
and brilliants.
Cartier (1939).
Cartier Archives.

Clip-brooch in the form of a flower opening around a
cluster of brilliants, mounted on platinum.
Cartier (1938).
Cartier Archives.

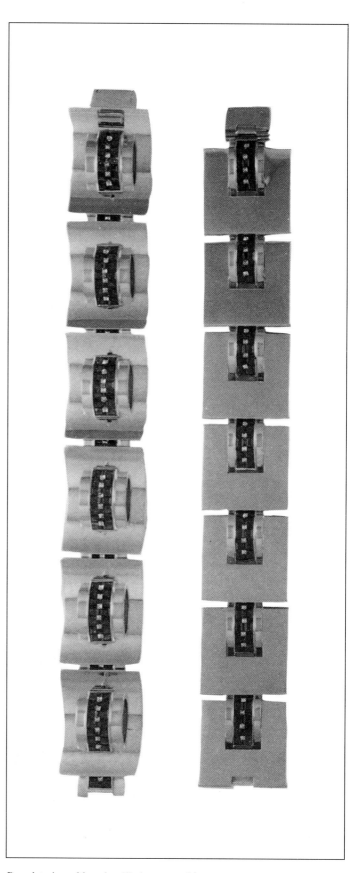

Bracelets in gold and calibré-cut sapphires.
Cartier (1938). Cartier Archives.

Design for a clip in yellow and red gold, brilliants and rubies.
Fasano Archives (Turin).

Gold was equally frequently used in the creation of brooches, clip brooches and clips. The clip brooch created by Cartier in 1936, in the form of a rectangular spatula decorated in the centre with two lines of calibré-cut topazes and rose shaped brilliants, was a design entirely characteristic of this generation of jewellery.

In 1935, Cartier launched a whole series of *épingles à nourrice* (safety-pins), entirely in gold; they were made of gold wire, with a cluster of mobile gold balls, each surmounted by a cabochon in lapis lazuli.

From the category of naturalistic brooches designed by Cartier came a 1938 clip brooch, mounted on platinum, in the form of an open rose, the petals of burnished yellow gold. The heart of the flower is composed of a group of antique cut, claw set brilliants.

A clip brooch in gold called *palmier* (palm-tree), with pliable trunk and rippling foliage, is also noteworthy.

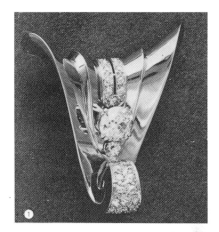

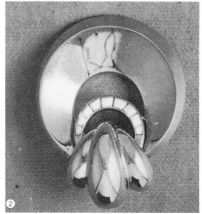

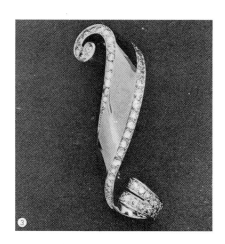

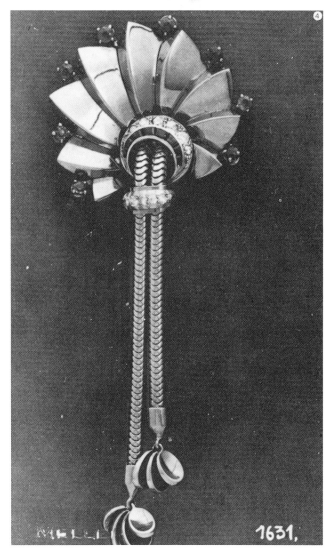

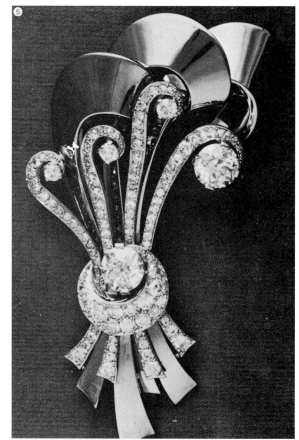

1. *Triangular clip in gold and brilliants.*
Mellerio dits Meller.

2. *Clip in red gold and turquoises.*
Mellerio dits Meller.

3. *'Turning' clip in gold and brilliants.*
Mellerio dits Meller.

4. *'Palette' clip in gold, rubies, brilliants and snake chains.*
Mellerio dits Meller.

5. *'Volute' clip in gold and brilliants.*
Mellerio dits Meller.

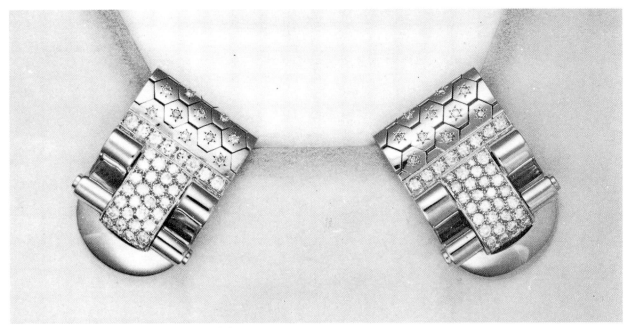

Pair of clips in yellow gold and star set brilliants.
Van Cleef et Arpels.

Series of rings with brilliants, rubies, topazes and sapphires, mounted on platinum.
Cartier (1937).
Cartier Archives.

Right:
'Strap and buckle' bracelet mounted on yellow gold with brilliants.
Photo: Routhier — Sotheby's.

Bracelet and ring in gold, diamonds and sapphires. Boucheron. Private Collection.

*Clip in gold and diamonds.
Private Collection.*

Within the repertoire of rings, designs in the signet-ring style became progressively more dominant. These were massive and imposing, decorated with diamonds and skilfully arranged coloured stones. But alongside these were other designs, lighter and airier, in which gold was substituted for platinum.

The July 1939 issue of *Femina* reported: 'The rings designed by Schlumberger, decorated with sapphires and rubies, are mounted on a flexible wire, which allows them to move slightly with each gesture of the hand. This added glitter lends a particular brilliance to these modern jewels.'

The year 1939 coincided with a particularly ostentatious period in the creation of French jewellery — the success of the New York Exhibition of French jewellery. Again in *Femina* we read: 'French jewellery has a special place at the New York Exhibition. Cartier is showing *parures* of great originality. For example, a shoulder clip in the form of a cluster of sapphires and emeralds, and a bracelet in yellow gold with mobile motifs of sapphires and rubies. Chaumet's *parure* takes the form of a superb necklace with three detachable motifs which can become three clips, each in the shape of a spiral set with brilliants and supporting a number of large pear-shaped brilliants...'

A diadem in brilliants in the form of stylised feathers had in the centre a large emerald. Mauboussin chose feathers and stars as themes for his gala head-dresses, all in diamonds and platinum. Van Cleef et Arpels showed *un chapeau en or tressé* (a hat in plaited gold), the same model which could be admired in the window of the place Vendôme premises at Christmas 1939, and of which the original sketch is shown here.

In 1939, the royal wedding of Mohammed Reza Pahlavi and H.R.H. the Princess Fauzia of Egypt offered French couturiers the opportunity of creating spectacular designs.

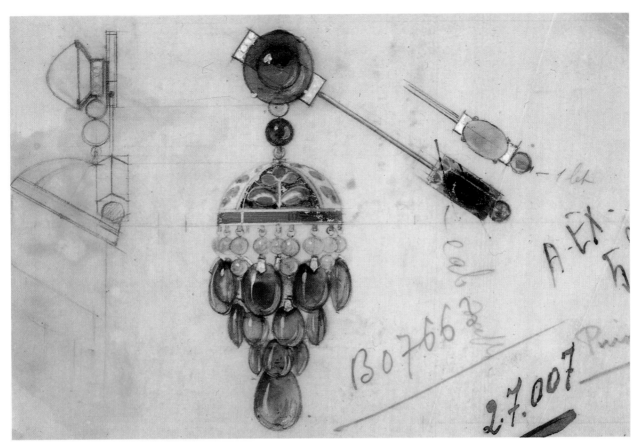

Workshop drawing for a brooch with Hindu style motif in sapphires and pearls. Cartier (1939). Cartier Archives.

Clip to match the 'Ludo' bracelet in yellow gold and star set rubies. Van Cleef et Arpels.

Clip in yellow and white gold, diamonds and synthetic rubies. Italy.

Design for a Van Cleef et Arpels window display in Paris, Christmas 1939.
Hat in woven gold, decorated with a bouquet of sapphires, rubies and brilliants, worn with matching bracelet, clips and necklace (on the right, a 'minaudière').

Femina comments on the occasion in the following terms: 'Teheran was the theatre for magnificent festivities... French good taste was combined with Oriental splendour. If many of the dresses had been conceived by our great designers, it is the famous Parisian jeweller Boucheron who was commissioned to execute most of the articles of jewellery ordered by the Imperial Court of Iran... Let us mention, amongst the most noticeable of the pieces created by Boucheron, two superb diadems and two splendid necklaces.'

Flexible bracelet in diamonds mounted on platinum.
Photo: Sotheby's.

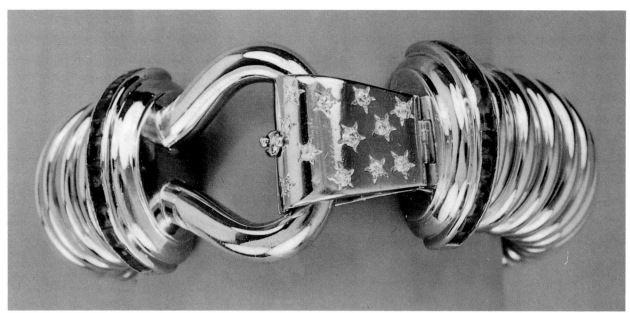

Flexible bracelet in gold and rubies with small diamonds. Van Cleef et Arpels.

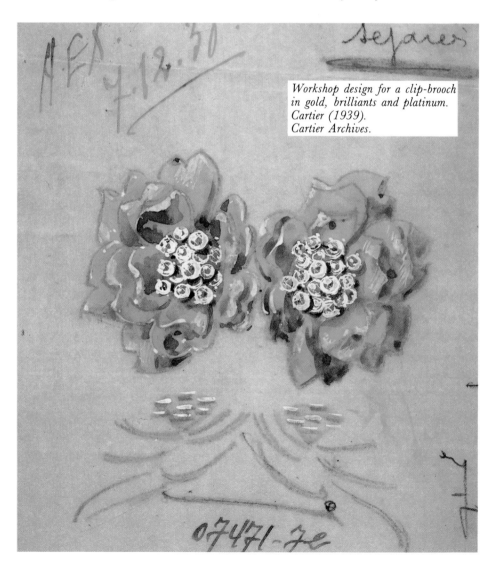

Workshop design for a clip-brooch in gold, brilliants and platinum. Cartier (1939). Cartier Archives.

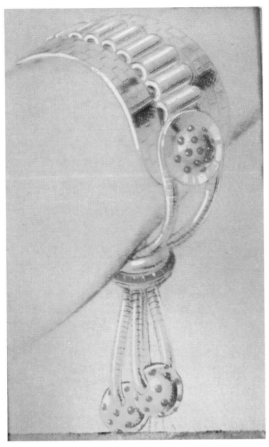

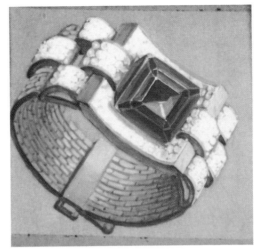

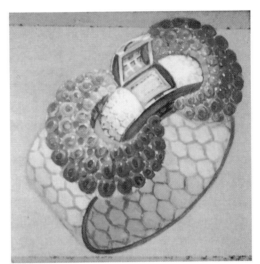

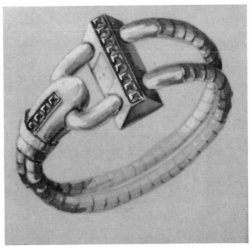

Workshop drawings for bracelet designs.
Van Cleef et Arpels (between 1937 and
1938).

Bracelet with detachable trapezoid clip-brooch in
gold and topazes. Cartier (1936). Cartier Archives.

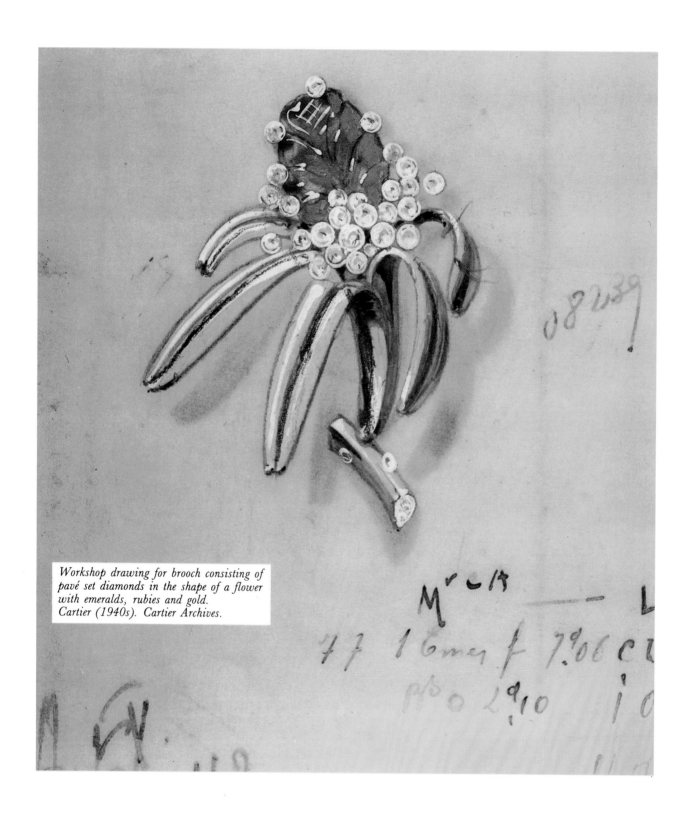

Workshop drawing for brooch consisting of pavé set diamonds in the shape of a flower with emeralds, rubies and gold.
Cartier (1940s). Cartier Archives.

CHAPTER VIII
JEWELLERY OF THE 1940S
FASHION

'The imminence of war is bringing to women's fashion a certain sense of dramatic foreboding and some informality' (*Album degli Anni Trenta*, by G. Massobrio and P. Portoghesi).

'In Paris, fashion design managed to keep going, for better or for worse', wrote Bruno de Roselle in his chapter on fashion during the Second World War.

For reasons of economy, skirt hems were raised to the knee. Shoulders, on the other hand, became extravagantly wide. The considerable success met by the tailored costume of masculine cut is well known. Skirts were short and tight, jackets long, covering the hips, and with very square shoulders.

To quote Roselle again: 'Uniform-style tailored costumes were also the general rule in Paris during the Occupation, with those bags with long shoulder straps which were worn slung across the back for cycling.'

Workshop drawings for two butterfly brooches with moving wings, in lapis lazuli and coral. Cartier (1944). Cartier Archives.

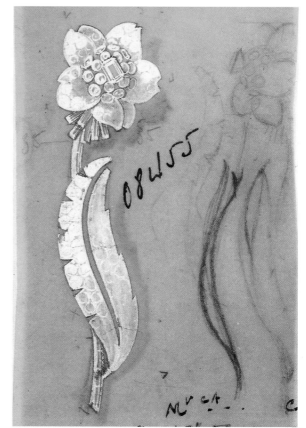

Workshop drawing for brooch consisting of pavé set diamonds in the shape of flower with emeralds, rubies and gold. Cartier (1940s). Cartier Archives.

Workshop designs for brooches of pavé set diamonds in the form of a flower. Cartier (1942). Cartier Archives.

As during the 1914-18 war, all over Europe women replaced the men who had gone to the front, as manual workers, office workers, managers.

These groups of women, conditioned by their economic role in society, naturally had new needs and demands in dress, and obviously jewellery had to accede to them. The productive woman, earning her living and that of her family, was no longer the fragile, dreamy creature of the past. Tailored jackets, modeled on men's jackets, became square cut, and trousers became more and

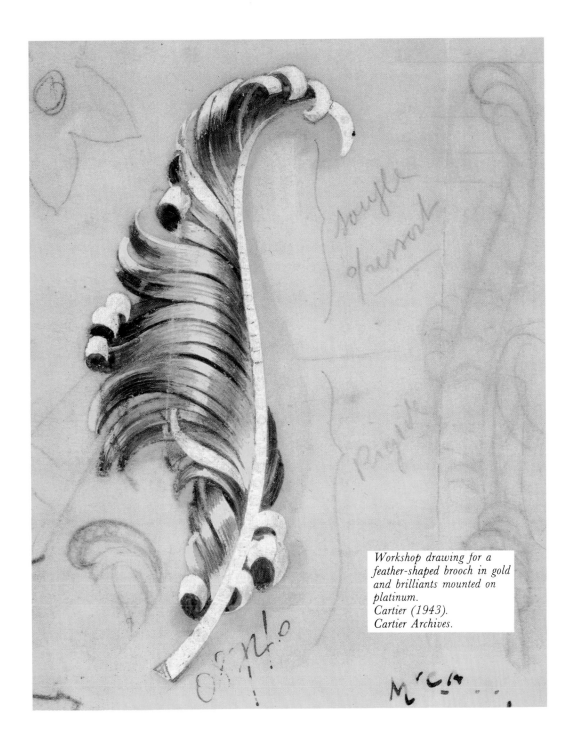

Workshop drawing for a feather-shaped brooch in gold and brilliants mounted on platinum.
Cartier (1943).
Cartier Archives.

more wide and loose. It might be said that women were requisitioned at the factory, as their husbands were at the front.

Probably as a form of compensation, for it is difficult to entirely abandon femininity, square, low-cut necklines were decorated with showy clips, and (Sunday best) hats took on a romantic air. They were embellished with extravagant decorations and sophisticated veils, and seemed to be perched on the head, as they had been in the Nineties.

Shoes were adapted to the necessities of work. They became more practical. Cork soles appeared, as a replacement for leather, which had become hard to

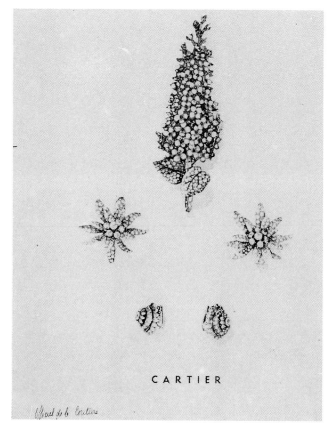

CARTIER

Plate showing Cartier jewellery published in the October 1941 issue of 'L'Officiel de la Couture'.

find. Confronted with these heavy blocked soles, it is tempting to refer to them as 'orthopaedic' shoes.

'It is quite evident that after six years of war, people had rather lost their taste for high fashion. Paris, in particular, suffered from the isolation in which it had been confined by the Occupation', reports Bruno de Roselle.

But high fashion soon began to take off again, and new names immediately began to appear. The new show took place in 1945 at the Museum of Decorative Arts, with models by all the great designers of the period: Jacques Fath, Balenciaga, Givenchy, Balmain, Lucien Lelong.

For afternoon dresses the fashion for short, full skirts was launched. But for evening wear, the top was a kind of very low-cut bodice, covered with a little bolero for outdoors.

The fashion show at the Museum of Decorative Arts was enormous. People came from everywhere to see it.

Christian Dior, father of the 'New Look', who took his first steps in the world of *haute couture* alongside Lelong, opened his workshop in 1947, and immediately showed himself to be among the greatest. The specific feature of his revolution was the lengthening of skirts, which came down to mid-calf. The waist remained pronounced, it was emphasised even more strongly. The straight skirt — one might even say, uniform skirt — gave way to fluted skirts, flared at the bottom. Shoulders were no longer emphasised, and lost their wartime squareness. Low-cut necklines became pointed in shape, thus giving prominence to the neck... and the cleavage.

Jewellery in France

The 1940s were indelibly marked by the Second World War, which broke out in September 1939. In the Europe invaded by Germany, destruction was rife. Soldiers and civilians alike perished, either at the front or under the rubble of bombed cities. The allies intervened, but not without heavy losses and a great deal of destruction. Peace returned in 1945. For a time Europe was overwhelmed with enthusiasm, then victors and vanquished set out to reconstruct their devastated continent and re-animate the industrial and commercial activities which had lain dormant for five years.

It is clear that a period of such turmoil hardly favoured the production of jewellery, which in wartime became a trivial pursuit. The reasons for its decline are both many and obvious, but are nevertheless worth stating: firstly, the destruction of factories and workshops; secondly, the desertion of the workshops which had been spared by the conscription of the workforce; finally, Europe was cut off from the rest of the world, and no longer received either stones or precious metals, the raw materials for jewellery production.

In 1942, Georges Fouquet noted: '...at the present time the jewellery being produced in Paris has lost its character of artistic composition by a return to the past. Let us hope that this is only temporary.'

Most works on jewellery have little to say about the jewellery produced in the 1940s, taking the war (which interrupted all activity in this field) as a pretext.

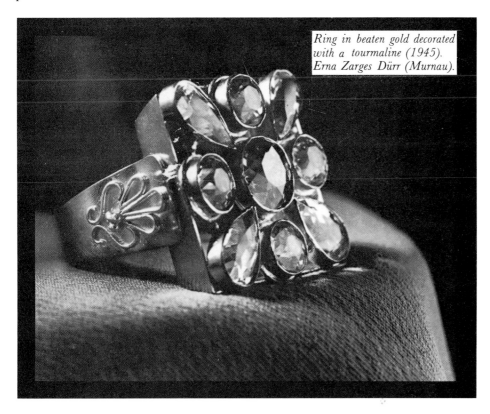

Ring in beaten gold decorated with a tourmaline (1945). Erna Zarges Dürr (Murnau).

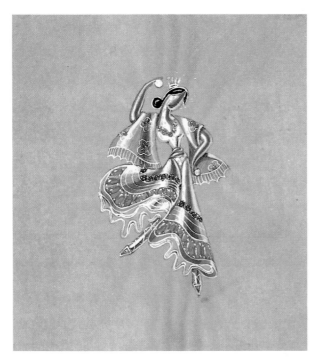

Designs for brooches.
Mauboussin.

Workshop drawing for an 'owl' brooch in gold, brilliants,
enamel, sapphires and turquoises.
Cartier (1945). Cartier Archives.

This interruption was not, however, total, even if, in some countries like Germany for example, there was a complete halt in production. But even so, in that country which suffered so much in the war, jewellers tried to carry on working, creating jewels out of weak alloys, and even out of iron.

In France, on the other hand, the situation was rather different. Destruction had been quite limited. Paris had been spared and the jewellers, once

Gold ring with cabochon-cut ruby presented to Chancellor Adenauer by the 'Deutsches Handwerk' in 1948. Erna Zarges Dürr (Murnau).

demobilised, had once more taken up their professional activities.

It is of course quite obvious that the evolution of style is related to the evolution of society. Although the jeweller's craft adapted itself to circumstances, the problem of raw materials was posed more acutely than ever.

In 1940 wholesale trade in gold was forbidden by the Bank of France. If a client wanted an object in gold, he had to supply the metal necessary for its manufacture. When platinum and gold were melted down, the State took its share: 20% of the value of the metal.

Moreover, precious stones had practically disappeared from the market. But, in spite of these difficulties, French jewellery was able to swim against the current. Some writers on the subject deny this vigorously, but need only be reminded of the article which appeared in May 1940 in the *Officiel de la Couture*: 'Not only in the domain of dress design and fashion is the French luxury industry carrying out a daily miracle of courage, will-power and energy, but also in the area responsible for the most traditional virtues of high taste and sober selectivity of jewellery... Eminently a luxury trade, French jewellery could not pretend to survive in these difficult times without modifying its aims and outlook. True, extremely valuable pieces are still to be seen in shop-windows ... But French men and women who, at the present time, feel the desire to cross the portals of the great jewellery houses which are the pride of our national trade, are rather looking for costume jewellery at a more easily accessible price. For this reason, Parisian jewellers have been above all orientated towards practical and decorative considerations in their creations.'

The raw materials most highly regarded remained gold, silver, platinum and precious stones, for the intrinsic value of the article of jewellery is a deeply rooted preference in our civilisation.

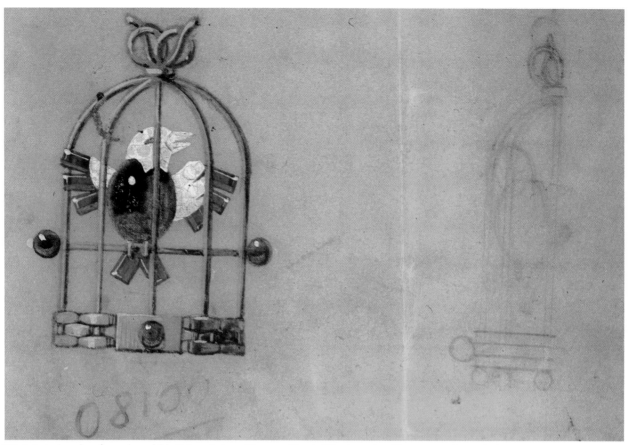

Workshop drawing for a 'caged bird' brooch in gold, emeralds, brilliants and rubies, mounted on platinum. Cartier (1942). Cartier Archives.

Various rings, including bridge, turban and open-book designs. Italy.

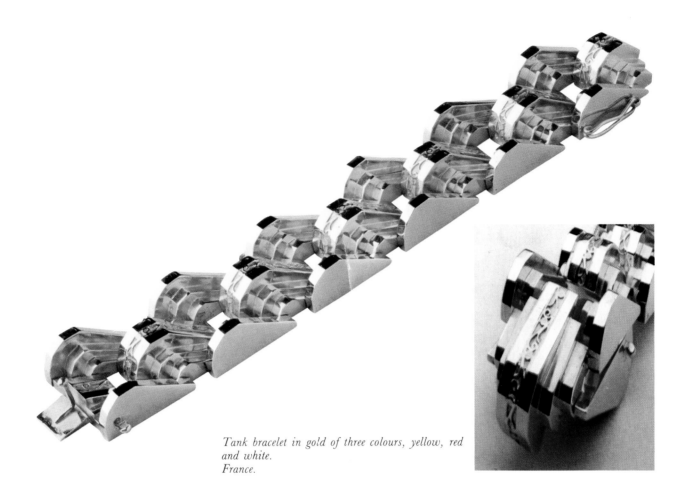

Tank bracelet in gold of three colours, yellow, red and white.
France.

The article quoted above was illustrated by the reproduction of two sumptuous earrings and an imposing brooch in platinum and brilliants.

But how was French jewellery able to retain its vitality in spite of the draconian restrictions imposed by the difficulty of the times? Probably the great houses had made substantial stockpiles of stones and precious metals. Jewellers we have asked maintain that the client usually arrived with antique jewellery to be transformed and updated.

Also, the government, in an attempt to encourage the activity of this important branch of French commercial activity, had decided to reduce the tax on jewellery (which thus went from 33% to 13%).

Then, as is suggested by the above article, the public was often persuaded to cross the jeweller's threshold by the desire to possess, in such a critical and uncertain period, 'under the mattress goods' which could be easily carried and hidden.

It is worth quoting a very forcible confirmation of this point by Georges Fouquet in 1942 in *L'Orfèvrerie, la Joaillerie*: ''Buyers, usually very recent jewellery fanciers, tend to turn their attention to stones of value. In this way jewellery is losing its artistic and decorative character, and becoming a 'solid investment', a 'form of capital' which has the special advantage of being 'readily transportable.''

For those who would claim that the war brought an almost complete halt to the jewellery trade, and above all that the archives of the big firms for this period show what might be called major gaps, we recall a text which appeared in *La Voix Française* of November 1941. Not without humour, it tells us that 'jewellers these days have no reason to complain'.

This is also confirmed by a number of other publications, like the *Officiel de la Couture et de la Mode de Paris* which, in June 1942, published reproductions of grandiose *parures* in platinum and diamonds produced by Boucheron, Cartier, Mellerio and many others. There is, however, more. Boucheron and Cartier's albums for the war years reveal an active production, although one which, it is true, was rather impoverished in terms of the birth of new forms. Mellerio's in particular shows — with the support of a number of dated photographs — an abundant prouction of new articles created precisely during the war period. In general, however, these were gold pieces rather than extravagant *parures* in platinum and brilliants.

In addition, the Cartier archives confirm the impression — however paradoxical it might seem — that if on the one hand there was less creation of new models, on the other, the workshop maintained its activities almost without interruption. The production of gold jewellery increased to such an extent that the use of gold in proportion to the use of platinum and brilliants went from a quarter to three quarters.

Nor should we limit our research to the production of the most famous jewellers, given that a large quantity of valuable and finely crafted objects were made, during and immediately after the war, by anonymous jewellers, both in France and the rest of Europe.

It might be deplored that these artisans, perhaps through excessive modesty, were not used to signing or initialling their works. But a number of the objects they produced have survived. They are to be found in private collections when they are not in circulation on the open market. And this is an irrefutable testimony to the vitality and fecundity of jewellers at this time.

It must be made clear that when we talk of the jewellery of the 1940s we are not referring exclusively to the specimens produced in the decade going from 1939 to 1949, but are thinking also of their precursors, the gold jewellery of the 1930s described in the previous chapter.

But how far is it legitimate to consider the latter to be closely linked from a stylistic point of view with the jewellery of the 1940s? Clearly it is, in so far as these models present the most marked characteristics of the style which was to develop and extend over the next ten years, although with certain substantial differences which it is useful to mention.

In the first place, the gold jewellery of the 1930s is notable for its abundant use of large precious stones, and for its geometrical style inherited from Art Deco (even though it is no longer flat, but contoured and in relief). In general, the creations of the 1940s are less rich in gemstones.

Other differences distinguish wartime production from that of the period to follow. The beginning of the 1940s was characterised by an abundance of hollow pieces, or by jewellery made of thin layers of gold soldered onto less

1. *Bridge ring in gold, rubies and brilliants.*

2. *Bow ring in yellow gold, emeralds and brilliants.*

3. *Turban ring in grey gold, sapphires and brilliants.*

4. *Ring in gold and brilliants.*

5-6. *Open-book ring in gold and brilliants.*

7. *Bridge ring in gold and brilliants.*

8. *Open-book ring in gold and brilliants.*

9. *Bridge ring in gold and rubies.*

Mellerio dits Meller Archives (Paris).

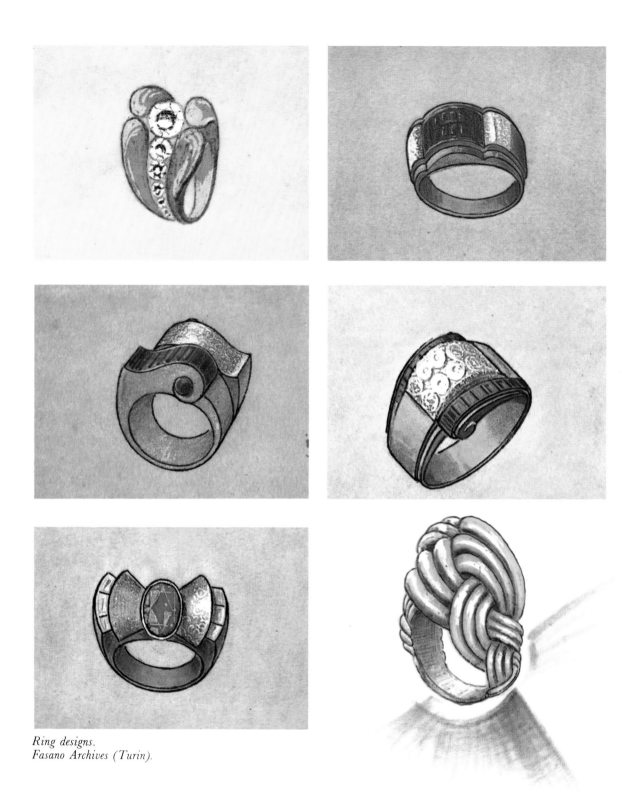

Ring designs.
Fasano Archives (Turin).

expensive metals. The aesthetic effect remained. The object retained its massive and voluminous appearance, but was much less heavy.

Economy was substantial. Precious stones were used parsimoniously. They were often replaced by semi-precious stones (aquamarines, topazes, citrines, amethysts) or by synthetic stones coloured like sapphires and rubies.

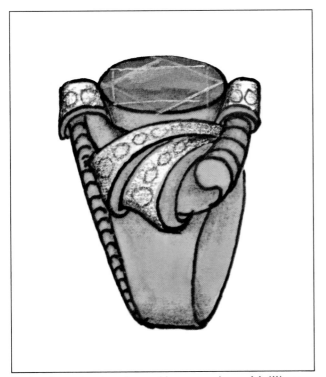

Design for a ring in yellow gold, aquamarine and brilliants.
Fecarotta Archives (Catane).

Design for a ring in yellow gold, with sapphire and brilliants.
Veneziani Brothers Archives (Milan-Rome).

Four types of bow ring. France.

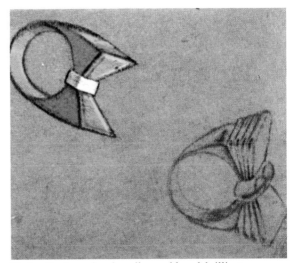

Design for bow ring in yellow gold and brilliants.
Bulgari Archives (Rome).

The post-war period saw a formal evolution characterised by an increase in the volume of articles of jewellery in gold, which now took on an extreme form of naturalism. At the same time, rich decoration in precious stones re-appeared. The working of the metal also became more complex, and fretted lacework and motifs recalling wrought iron became more and more prevalent. In short, the structure of articles of jewellery became richer and more elaborate.

We should, however, examine the character of the jewellery of the 1940s and the decorative themes most frequently used. From an aesthetic point of view,

Signet-style ring, decorated in the centre with an emerald surrounded by sapphires and brilliants. Cartier (1945). Cartier Archives.

Ring in gold, diamonds and rubies (1940). Private Collection.

Ring in yellow gold, white gold, diamonds and emeralds. Dusausoy (Private Collection).

Spatula-shaped ring with alternating braids in gold and rubies and an emerald in the centre. Cartier (1946). Cartier Archives.

Turban ring in gold and diamonds. Private Collection.

Signet-style ring in gold and diamonds. Mellerio dits Meller (1941). Mellerio dits Meller Archives.

the plasticity and three-dimensionality of an article of jewellery became noticeable, giving it a sculptural quality which was contrary to the principles of Art Deco, based on linear or 'flat' forms.

The break with symmetry and absolutely geometrical forms was now fully accomplished. The period saw the triumphant return of curved lines, circles, volutes, natural and asymmetrical designs. The thematic repertoire derived from nature, and flowers, bouquets, birds, plumage, bows, snowflakes, as well as pleats, turnings and curls, were legion, but in a realist rather than a symbolist manner.

Gold now replaced platinum. But it was a gold which took on whimsical tints — red, pink, green, yellow, white or grey, according to the proportions in which it was alloyed with copper or silver. It became the principle basis of and framework for the article of jewellery. It was used for smooth or fluted motifs, in perforated plaques, in single or multiple strands, plaited or cross-wired.

The stone most frequently used remained the diamond, often small in dimension, preferably square cut or rectangular, combined with coloured stones, usually square in shape.

The most frequent combination was one involving sapphires and rubies (sometimes even synthetic ones), used alone or in conjunction with diamonds. Semi-precious stones such as topaz, aquamarine, turquoise, citrine and amethyst, were also used. It was all produced with a fantasy and a variety of forms and structures which gave rise to the most unusual specimens of the century.

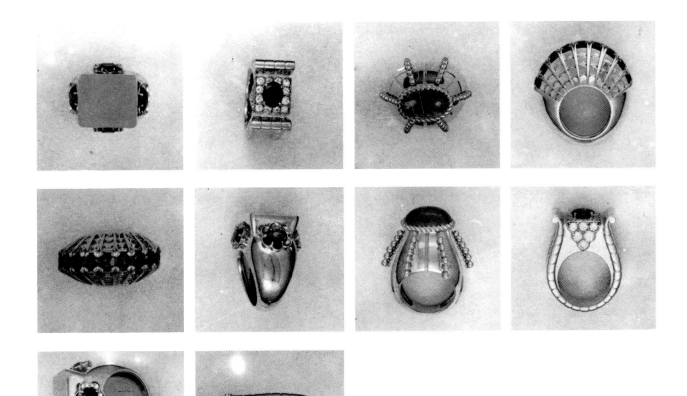

Series of signet-style rings in gold and precious stones. Cartier (1945). Cartier Archives.

Harmony was the rule in design, as in the choice of materials for *parures,* which consisted of bracelets, brooches and earrings.

Bracelets were certainly the most characteristic articles of jewellery of this period. Made of gold, often articulated, they were composed of elaborate motifs, angular or pleated according to formulae which were intended to make them appear larger. The motifs could be square, rectangular, hexagonal, round or trapezoid — shapes undeniably inherited from the geometrical tradition.

Jewellers of the period gave a free rein to their imaginations as far as motifs were concerned. These were joined by bulky links, bridges or medallions, which accentuated the relief of the piece.

The most characteristic models were those which imitated bicycle chains or moving staircases, inspired by industrial design. There also existed a design which presents alternating grooves and projecting angles strongly suggesting the caterpillars of a tank. These bracelets were, in fact, called 'Tank bracelets'. In 1917 Louis Cartier had already given the name 'tank watch' to a model inspired by the tanks which appeared during the First World War. But the term 'tank', which appeared so appropriate, had already become a household word.

There were other forms of bracelet fashionable in the 1940s, like the Ludo bracelet, the bridge bracelet, the snake bracelet or the rat's tail, which had begun to be produced towards the end of the 1930s, and which we have already discussed in the preceding chapter.

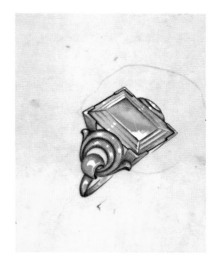

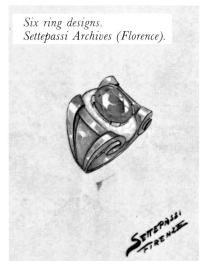

Six ring designs.
Settepassi Archives (Florence).

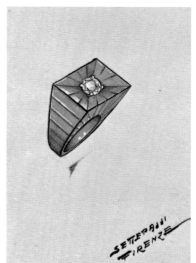

Design for a ring.
Settepassi Archives (Florence).

We should now describe some of the most typical designs, drawn from the archives of the principal Paris firms.

Boucheron's 1940 design album shows a gold bangle, composed of two curved feathers ruffled at the bottom. The following year's production includes a classic tank bracelet.

Another style of bracelet very fashionable around 1942 was decorated with a series of arrow flight motifs. This design was also used for watch straps.

Again by Boucheron (1942), was a type of band bracelet created in interlaced tightly woven gold wire, with a cylindrical clasp decorated with two lines of rubies alternating with a line of brilliants.

In the same year Mellerio launched the pennant bracelet composed of a series of banderoles in gold.

Different versions of the strap and buckle bracelet were also very fashionable. One was decorated with fish scales, another in woven gold links, with the loop of the buckle decorated with rubies and brilliants.

Mellerio inserted on a gold strap and buckle bracelet, decorated with a fish-scale pattern, a bouquet of flowers with corollae in gold and pistils in brilliants and coloured precious stones.

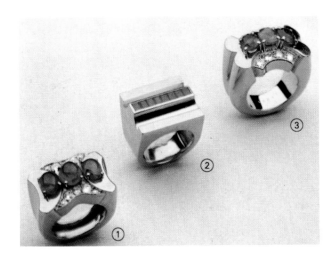

Turkish ring in yellow gold
and star set sapphires.
Cartier.

Ring in wrought iron style
with brilliants. France.

1. *Bridge ring in yellow gold, brilliants and cabochon-cut rubies. Mauboussin.*

2. *Signet-style ring in yellow gold and synthetic rubies. France.*

3. *Bridge ring in yellow gold, brilliants and rubies. Mauboussin.*

4. *Ring in yellow gold and sapphires. Cartier. Photo: Sotheby's.*

5. *Ring in yellow gold and sapphires incorporating a watch. Cartier. Photo:Sotheby's.*

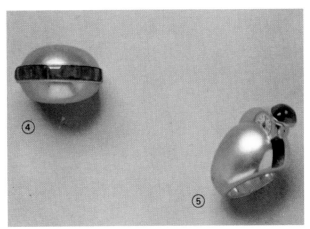

A series of flexible bracelets by Cartier dates from 1946. One is in the 'gas-pipe' style, with an oval cross-section, and motifs in interlaced gold wire, decorated with small sapphires and brilliants.

Two similar gas-pipe models were created in the same year (1946). The first, with double coil, loop and clasp in gold wire, has in its centre a sapphire surrounded by six rubies. The second has an emerald clasp.

In 1947, Cartier launched a fluted bracelet with lozenge motifs in gold wire and sapphires, with, in the centre, an oval cabochon-cut ruby surrounded by brilliants.

In 1947-48, gold wire bracelets in the shape of springs became fashionable. Most often these consisted of two strands of gold wire in the shape of springs with a decoration of brilliants between the two. The bottom part of the bracelet was formed of woven gold wire. Another design in gold of the same period suggests a braid of wavy hair.

At the end of the 1940s (1947-48), the strap and buckle bracelet in woven gold wire was often decorated at the end with fringes and pompoms.

Wrist-watches also occupied an important place in the arsenal of jewellery of this decade. Watches were mostly small, with heavy straps in gold. The dial, which was usually square, was often hidden beneath a lid. The straps were in the mode of the times, consisting of articulated motifs, metal ribbons, rat's-tail structures, braids of gold wire, or openwork bands with motifs deriving from

*Platinum ring with emeralds
and brilliants.
Bulgari (Rome).*

239

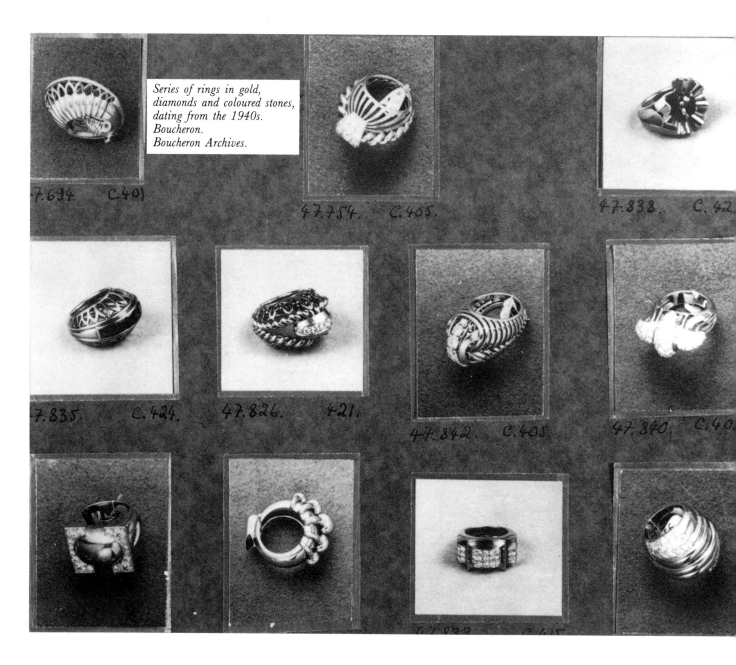

Series of rings in gold, diamonds and coloured stones, dating from the 1940s. Boucheron. Boucheron Archives.

wrought iron work. The lid of the dial was usually set with precious stones. Many watches had leather straps. Where this was the case the dial and fastenings were decorated with ornamental motifs.

But what was the elegant way to wear a wristwatch? The October 1947 issue of *Femina* offers the following advice: 'This is the secret: Wear it over beautiful black gloves with slightly ruched cuffs, to show off the lustre of the metal.'

A special place was reserved for rings, which have always been the pride of jewellers. The rings of the 1940s were of massive, heavy structure, in the signet-ring style. They were usually in solid gold, decorated with brilliant-cut diamonds, calibré-cut coloured stones, or synthetic stones. They can be categorised in five groups, the designations of which became classic from that period onwards: — *bague à pont* (bridge ring): the two ends of the ring are linked by a motif with a flat surface, usually decorated with precious stones; — *bague 'livre ouvert'* (open-book ring): the ends are here linked by a two-facetted motif

'Liberated bird' brooches of gold, coral, lapis lazuli and sapphires mounted on platinum and gold. Cartier (1944). Cartier Archives.

reminiscent of an open book; — *bague à la turque* (Turkish ring): directly inspired by the fez; — *bague turban* (turban ring): spiralled in the shape of the famous Oriental headpiece; — *bague noeud* (bow ring): represented by different, often stylised forms of knot or bow, decorated in the centre (and sometimes on the sides) with precious stones.

The Boucheron album for 1940-41 shows an important series of bridge rings. This jeweller produced at the same time rings with motifs in the form of 'melon slices', in which lines of brilliant-cut diamonds were alternated with lines of coloured stones. Although, in 1942 and 1943, women showed a marked predilection for turban shapes, Dusausoy nevertheless created a signet-style ring in gold, decorated with two semi-circles in emeralds, butted against each other to form an X shape, and contrasting with a surround of brilliant-cut diamonds.

There were also mobile rings, like one by Mellerio in yellow gold decorated with two mobile spheres embellished with calibré-cut rubies and sapphires.

In October 1947, the review *Femina* remarked: 'Mixtures of stones are in fashion. Thus, the combination of rubies, gold and diamonds is always extremely elegant. This was a must for Cartier in creating this ring, which goes marvellously with a fine gold bracelet enriched with precious stones.'

At the end of the 1940s Boucheron presented a series of light, open-work rings, following the style of wrought iron work, and made out of a sheet of gold cut and fretted like a piece of lace. They were all decorated with brilliant-cut diamonds and coloured precious stones.

During the 1940s brooches and clips enjoyed unprecedented success. Their size and volume had nothing in common with their ancestors of the Art Deco period.

To attract attention, gold jewellery without the advantage of glittering stones had to count on volume, which became considerable. This kind of consideration gave birth to the large bows, the imposing bouquets, the huge

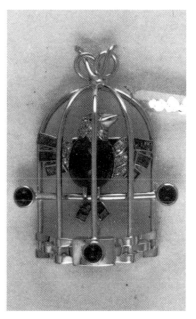

'Caged bird' clip-brooch. The cage is in gold wire and cabochon emeralds, the bird in emeralds, brilliants and calibré-cut rubies, with an onyx eye (1942). Cartier Archives.

241

Ring in gold, diamonds and sapphires.
Gübelin (1940).
Franco Bernardini Collection.

Ruby ring mounted on yellow gold. Photo: Laurent Sully-Jaulmes.

Ring in gold, diamonds and sapphire.
Private Collection.

Gold ring consisting of two mobile balls in calibré-cut sapphires, rubies, topazes and emeralds.
Mellerio dits Meller.
Mellerio dits Meller Archives.

Bridge ring in gold and brilliants.
Signed: Boucheron.
Private Collection.

Watch-ring in gold: dial hidden under a ribbed lid.
U.T.I. Paris.
Private Collection.

1. Gold and diamond ring.
Private collection.

2. Bridge ring in gold, diamonds and sapphires.

3. Gold and diamond ring, decorated in the centre with a large sapphire. Private Collection.

flowers with wide corollae, the masses of foliage and greenery which at this point began to invade the lapels of tailored costumes and the low-cut necklines of evening dresses.

In Boucheron's album for 1939-40 there is a gold brooch in the form of a feather with the veins in brilliants. This album reveals many specimens of brooches with motifs deriving from the bestiary. It is interesting to note that the 1940s exploited to the full this form of imagery, which is to be found in practically all periods of the art of jewellery.

But the stylisation of Art Deco was a thing of the past, and the tiny animals of the post-war period were simultaneously realistic, plastic (in the sculptural sense), strongly designed, and dynamic. They were decorated with emeralds

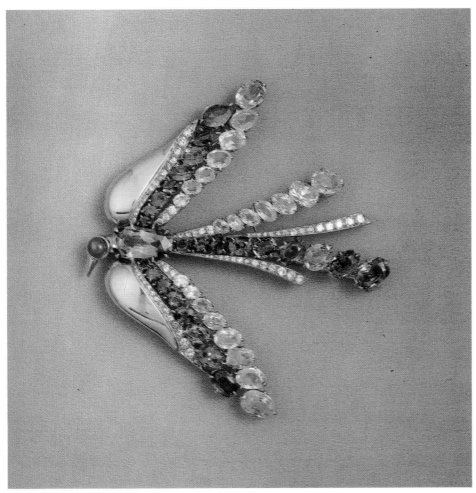

'Bird of Paradise' brooch in yellow gold, yellow and blue sapphires, brilliants and cabochon rubies. Van Cleef et Arpels. Photo: Laurent Sully-Jaulmes.

or combinations of stones. They were all either domesticated animals (dogs, horses, farmyard animals) or exotic birds and mammals (birds of paradise, pink flamingoes, monkeys, tigers, lions, panthers and leopards) or even reptiles and camels.

Cartier displays a remarkable example of this taste for zoology, with what we might call a 'nature reserve', as astounding for the animal specimens it contains as for the rarity of the materials used.

The credit for developing this aspect of production must go to Jeanne Toussaint, assisted by the Cartier designer Peter Lemarchand, who shared her love for animals. The most shining example of all was the flamingo brooch in rubies, sapphires, emeralds, citrines and diamonds, commissioned from Cartier by the Duke of Windsor in 1940.

Lemarchand was inspired by the deprivations of wartime, which for some involved captivity, to create the lyrical image of a caged nightingale, the symbolism of which requires no comment. In 1945, he offered a new version of the same theme, representing the tiny bird liberated, joyously singing at the open door of its cage.

Peter Lemarchand must also take credit for having created the model of the panther, so often present in the 1940s production. In truth, this was a subject

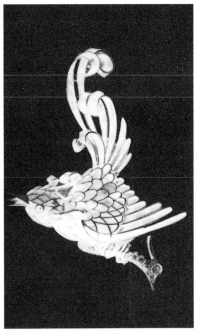

Bird clip in gold, translucent enamel and brilliants. Exhibited in Lyons in October 1941, Mellerio dits Meller. Mellerio dits Meller Archives.

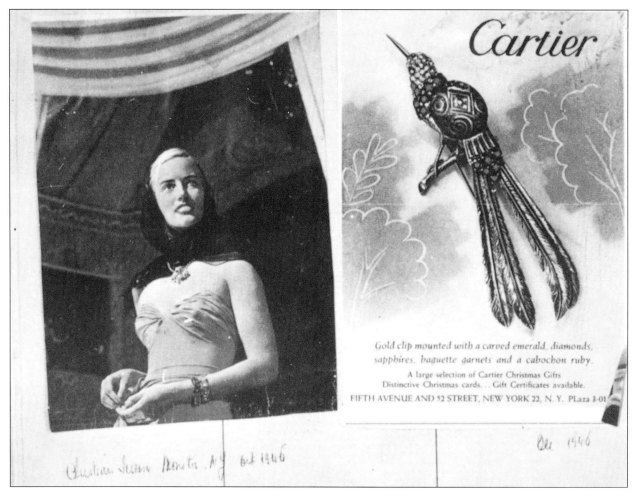

Advertisement for Cartier jewellery, published in December 1946.

Bird brooch in topaz, sapphires and coral.
Cartier (1943).
Cartier Archives.

in which Cartier had always been interested. Towards 1914, the markings on the coat of the big cat had inspired the abstract decorations, in brilliants and onyx, of strap bracelets and wrist-watches. But the prototype of the panther in its three-dimensional version dates from the 1940s generation of jewellery. It was commissioned from Cartier in 1948 by the Duke of Windsor. The piece was composed of a cabochon emerald of 116.74 carats, on which was laid a panther whose body was set with brilliants and spotted with onyx.

This panther brooch had such a lively success that it was soon followed by innumerable replicas in which the big cat was represented in every imaginable posture (lying down, playing, ready to fight).

The floral repertoire, that other favourite of the jewellers of the 1940s, was made up of roses, lilies of the valley, buttercups, asters, anemones and dahlias. Sometimes the bouquet of flowers, in gold embellished with coloured stones, was tied, at the top of the stems, with a large-looped bow. Boucheron's favourite flowers were lucky lilies of the valley (leaves in gold and trumpet in brilliants), anemones and lilac.

A 1941 brooch by Cartier was composed of a bunch of lilac in gold with petals set with brilliants and coloured stones, and strangely recalled the famous sprig of lilac, enamelled and beaded with dewdrops in brilliants, shown by Mellerio at the Universal Exhibition of 1862.

Carved and chased kitten brooch with diamond set eyes and purple enamel bow collar playing with a ball formed from a baroque pearl. *Circa 1945.*

'Bullrush' brooch: the nest in gold, the eggs in pearls, the bird in brilliants, with an emerald for the head. *Cartier (1943). Cartier Archives.*

Left:
Bird-shaped brooch in emeralds, brilliants and gold, mounted on platinum.
Cartier (1942).
Cartier Archives.

Owl brooch in topaz, sapphires and coral. *Cartier (1943). Cartier Archives.*

The 'Hawaii' brooch by Van Cleef et Arpels consisted of a bouquet of small flowers set with rubies, brilliants and sapphires, with lanceolate leaves in gold.

The range of bouquets of flowers created by Van Cleef et Arpels towards the end of the 1930s and throughout the 1940s was enormous. It included the simple open rose with petals and leaves in yellow gold and pistils in brilliants, and — at the opposite extreme — a composition of red and blue forget-me-nots corresponding to the decoration of the *parure,* with a basic gas-pipe structure. This was shown in the jeweller's shop window in 1939. The specimen which adorned the tailored costume of the Duchess of Windsor belonged to the series

Ruby, sapphire, emerald, citrine and diamond flamingo clip from the collection of the Duchess of Windsor.
Cartier (1940).
Photo: Sotheby's.

Invisibly set ruby and diamond 'holly leaves' clip from the Duchess of Windsor's collection.
Van Cleef et Arpels, 1936.
Photo: Sotheby's.

Invisibly set sapphire and diamond bracelet created in 1937 by Van Cleef et Arpels for the Duchess of Windsor.
Photo: Sotheby's.

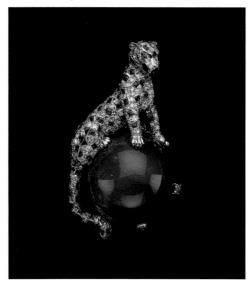

Left: Sapphire and diamond panther clip, the panther pavé set with diamonds and calibré-cut sapphire spots with pear-shaped yellow diamond eyes, crouched on a large cabochon sapphire.
Created for the Duchess of Windsor by Cartier (1949).
Photo: Sotheby's.

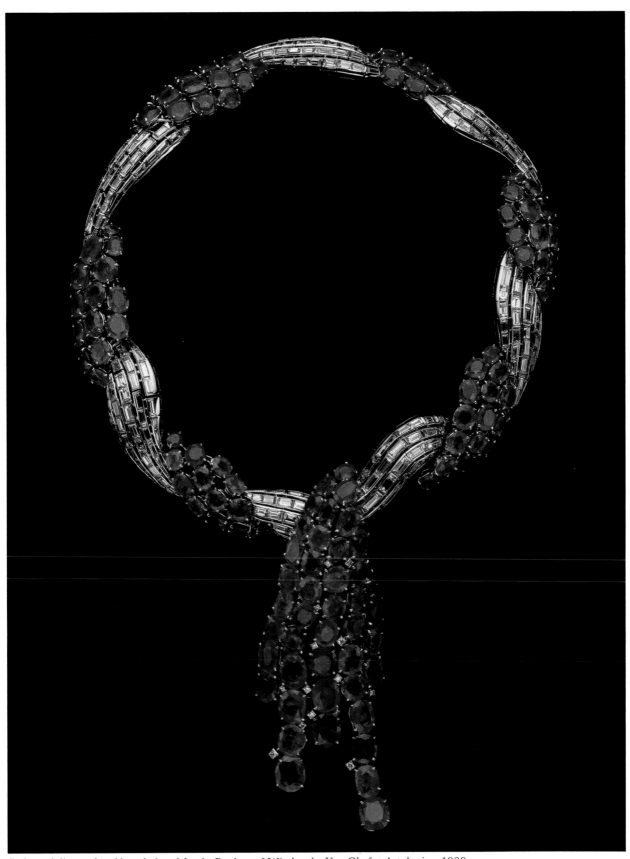

Ruby and diamond necklace designed for the Duchess of Windsor by Van Cleef et Arpels circa 1939.
Photo: Sotheby's.

*Bird-shaped brooch in gold,
emeralds, rubies and brilliants.
Cartier (1945).
Cartier Archives.*

of small bouquets of multicoloured flowers in yellow gold with petals and leaves set with sapphires of varying tones and topazes.

The same design was repeated with infinitely varied combinations of stones (emeralds and brilliants, for example).

Also signed by Van Cleef et Arpels was the pair of clips with two leaves in the shape of elongated hearts in yellow, red and green gold, with a central vein in calibré-cut sapphires.

The flower jewellery produced by Mellerio in the spring of 1941 included an open flower brooch with cabochon-cut rubies and luxurious foliage in gold, as well as an amusing brooch in yellow gold in the form of an Italian straw hat, decorated with a bunch of multicoloured flowers and feathers in cabochon-cut coloured gemstones.

Advertisement for Cartier bird jewellery published in the October 1947 number of 'Femina'.

The bow, another theme exploited in brooches, was used in an infinite series of variations, with larger or smaller loops, solid or in openwork, rigid or flexible, decorated with the usual precious stones.

Boucheron's album for 1941 contains the design for a typical bow brooch in lacy gold openwork embellished with diamonds. Alongside bows, we should mention the brooches in gold mesh.

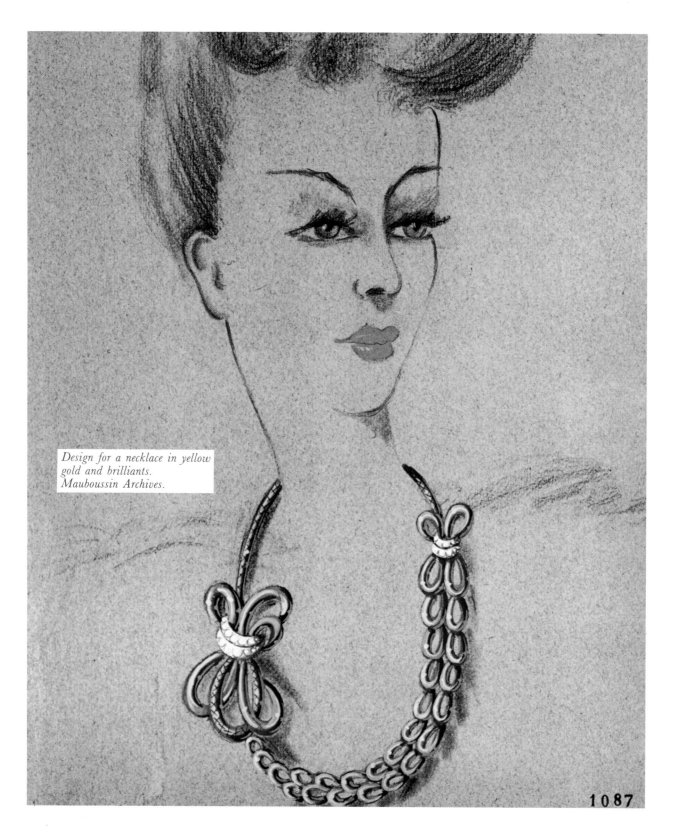

Design for a necklace in yellow gold and brilliants. Mauboussin Archives.

1087

Other shapes served as motifs for brooches and clips: turnings, drapes, cords and question marks, to cite only a few.

In about 1944, Boucheron created a piece in gold in the form of a question mark. It was composed of articulated segments and finished in two mobile

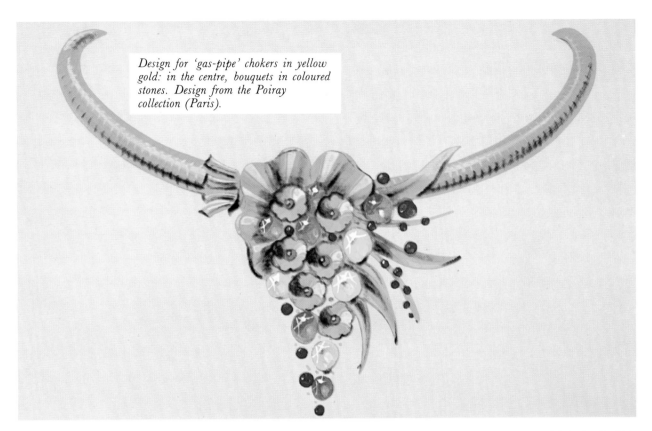

Design for 'gas-pipe' chokers in yellow gold: in the centre, bouquets in coloured stones. Design from the Poiray collection (Paris).

tassels set with coloured precious stones. Another variant on the *cordelette* has a bow-shaped upper part, finishing in a kind of ram's horn.

Some brooches represented a painter's palette, for example the Boucheron model of 1946, complete with brushes. The dabs of colour are rendered by cabochon-cut engraved gemstones.

Between 1941 and 1947, Boucheron created a curious series of brooches representing figures in regional costume (Brittany, Normandy, Périgord,

Photograph of gold jewellery by Cartier published in the 'Officiel de la Mode et de la Couture' for Christmas 1946.

etc.), worked in gold and enamel, and also a series of brooches representing French landscapes or village scenes, again in gold and enamel. Finally, brooches representing members of the different branches of the armed forces in uniform. The reservoir of images seemed to be inexhaustible...

The necklace of the 1940s was a gold choker, usually composed of chains in the gas-pipe or rat's tail style, or of intertwined gold wire, of which the visible

Necklace consisting of gold cord and an assembly of gold discs with emeralds, rubies, sapphires and brilliants. Cartier (1946). Cartier Archives.

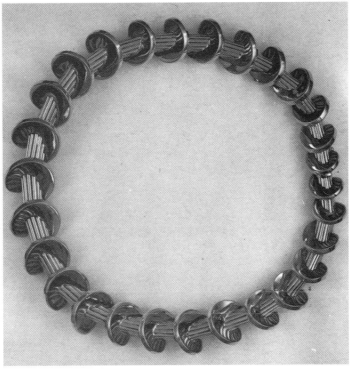

Gold necklace with sequence of motifs on fluted choker. Cartier (1946). Cartier Archives.

part was often embellished with decorative motifs forming collarettes, sometimes detachable. They took the form of massive volutes in gold with motifs drawn from the natural world, or folds and pleats, always produced in gold (of different tones), sometimes set with precious stones.

A series of Boucheron necklaces of 1947 take the form of gold coils finishing in tassels, which are in turn embellished with gold balls.

A very elegant necklace by Van Cleef et Arpels consists of a two-tone choker, of which the left-hand side is made up of small articulated plaques in yellow gold joining up at the front with the right-hand side which is set with calibré-cut citrines.

Clearly, earrings continued to be produced in the 1940s.

The most current form of earring was the clip version: ornamental themes

Gold plaited necklace: in the centre a detachable clip in brilliants and sapphires. Design from the Poiray Collection (Paris).

Design for a spiralled choker with bow in yellow and red gold, brilliants and rubies. Fecarotta Brothers (Catania).

Necklace in yellow gold with descending plaquette motifs. Cartier (1946). Cartier Archives.

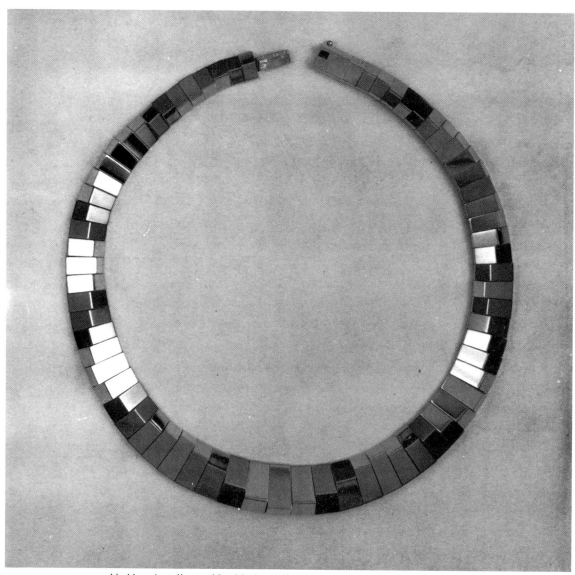

Necklace in yellow gold with descending plaquette motifs. Cartier (1946). Cartier Archives.

were very varied, and noticeably echoed those of brooches and clips (bows, ribbons, fans, bouquets of flowers, small shells, volutes, loops).

A classic design by Cartier (1941) is in the form of an edelweiss made of gold.

We also find pendant earrings composed of fringes of small chains in gold, hanging from tassels or other, varied motifs already listed in our discussion of other forms of jewellery.

The years immediately following the war were marked by a vigorous development of the goldsmith's craft. Indeed, when armed conflict came to an end in 1945, everything had to be recreated. The countries of Europe threw themselves into the adventure of reconstruction, and this was of great benefit to new techniques deriving from war industry. The strong renewal of international exchange created everywhere a climate of enthusiasm and optimism. Indeed, the immediate aftermath of the war saw the emergence of

Necklace in plaited gold wire. Boucheron. Boucheron Archives.

new demands for material goods and luxury products, a very natural reaction after the deprivation of the preceding years.

Out of the debris of war there arose a class of *nouveaux riches*, lacking in cultural and artistic traditions, but with a thirst for opulence and a taste for ostentation, in short a class for which gold was the symbol of new wealth. The gold jewellery of the 1940s often bears the mark of these origins.

Needless to say, things were not the same in every country, partly because of differences in the socio-political climate, partly because of the diversity of traditions.

Moreover, in territories spared by the war, like the United States and Switzerland which, in fashion, followed the precepts deriving from Paris, the uncontested leader of taste, there developed, during the 1940s, a style of gold jewellery born in France several years earlier.

*Parure with bouquet motifs
in yellow gold with
sapphires and rubies.
Van Cleef et Arpels.
Photo: Sotheby's.*

*Gold 'gas-pipe'
necklace with
brilliants.
France (1940).
Private Collection.*

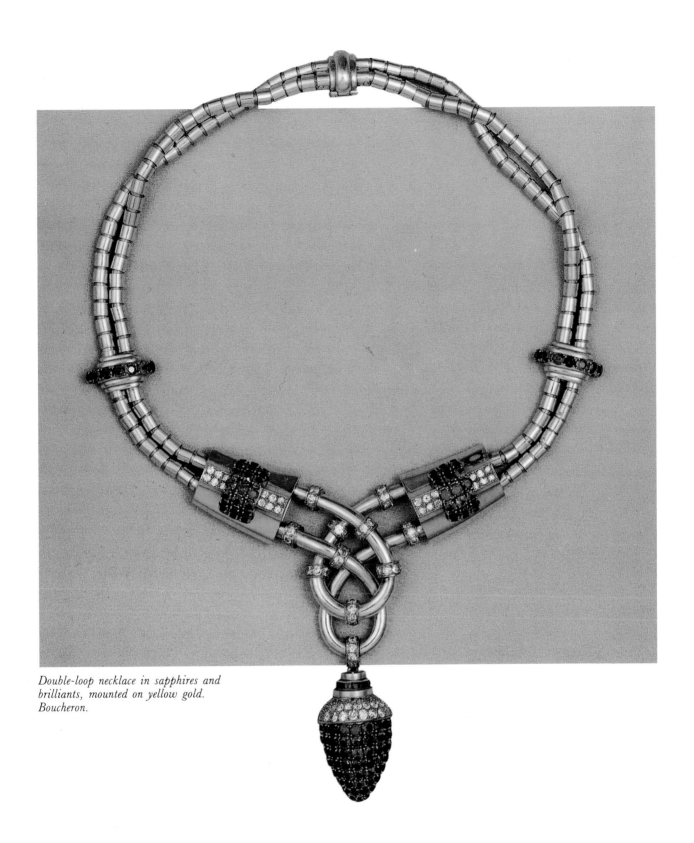

Double-loop necklace in sapphires and brilliants, mounted on yellow gold. Boucheron.

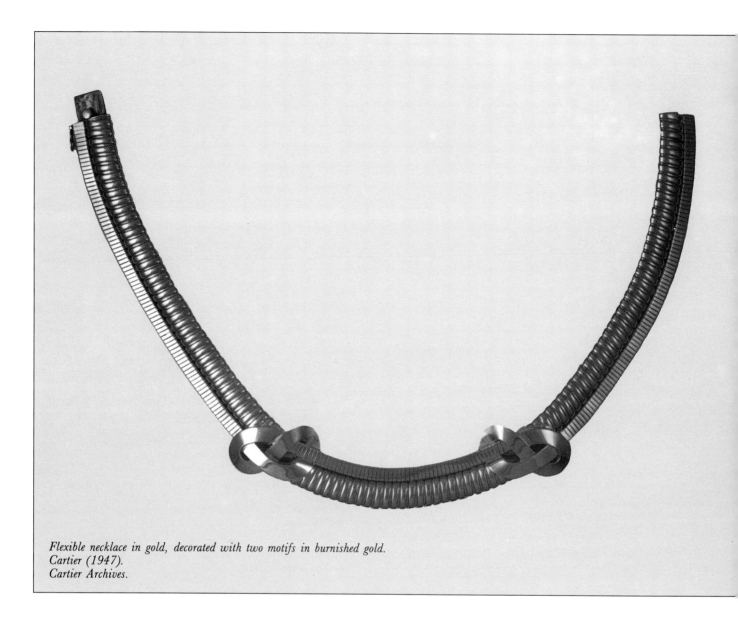

Flexible necklace in gold, decorated with two motifs in burnished gold.
Cartier (1947).
Cartier Archives.

Yellow gold and diamond necklace, signed: Golay fils et Sthal.
Geneva.
Sold in March 1945.

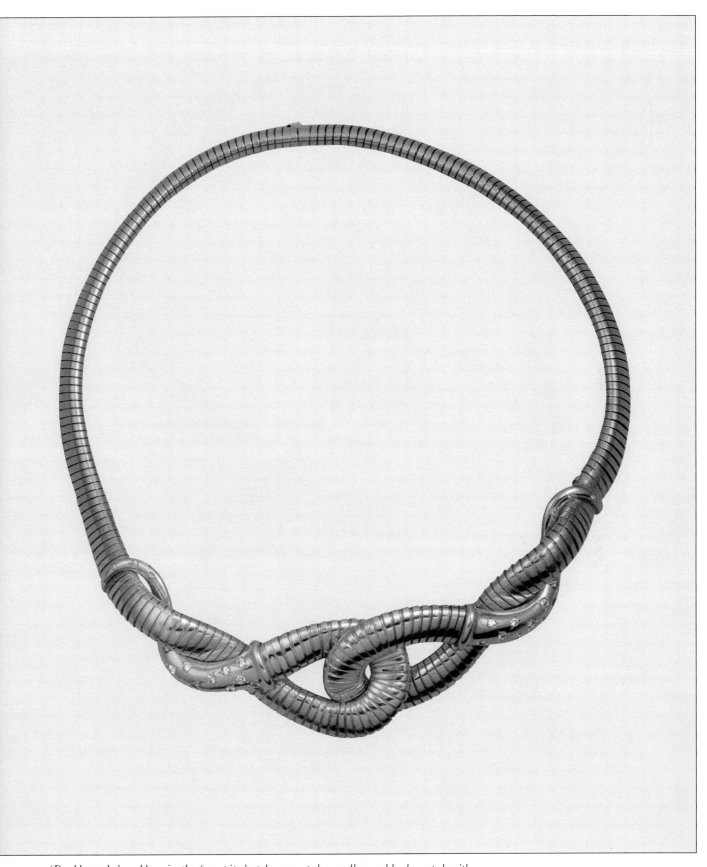

'Double snake' necklace in the 'gas-pipe' style, mounted on yellow gold, decorated with diamonds. Mauboussin. Photo: Laurent Sully-Jaulmes.

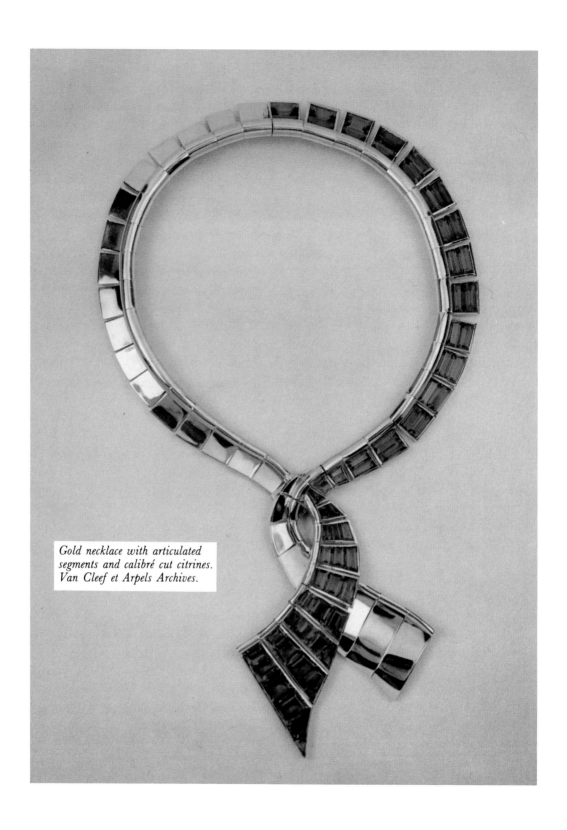

*Gold necklace with articulated
segments and calibré cut citrines.
Van Cleef et Arpels Archives.*

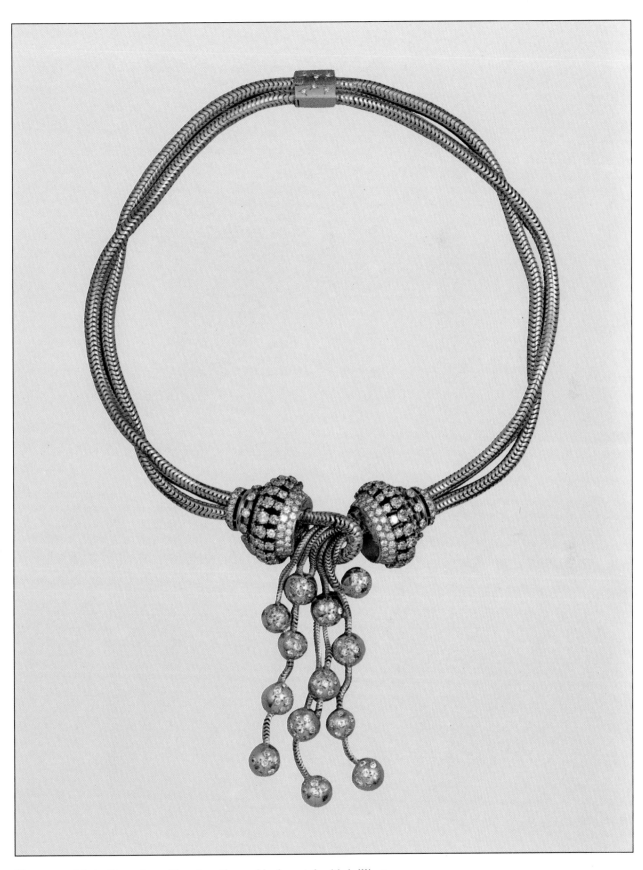

'Passementerie' double snake necklace in yellow gold, decorated with brilliants.
Van Cleef et Arpels.

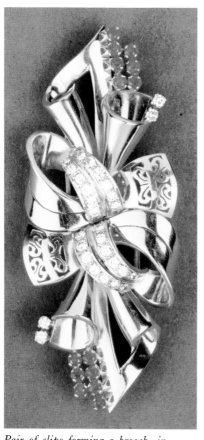

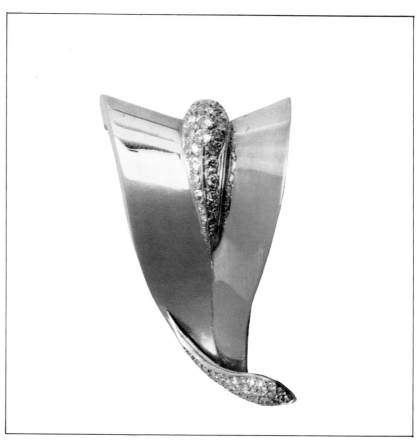

Pair of clips forming a brooch, in yellow gold, white gold, diamonds and rubies. Italy (1940). Private Collection.

Clip in yellow gold and brilliants, Mellerio dits Meller.

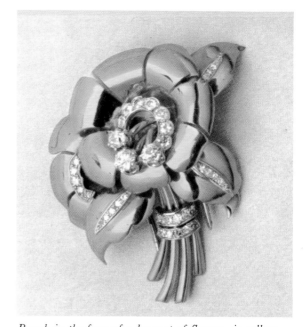

Bouquet brooch in yellow gold, brilliants and emeralds. Van Cleef et Arpels.

Brooch in the form of a bouquet of flowers, in yellow gold and brilliants. Van Cleef et Arpels.

264

Brooch in yellow gold, moonstones, brilliants and rubies. Boucheron.

Flower brooch in platinum and brilliants. Boucheron.

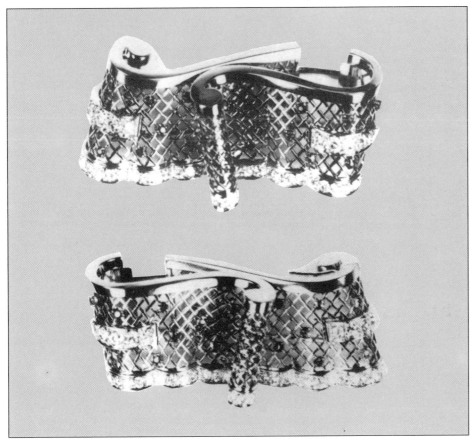

Brooches in gold, brilliants and coloured stones. Boucheron. Boucheron Archives.

Brooches in the form of bouquets of flowers in yellow gold, rubies, topazes and sapphires.
Van Cleef et Arpels.

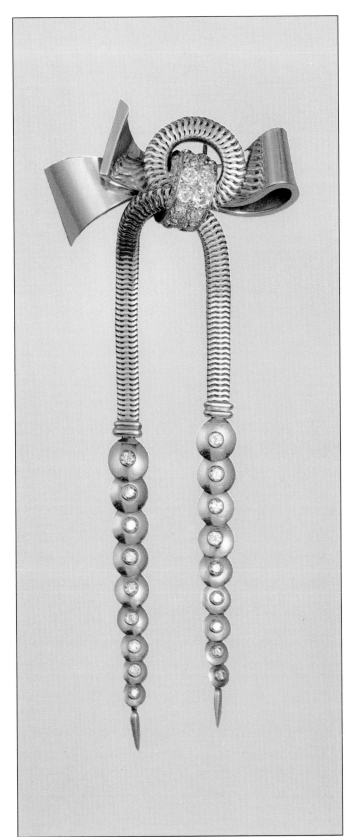

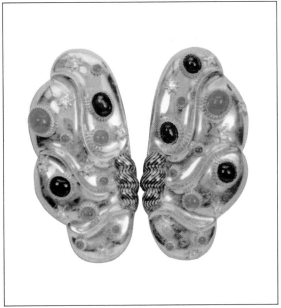

Pair of clips in gold, enamel, diamonds, rubies and sapphires, signed: Margherita (Milan). Photo: Christie's.

Bow brooch in pierced yellow gold and brilliants.
Regner (Paris).
Photo: Christie's.

Brooch in the shape of a bow, mounted on yellow gold and decorated with brilliants. Van Cleef et Arpels.
Photo: Laurent Sully-Jaulmes.

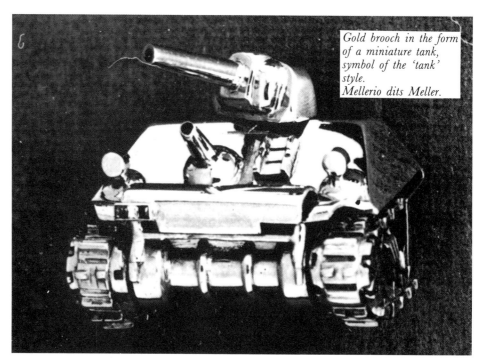

Gold brooch in the form of a miniature tank, symbol of the 'tank' style.
Mellerio dits Meller.

Snowflake clip in gold and brilliants.
Van Cleef et Arpels.

'Hawaii' clip in gold, rubies, brilliants and sapphires.
Van Cleef et Arpels.

Bow and flower brooch in yellow gold and brilliants.
Wolfers (Brussels).

'Wheatear' brooch in platinum and brilliants.
Wolfers (Brussels).

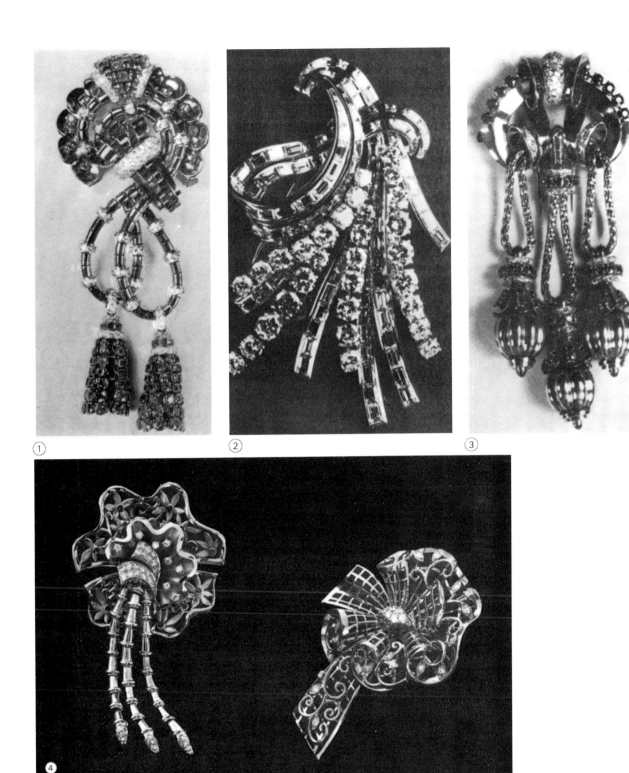

1. *Clip in yellow gold, brilliants and coloured stones. Boucheron.*

2. *Clip in platinum and brilliants. Boucheron.*

3. *Clip in yellow gold, brilliants and rubies. Boucheron.*

4. *Left: Bow brooch in gold, brilliants, rubies and enamel.*

Right: Brooch in pierced gold and brilliants. Gübelin (Lucerne).

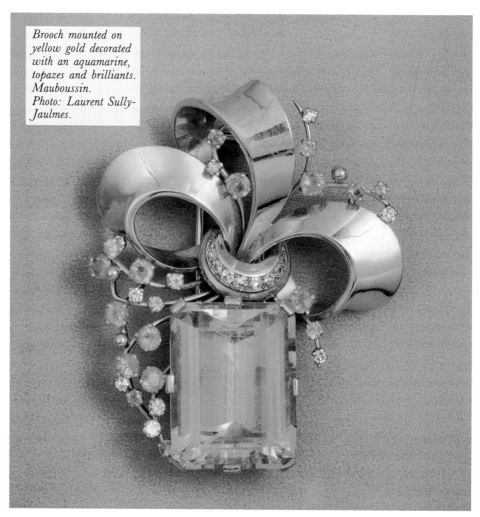

Brooch mounted on yellow gold decorated with an aquamarine, topazes and brilliants. Mauboussin. Photo: Laurent Sully-Jaulmes.

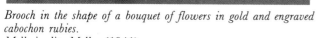

Brooch in the shape of a bouquet of flowers in gold and engraved cabochon rubies.
Mellerio dits Meller (1941).
Mellerio dits Meller Archives.

Bow brooch in gold and brilliants.
Private Collection.

*Above left: bow brooch in
yellow gold and brilliants.
France.*

*Above right: bow clip in
yellow gold and brilliants.
France.*

*Right: Design for a gold-mesh bow brooch with
brilliants and rubies.
Fecarotta Brothers Archives (Catania).*

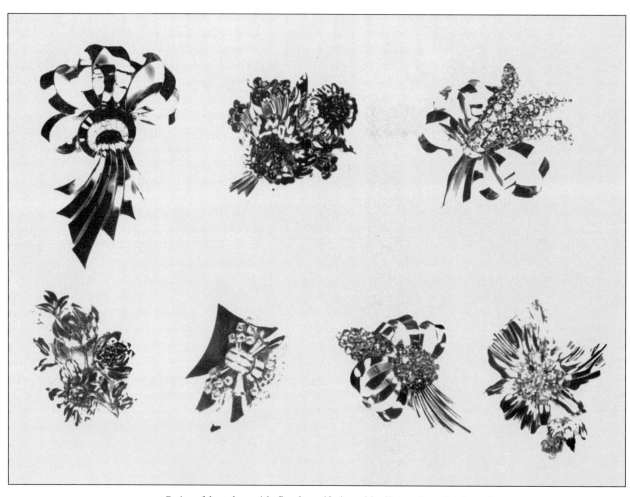

Series of brooches with floral motifs in gold, diamonds and coloured stones. Boucheron.
Boucheron Archives.

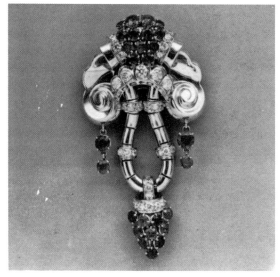

Gold, diamond and emerald brooch. Boucheron (1943).
Photo: Routhier - Sotheby's.

Clip in gold and brilliants.
Mellerio dits Meller (1941). Mellerio dits Meller Archive.

Bow-shaped brooch and earrings in yellow and white gold and diamonds. Private Collection.

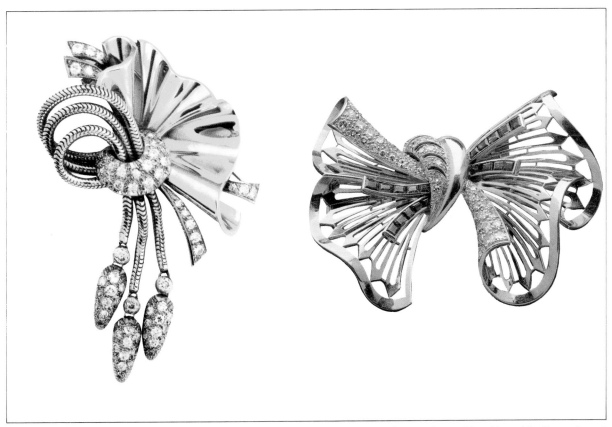

Bow brooch in yellow gold, white gold and diamonds. Private Collection.

Bow-shaped brooch in yellow gold, white gold, diamonds and calibré-cut sapphires. Bucherer (Zurich). Private Collection.

273

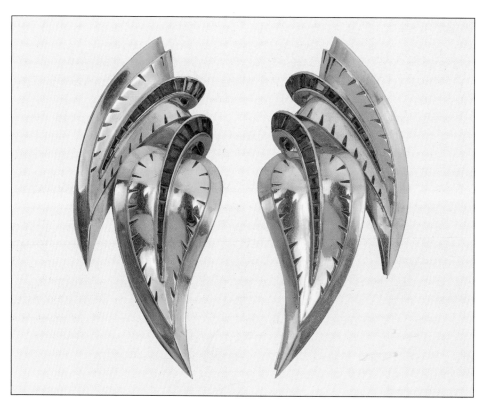

Clips in pink and yellow gold with calibré-cut sapphires. Van Cleef et Arpels. Private Collection.

Brooch mounted on gold, decorated with emeralds and diamonds. Van Cleef et Arpels. Private Collection.

274

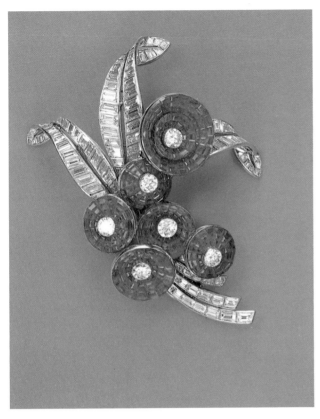

Pair of invisibly set ruby and diamond flower-head ear clips. Van Cleef et Arpels. Photo: Christie's.

Left: Invisibly set ruby and diamond floral spray clip brooch. Van Cleef et Arpels. Photo: Christie's.

Leaf-shaped brooch in gold with central vein in calibré-cut emeralds. Van Cleef et Arpels (1943). Van Cleef et Arpels Archives.

Invisibly set ruby and diamond leaf clip brooch. Van Cleef et Arpels. Photo: Christie's.

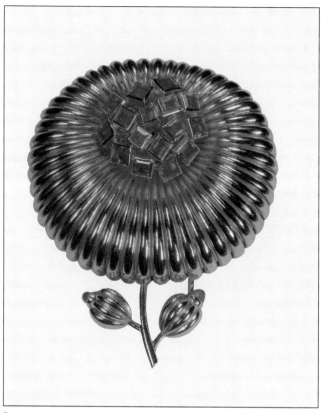

Brooch mounted on yellow and white gold with brilliants and square sapphires. France (1946). Franco Bernardini Collection (Milan).

Brooch in the shape of a bouquet of flowers in gold and engraved cabochon rubies. Mellerio dits Meller (1941). Mellerio dits Meller Archives.

Gold brooch with coloured stones and an engraved cabochon. Mellerio dits Meller Archives.

'Animalier' brooch in yellow gold, brilliants, rubies, emeralds and sapphires. Lacloche Freres.

Butterfly clip in gold, brilliants and emeralds.
Mellerio dits Meller.

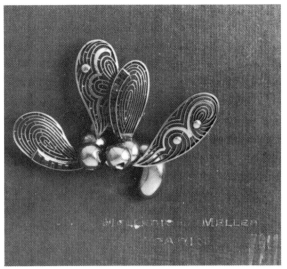

'Animalier' style brooch in gold and sapphires.
Mellerio dits Meller.

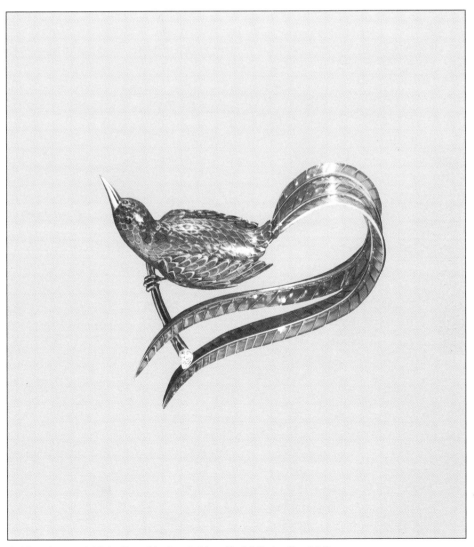

Gold and enamel bird clip with detachable tail. Mellerio dits Meller.

'Animalier' style brooch in gold and
rubies. Mellerio dits Meller.

277

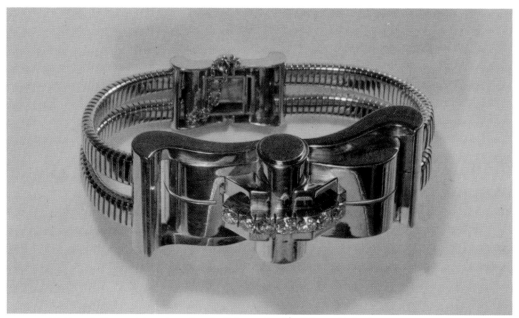

Gold and diamond bracelet, signed: Régner. Paris. Private Collection.

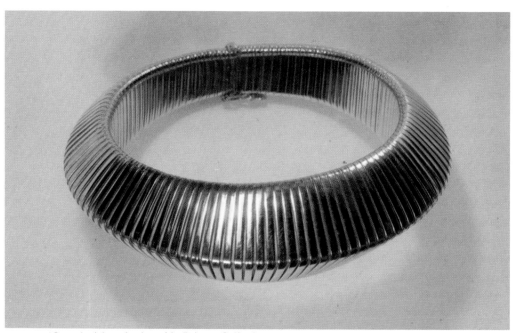

'Gas-pipe' bracelet in gold. Private Collection.

Articulated bracelet
in gold.
Private Collection.

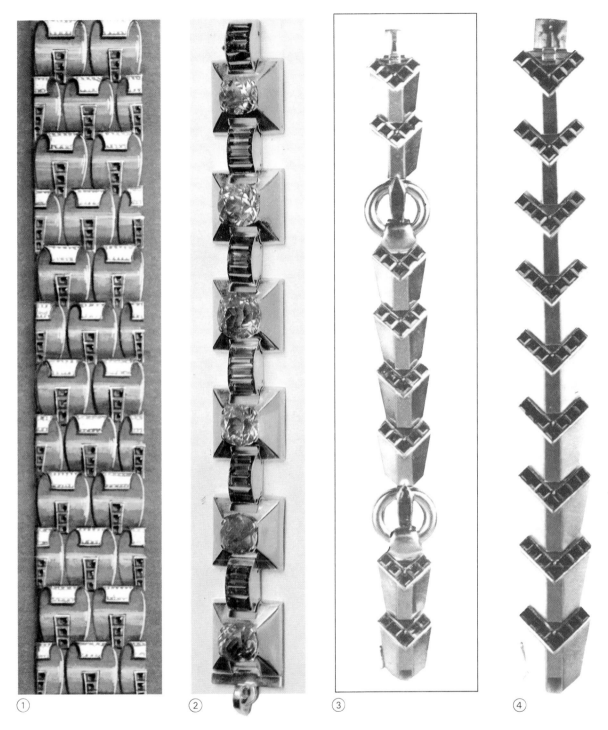

1. *Design for a 'tank' style bracelet in gold, brilliants and rubies. Bulgari (Rome).*

2. *Bracelet in pink gold and amethysts. Italy.*

3. *and 4. Articulated bracelets in gold and sapphires. Private Collection.*

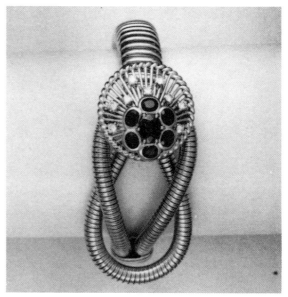

Gold bracelet forming a double loop, with a fastening consisting of a round motif in brilliants, sapphires and rubies. Cartier (1946). Cartier Archives.

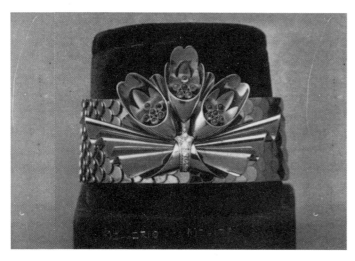

Right:

Fluted bracelet in gold, with lozenges in gold wire and sapphires, enhanced with brilliants and a ruby. Cartier (1947). Cartier Archives.

Gold fish-scale bracelet, decorated with a bouquet of flowers in brilliants and sapphires. Mellerio dits Meller (1940). Mellerio dits Meller Archives.

Fish-scale bracelet in gold, with stylised floral motif decorated with diamonds and rubies. Mellerio dits Meller (1941). Mellerio dits Meller Archives.

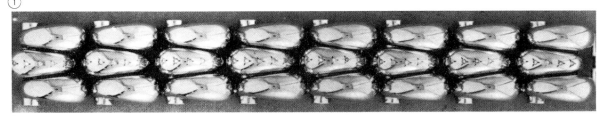

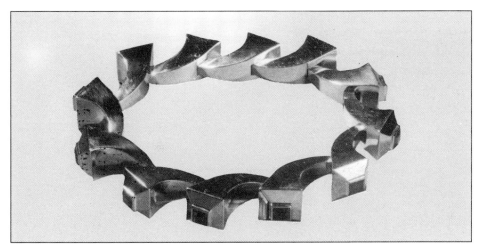

1. *Gold bracelet with hexagonal segments. Mellerio dits Meller.*

2. *Bracelet with segments in yellow gold and brilliants. Mellerio dits Meller.*

3. *Bracelet in gold, with brilliants and sapphires. Mellerio dits Meller.*

4. *'Tank' style bracelet in gold with rubies. Mellerio dits Meller.*

Bracelet in yellow gold and coloured stones. Mellerio dits Meller (1940).
Mellerio dits Meller Archives.

'Etruscan' bracelet in gold with cabochons of lapis lazuli.
Mellerio dits Meller.
Photo: Laurent Sully-Jaulmes.

Bangle in yellow gold decorated with rubies.
Van Cleef et Arpels.
Photo Laurent Sully-Jaulmes.

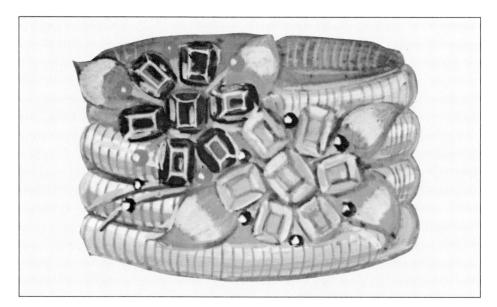

Design for a 'gas-pipe'
bracelet with a flower motif
in coloured precious stones.
Bulgari Archives (Rome).

Bracelet in pink gold consisting of a series of stylised bows.
Beszanger (Geneva).

Chain bracelet in pink gold.
Great Britain.

Gold 'tank' style bracelet. France.

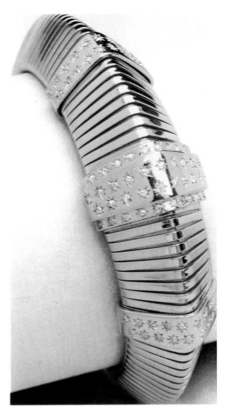

'Gas-pipe' bracelet in gold and star set brilliants. Private Collection.

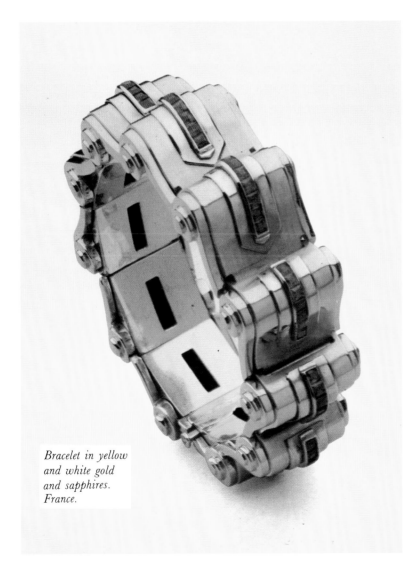

Bracelet in yellow and white gold and sapphires. France.

Gold rice-pattern bracelet. Italy.

Plaited 'gas-pipe'
bracelet in gold.
Mellerio dits Meller.

Gold bracelet with articulated segments.
Boucheron (1941).
Boucheron Archives.

Articulated gold bracelet.
Boucheron (1941).
Boucheron Archives.

Pennant bracelet in yellow gold.
Mellerio dits Meller (1941).
Mellerio dits Meller Archives.

Fish-scale bracelet in gold, with clasp in brilliants and rubies. Mellerio dits Meller.

Bicycle chain bracelet in gold of two colours. Mellerio dits Meller.

Flexible gold bracelet with oval cross-section and motifs consisting of discs in gold wire, sapphires and brilliants. Cartier (1946). Cartier Archives.

Bracelet with floral motifs in
yellow gold and topazes.
Masenza (Rome).

'Strap and buckle' bracelet mounted on yellow gold with
detachable clip in yellow and blue sapphires.
Photo: Laurent Sully-Jaulmes.

Articulated bracelet in
gold. Private Collection.

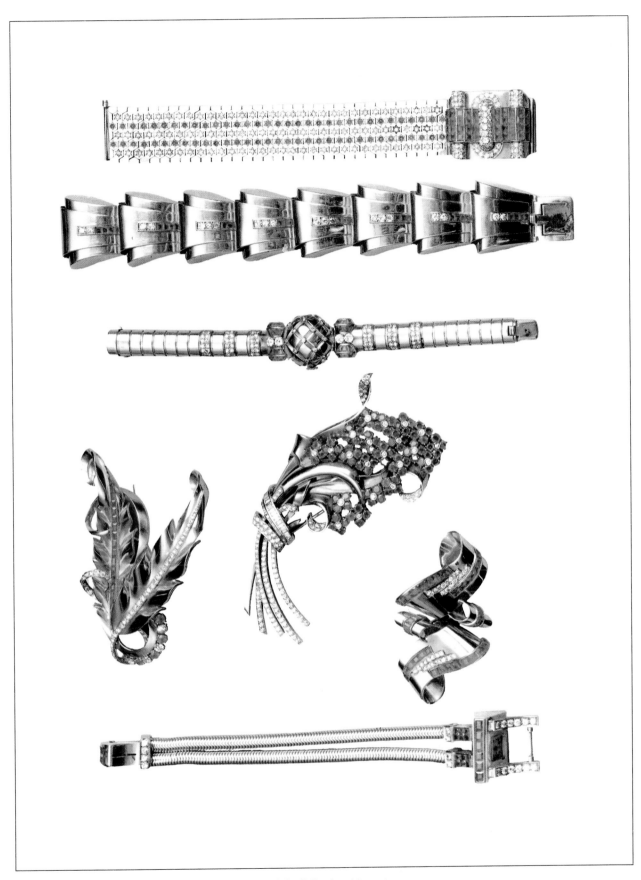

Jewellery in gold, rubies and diamonds. Nicoletta Lebole Collection (Arezzo) .

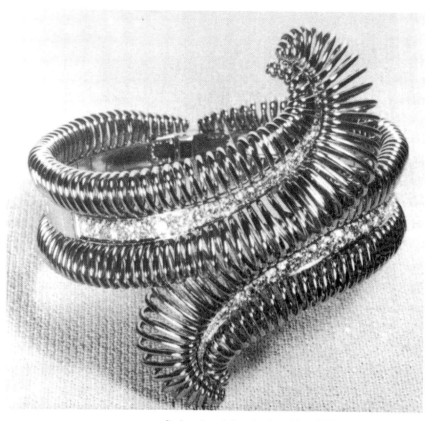

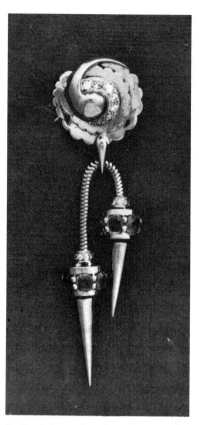

*Spring-shaped bracelet in gold and diamonds.
Boucheron (1948).*

*Snake-chain earrings in yellow gold,
sapphires and brilliants.
Mellerio dits Meller.*

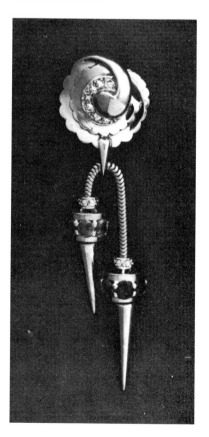

*Spring-shaped bracelet in gold and diamonds.
Boucheron (1947-48).
Boucheron Archives.*

Snake-chain earrings in gold and brilliants. Mellerio dits Meller.

Snake-chain earrings in gold, with rubies. Mellerio dits Meller.

Earrings in the wrought-iron style, in yellow gold and rubies. Mellerio dits Meller.

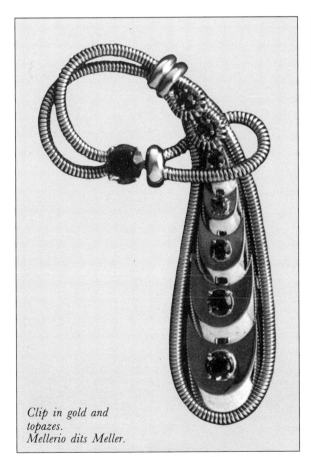

Clip in gold and topazes. Mellerio dits Meller.

Pendant earrings in red gold and rubies. Italy (circa 1940). Private Collection.

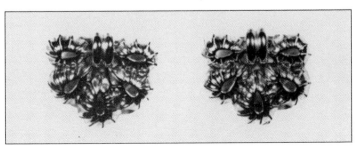

Earrings in red gold. Italy (circa 1940). Private Collection.

Parure in yellow gold and brilliants, comprising a pair of clips and earrings. France. Photo: Christie's.

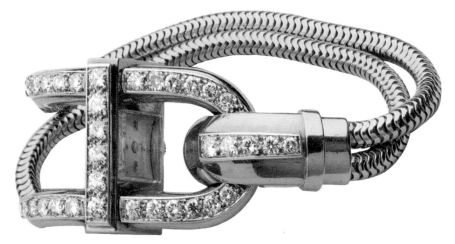

Wrist-watch in yellow gold and brilliants: double snake-chain and vertical dial. Van Cleef et Arpels.

"SYMPHONIE" Gros serpent d'or rose et couvercle mobile-sertis de diamants.

L'ÉVENTAIL

Ce blanc vol fermé que tu poses
Contre le feu d'un bracelet.
                    Mallarmé.

A quoi sert-il ce masque sur vos lèvres, qui ne laisse parler que vos yeux ? A déplacer un peu d'air, à dissimuler un sourire, à faire jouer la lumière sur les pierreries de votre montre, ou à faire croire que vous êtes timide ?

Vous jouez avec votre éventail comme l'hirondelle avec le vent ou le flot. Mais quand j'ai voulu vous prendre la main, vous avez replié brusquement les plumes légères et j'ai reçu un coup sec sur les doigts.

J'ai compris maintenant son utilité.

Pourtant vous savez bien qu'on ne frappe pas un homme même avec un éventail.

Page from an Omega catalogue, 1947.

Wrist-watch in gold of two colours and brilliants: typical convex glass.
France.

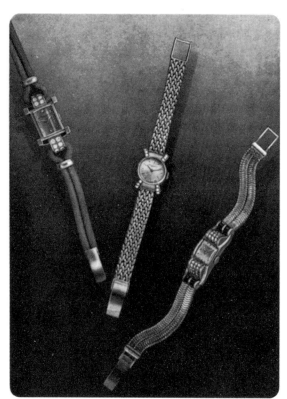

Reproduction of a page from the review 'Pro Arte', Geneva, 1947.
Baume et Mercier (Geneva).

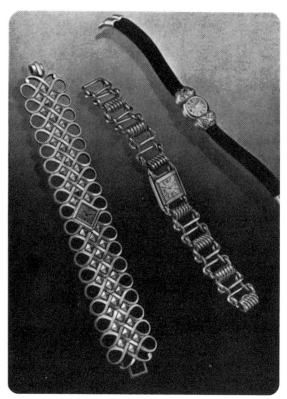

Reproduction of a page from the review 'Pro Arte', Geneva, 1947.
Jaeger-Le Coultre (Geneva).

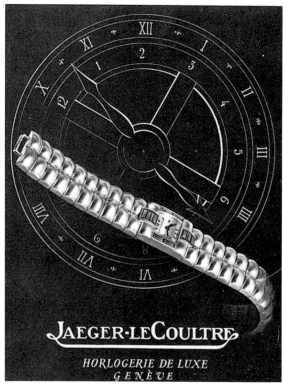

Reproduction of pages from the review 'Pro Arte', Geneva, 1947.
Jaeger-Le Coultre. Baume et Mercier (Geneva).

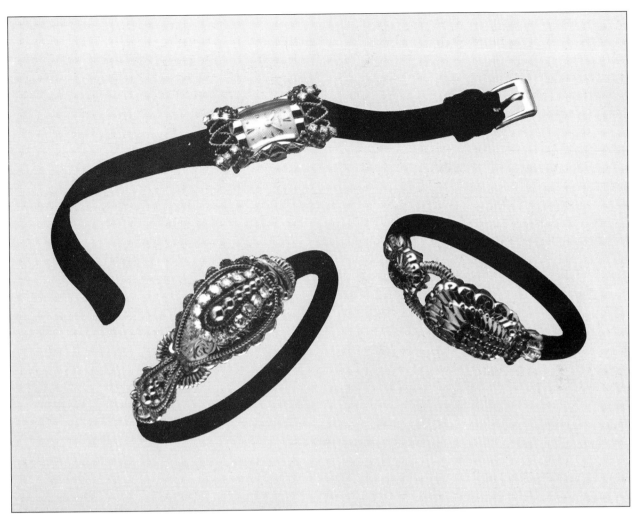

Top to bottom, clockwise:
Watch in gold and brilliants, with suede strap.

Watch with covered face in gold, brilliants and rubies, with suede strap.

Watch in gold, brilliants and rubies, with suede strap.
All by Gübelin (Lucerne).

Reproduction of a page from the review 'Pro Arte',
Geneva, 1947.
Patek Philippe & Co. (Geneva).

Wrist-watch with flexible segments in yellow gold. Lid in sapphires and gold studs. Lacloche.

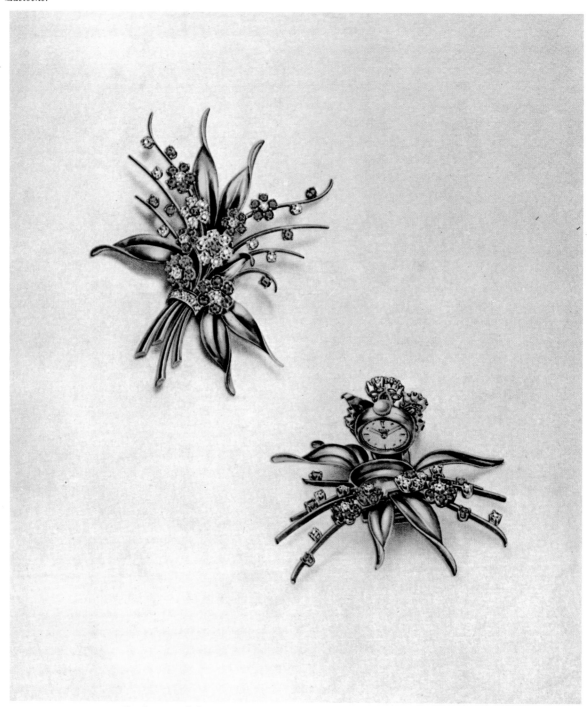

Pendant watch in yellow gold, rubies, sapphires and brilliants. Rolex (Geneva).

Wrist-watch in red gold: lid in brilliants and rubies, with double rats-tail strap.
Mauboussin.

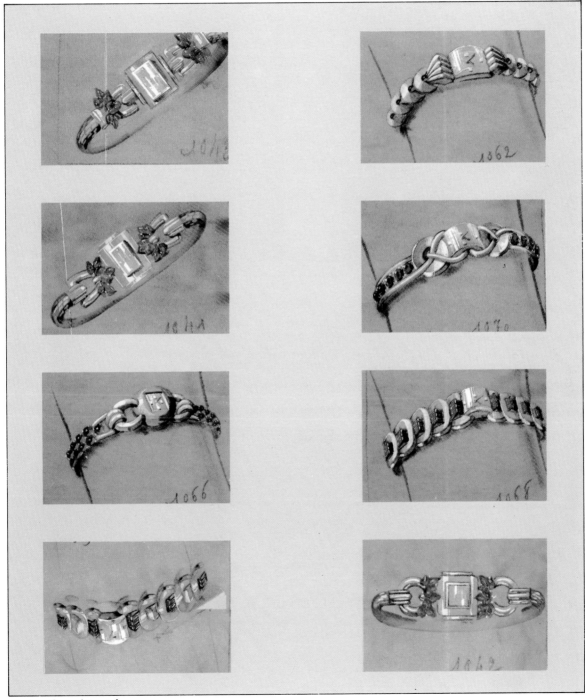

Designs for wrist-watches.
Mauboussin Archives.

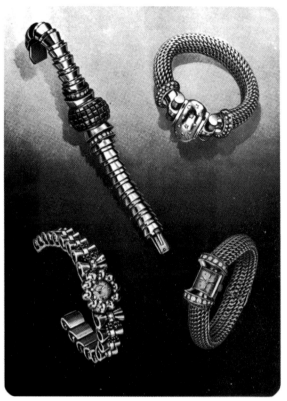

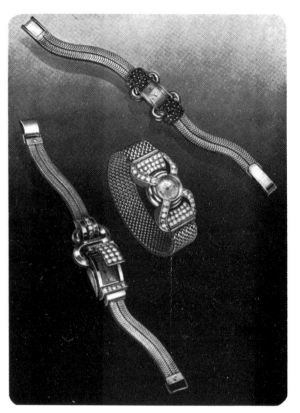

Reproduction of a page from the review 'Pro Arte', Geneva, 1947.
Patek, Philippe & Co. (Geneva).

Reproduction of a page from the review 'Pro Arte', Geneva, 1947.
Rolex (Geneva).

Gold wrist-watch with black lizard-skin strap.
U.T.I. Paris (1940).
Private Collection.

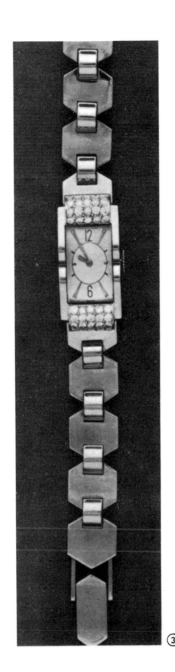

1. Gold wrist-watch in the wrought-iron style. Mellerio dits Meller.

2. Gold wrist-watch in the wrought-iron style. Mellerio dits Meller.

3. Wrist-watch with hexagonal segments in gold and brilliants. Mellerio dits Meller.

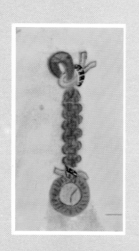

*Designs for pendant
watches.
Mauboussin Archives.*

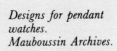

Gold wrist-watch with hidden dial.
Cyma (1940).

Pendant watch in gold and brilliants.
Gübelin (Lucerne).

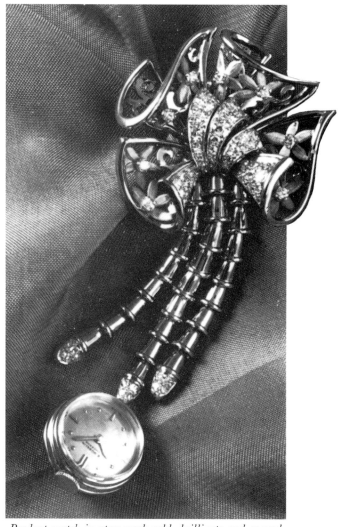

Pendant watch in open-work gold, brilliants and enamel.
Gübelin (Lucerne).

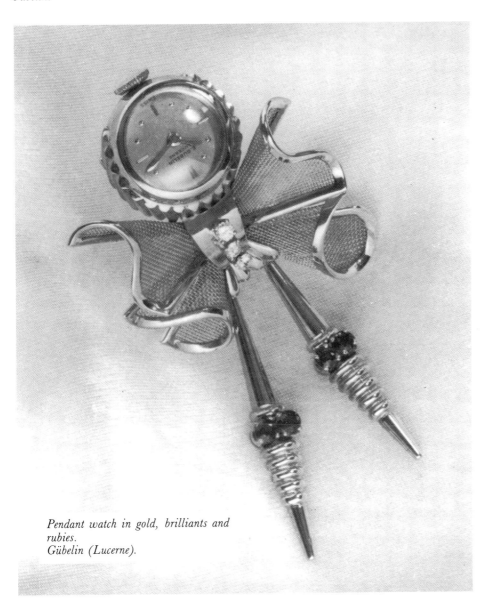

Wrist-watch with articulated segments in pink gold.
Gübelin.

Pendant watch in gold, brilliants and
rubies.
Gübelin (Lucerne).

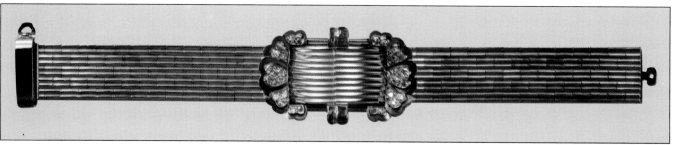

Wrist-watch in yellow gold: lid in brilliants and rubies.
France.
Photo: Christie's.

Pendant watch in gold. Mauboussin.
Watch in gold and topazes, strap in crocodile skin.
Mauboussin.

Wrist-watch in gold, rubies and brilliants.
Rolex (Geneva).

Wrist-watch in gold and star set sapphires.
Private Collection.

Wrist-watch in yellow gold and brilliants: veined lid and double rat's-tail strap. France.

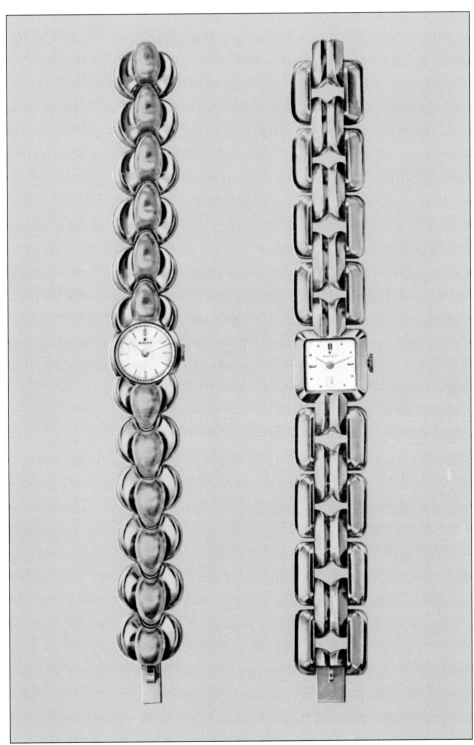

Wrist-watches in yellow gold. Rolex (Geneva).

Wrist-watch in gold and brilliants.
Gübelin (Lucerne).

Wrist-watch in gold and rubies.
Gübelin (Lucerne).

Gold wrist-watch decorated with coloured stones.
Gübelin (Lucerne).

Wrist-watch in gold and diamonds.
Private Collection.

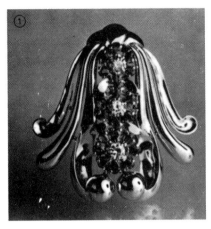

1. Clip in yellow gold, diamonds, sapphires and rubies.
Wolfers (Brussels).

2. Clip in yellow gold, brilliants and aquamarine.
Wolfers (Brussels).

3. Clip in yellow gold and brilliants.
Wolfers (Brussels).

4. Bow-shaped brooch in yellow gold and rubies.
Wolfers (Brussels).

5. Bow-shaped brooch in yellow gold and brilliants.
Wolfers (Brussels).

6. Bow-shaped brooch in red gold and rubies.
Wolfers (Brussels).

7. Clip with double bow in gold, platinum and
brilliants.
Mellerio dits Meller.

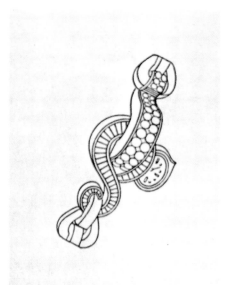

*Above and left: Wrist-watch in yellow
gold, brilliants and sapphires.
Rolex (Geneva).*

*Above and right: Wrist-watch in yellow
gold: lid set with brilliants.
Rolex (Geneva).*

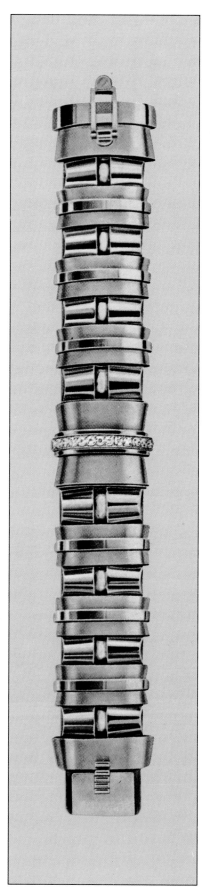

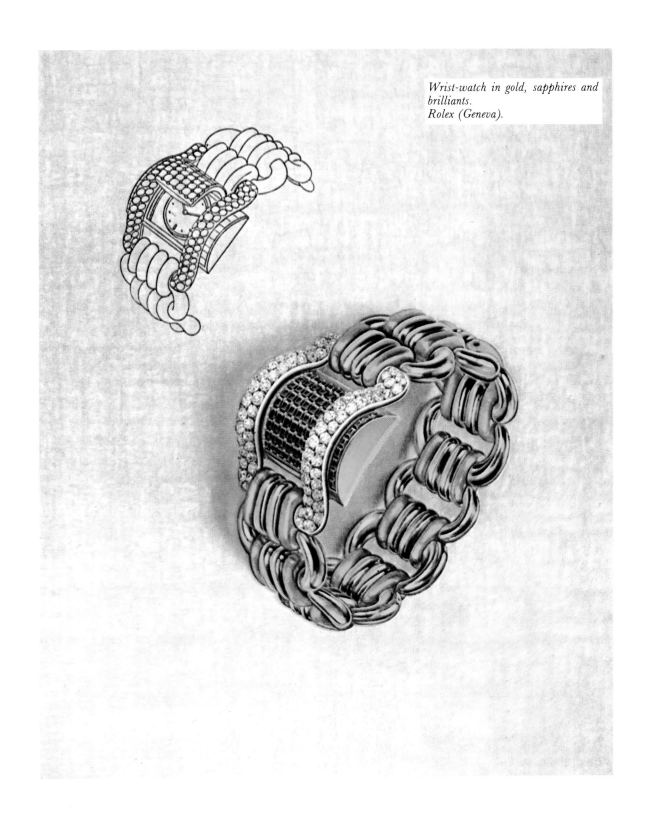

Wrist-watch in gold, sapphires and brilliants.
Rolex (Geneva).

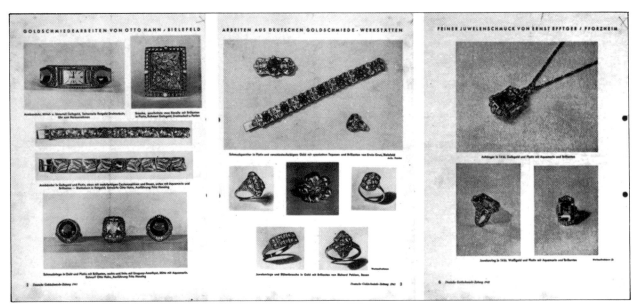

Pages from the review 'Deutsche Goldschmiede Zeitung', 1941.

Jewellery in Belgium

The goldsmith's craft in Belgium, traditionally linked to French taste, suffered particularly from the vicissitudes of war. The penury of materials had a disastrous effect on the fertile imagination which had characterised Art Nouveau and Art Deco in that country. The Wolfers dynasty was maintained by neo-baroque creations (bows, volutes, flowers, set with precious and semi-precious stones). Leysen Frères, Altenloh, and Sturbelle also continued production.

Jewellery in Germany

The ideological demands of the Nazi regime, which affected all areas of German art, did not spare artisanal activity, including of course, jewellery.

In the 1930s Parisian influence was preponderant, although adapted to the Germanic taste. The appearance of Nazism corresponded, however, with a rejection of French influence. The new jewellery lost a part of its ornamental character. Its design took on a more dynamic and geometrical style.

At that time there co-existed two well-known centres of jewellery production: Hanau, specialising in high fashion jewellery, and Pforzheim, specialising (with firms such as Braendler, Fahrner, Knoll, etc.) in mass-produced jewellery.

The great names in German jewellery were, in Berlin: Lettré, Sy-Wagner, Wilm and the Deutsche Werkstätte; in Frankfurt: Robert Koch; in Cologne: Dix; in Stuttgart: Menner; in Leipzig: Troesch; in Hamburg: Wilm (this company is still active).

The war put an end to creative jewellery as well as to industrially produced jewellery. The artisans were at the front. Hanau and Pforzheim were completely destroyed. Factories, archives, designs and documents all disappeared. The shortage of precious materials forced German jewellers to fulfil only official commissions. Gold was progressively replaced by silver and other alloys. From now on, jewellery was produced 'with base metals (iron sheeting, cast iron), decorated with coloured enamel or burnished,' as Rücklin wrote in the specialist review *Deutsche Goldschmiede Zeitung* (no. 43) in 1941. The working of these metals imposed new techniques. The design of leaves and flowers became rigid and stylised. In the Pforzheim Museum are exhibited two rings created by German soldiers in 1939-40 out of metal from barbed wire defences. These rings served as prototypes for rings produced on a large scale during the war. Industrially they were made of steel.

Gold was used in very small quantities, in the form of thin sheets, interlaced wire and small chains. Tourmaline, onyx, rock crystal and aquamarine became, in Germany as throughout Europe, the favourite stones of the period. The few pieces which have come down to us do not correspond to any well defined style. Their forms are diverse, but always strongly impregnated with Germanic tradition.

According to the accounts of certain German jewellers, it was also possible, during the first phase of the war, to obtain jewellery coming from Occupied France.

After the war, German jewellery production did not get under way again until the 1950s, and it was, at that time, principally intended to satisfy the demands of the occupying forces.

Austrian jewellery, marked by the *Jugendstil*, which was at the height of its splendour in Vienna in the 1930s, declined during the war, closely following the fortunes of its neighbouring country.

Necklace with 'pip' segments. In the centre an aquamarine and zircons. 1942. Erna Zarges Dürr (Murnau).

310

Jewellery in Switzerland

Switzerland, spared by the war, nevertheless had monetary problems and difficulties in obtaining supplies. Activities were maintained on a reduced scale.

It is interesting to note that it was outside the frontiers of the German speaking countries, in Scandinavia, that the style deriving from the Bauhaus bloomed. This new style, austere and pure, was later to return to its native land, but renamed the Scandinavian style.

Walter Gübelin, the celebrated jeweller from Lucerne, recalled the influence of the Parisian style on pre-war Swiss jewellery.

A few weeks before the outbreak of hostilities, in September 1939, the Swiss National Exhibition opened in Zurich. The Lucerne firm took part, with a jewellery pavillion created by the Zurich architect K. Egender and Edouard Gübelin senior. Here was shown a new concept in jewellery inspired by the sober Scandinavian style and by the Chinese art dear to Edouard Gübelin. This style, christened *style nuage* (cloud style), was dominated by large volutes in gold, which provided the basic element for clips, brooches, rings and bracelets.

Affected by the backlash of the European war, Swiss jewellery gradually adopted a certain sobriety and austerity. Pieces of jewellery were poorly endowed with precious stones (synthetic stones were hardly used), but rich in gold, and sometimes decorated with enamel work and miniatures, using motifs

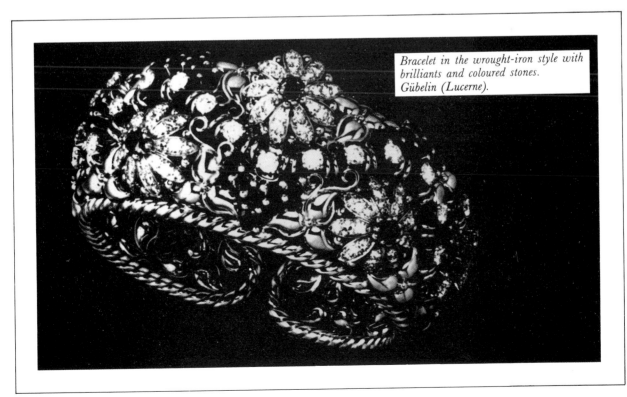

Bracelet in the wrought-iron style with brilliants and coloured stones. Gübelin (Lucerne).

inspired by medieval and Persian painting. The decorative techniques of enamelling had always been characteristic of this country (Geneva enamels), and lent themselves very well to the decoration of brooches, pendants, boxes and cases.

During the war, cheap objects imported from Pforzheim and Valenza (Italy) no longer came into Switzerland, and the Swiss were obliged to take the production of flowers, bows, loops and shells in simple sheets of laminated gold into their own hands. In March 1945 Golay fils et Stahl of Geneva were selling a necklace in yellow gold richly set with diamonds.

At the end of the war forms became softer. From 1946 onwards mesh-work metal made its appearance, taking the form of wispy veils. At the same time, pieces of classic high fashion jewellery were re-created, in platinum, grey gold and palladium, with finely worked surfaces, decorated with precious stones.

Bracelet in yellow gold and brilliants, sieve style.
Gübelin (Lucerne).

Echten Gefühlen gibt man mit echtem Schmucke Ausdruck

Reproduction of a page from the review 'Pro Arte' (Geneva), 1947.

Spiral necklace in yellow gold: wrought-iron style pendant with brilliants and rubies. Gübelin (Lucerne).

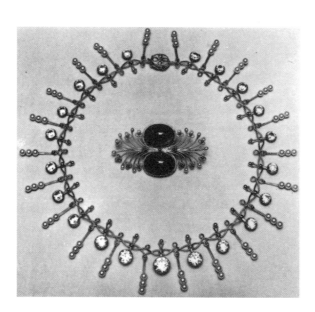

Choker in gold wire with pearls and zircons, 1946. In the centre: brooch in gold wire, tourmalines and pearls. 1943. Erna Zarges Dürr (Murnau).

Necklace in gold and diamonds with bow motif. Gübelin (Lucerne).

The great jewellers of that period are almost all still in business. They are as follows: in Zurich, Bucherer and Meister; in Lucerne, Gübelin; in Geneva, Beszanger; elsewhere, Weber, Ponti-Gennari, Wegner, Bonnard, Bergerious.

It is impossible to speak of Swiss jewellery without mentioning the wristwatch (which was the subject of the Geneva exhibition of 1940). The Swiss wrist-watch seemed to refuse to fulfil a simple practical function, and rivalled in opulence the most sumptuous bracelets of the period. The tiny dial, usually square in shape, was hidden by a lid which was often decorated with precious stones. In some cases it was even hidden in the petals of a flower. But there were also watches with open faces or models with leather straps. Here the face and the fastenings were composed of decorative motifs. Most of the big houses have maintained their past reputation. This is the case with Baume-Mercier, Jaeger-le-Coultre, Omega, Patek-Philippe, Piaget, Rolex, Solvil, Universal, Vacheron and Constantin.

Jabot pin, pendant earrings, pendant brooch, ring and bracelet in platinum, brilliants, onyx and emeralds.
Cigarette box in platinum, black enamel and diamonds.
Adler Collection (Geneva).

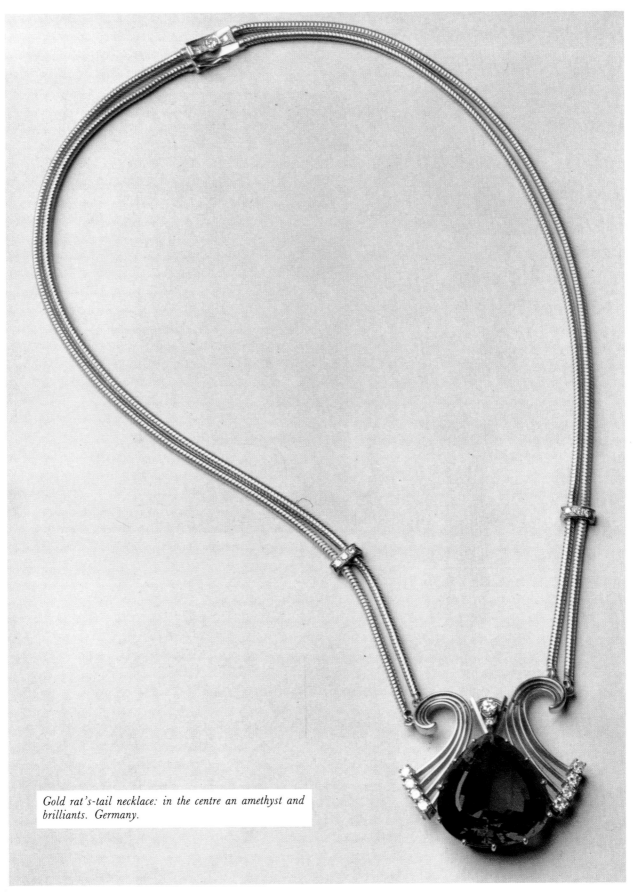

Gold rat's-tail necklace: in the centre an amethyst and brilliants. Germany.

Jewellery in Great Britain

English jewellery, which had been seriously weakened by the economic crisis of the 1930s, was just beginning to raise its head above water when war broke out.

In England it had not been usual to invest in jewellery, which had merely had a decorative value. In the 1940s, this attitude changed. Motor-car production was interrupted, and bombing made property investment uncertain. Jewellery thus acquired the safety net value it had everywhere else.

But raw materials were only obtainable with difficulty. The production of jewellery was slowed down (as Garrard's of London, official suppliers to the Royal Family, recall) by the introduction of a tax on the purchase of new articles of jewellery which went from 10% in 1943 to 125% in 1947! This tax also applied to wedding rings. But the antique or second hand jewellery market escaped. The supply of diamonds from South Africa was very irregular, and Antwerp, the centre of the diamond cutting industry, was in an occupied country, separated from England by a sea controlled by the enemy.

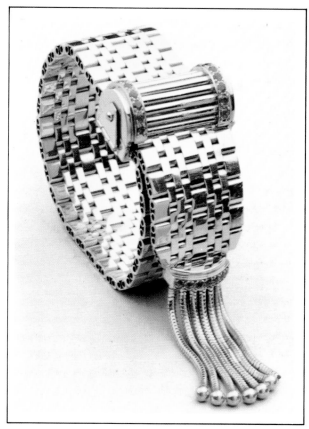

'Strap and buckle' bracelet in yellow gold and rubies.
Garrard (London).

The English jewellery trade lived above all on remodelling and on the second hand market. Articles created in England were usually in gold, which was preferred to platinum or palladium (which had fallen into disfavour on account of its greyish colour). Forms tended to be geometrical, in harmony with the square lines of wide-shouldered dresses. This was a style which hardly survived, for, according to Garrard's, it was heavy and lacking in femininity. In addition to Garrard's, the best known jewellers of the period were Asprey, Collingwood, Drayson and Mappin & Webb. Documentation on this period is very limited, since English jewellers found it a waste of time drawing up catalogues in these difficult times.

Jewellery in Italy

The triumph of bad taste. This is the way in which 1940s jewellery was defined in Italy. The time had perhaps come to rehabilitate and rescue it from oblivion.

But the discredit into which it has fallen is probably originally due to the poverty of the archival documents (specimens, photographs, designs) which might have enabled us to understand this period properly. Most pieces were melted down or destroyed for their gold or precious stones. The jewellers' archives were destroyed by bombing, or simply not kept up. It is therefore very difficult to identify pieces, since few goldsmiths signed their works. The authorship of some pieces can, however, be recognised thanks to sketches left in workshops or the direct evidence of artisans or purchasers.

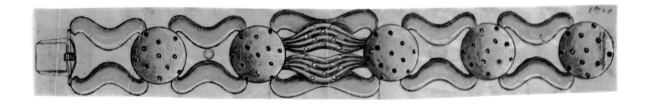

Design for a bracelet in red gold and sapphires, 1948.
Illario (Valenza).

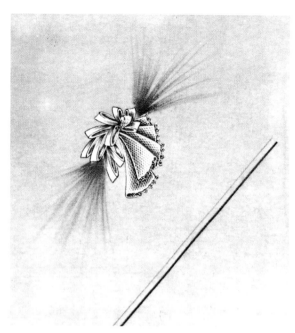
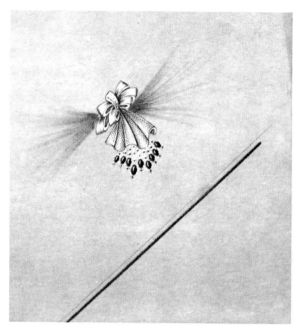

Designs for bow-shaped brooches.
Fratelli Veneziani Archives. (Milan-Rome).

In September 1942 a decree was issued forbidding the sale of precious articles. But well before this, the slogan 'Give your gold to the Fatherland' launched by the Fascists had already played its part in divesting private citizens of their wealth.

Remodelling was the only work officially authorised. Nevertheless some limited creative activity was clandestinely maintained. But many jewellers closed down their workshops, in the hope of better times to come.

Cesare Settepassi, still today a jeweller on the Ponte Vecchio in Florence, recalls that during the war his father-in-law carried on paying his artisans, although he had given up all activity, in order not to lose them.

Giovanni Illario of Valenza notes: 'In 1939, we had a workforce of eighty and an annual production of a thousand hand-made pieces. Between October 1940 and May 1945, our manufacture had to be limited to three thousand one hundred pieces.' However, the jewellery trade did not cease completely, for the public saw in it a means of hoarding.

There were two categories of production. The first, aimed at mass distribution, was already provided for by Valenza (although articles like small chains and medallions also came in from Pforzheim). The other was that of the artisanally produced article of jewellery, a unique object, the privilege of the monied classes.

'In general', recalls Stella Fasano, who was at that time installed on the piazza Castello in Turin: '..Italian jewellery traditionally took its inspiration from French taste.'

Indeed the forms and decorative motifs of French jewellery had been adopted: the emphasis on relief, the classic moving staircase designs; the buckle, snail, shell, and curtain structures; the honeycomb settings; the panier, bouquet, horn of plenty, wheat-ear brooches, and the famous little dogs...; the dice rings and the rings with three flowers or heavy, prominent bows. Gold and

Design for a bow-shaped brooch.
Fratelli Veneziani Archives.
(Milan-Rome).

coloured stones, often synthetic, given the times, were abundantly used. Brilliants were round or baguette-cut.

Apart from the names already referred to, the following jewellers also adopted the new style: Cusi, Castelli, 'Margherita', Veneziani in Milan; Bulgari, Masenza, Ventrella in Rome; Chiappe, Cipollina in Genoa; Janesich in Trieste; Night in Naples; Veronese in Bologna; Trizio in Bari; Missiaglia in Venice; Pietro Capuano known as 'Chantecler' in Capri. The classic line of jewellery was maintained by, for example, Buccellati in Milan.

In Sicily the Fecarotta brothers of Catana recall: '...Art Deco jewellery arrived here late, above all as a result of the German production. It was accepted by a few sophisticated clients, always ready to adopt the novelties of high society.' Thus there developed a modest local production of 1940s jewellery, disdained by the Sicilian aristocracy, which had always preferred diamonds and pieces in the eighteenth and nineteenth century styles, ignoring coloured stones and the new fashions, thought to be extravagant.

But in Sicily it was a tradition, even in the war years, to give presents of jewellery for engagements, births and weddings. This habit prevented the complete stoppage of production, although it remained feeble and rarely offered prototypes of a high standard. Since precious stones were lacking, amber, thought of from time immemorial on the island as being lucky, came back into use.

Design for a gold and sapphire bracelet. Fasano (Turin).

Design for a bow-shaped bracelet in yellow gold, brilliants and rubies. Fasano (Turin).

Design for a necklace in gold and brilliants.
Fratelli Veneziani Archives (Milan-Rome).

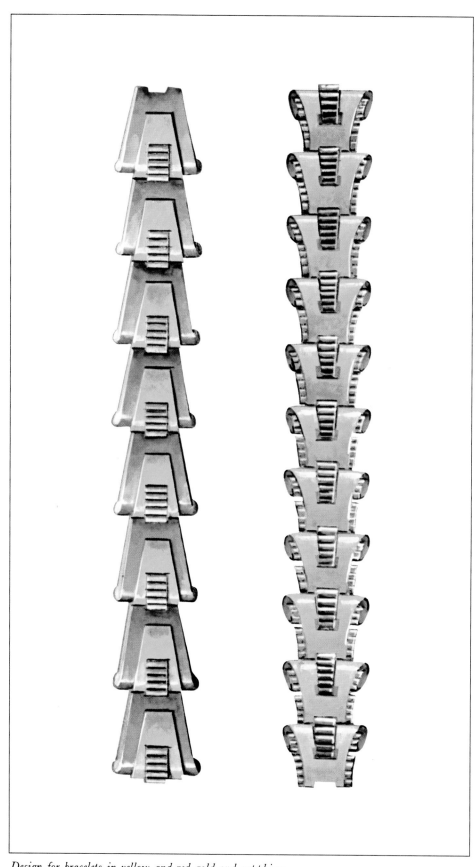

Design for bracelets in yellow and red gold and sapphires.
Bulgari Archives (Rome).

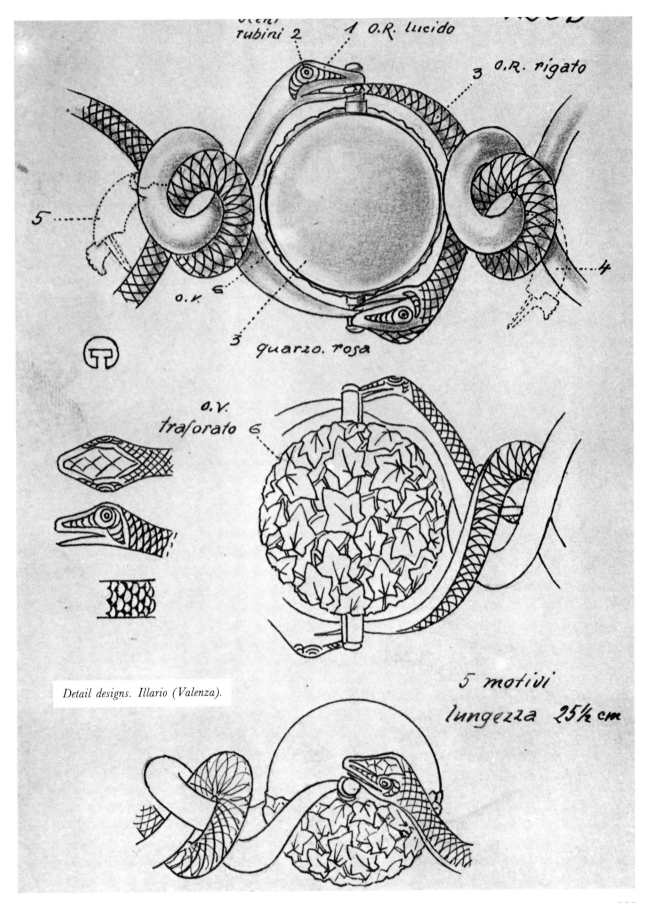

occhi tubini 2
1 O.R. lucido
3 O.R. rigato
5
o.v. 6
3 quarzo. rosa
4

O.V. traforato 6

Detail designs. Illario (Valenza).

5 motivi lungezza 25½ cm

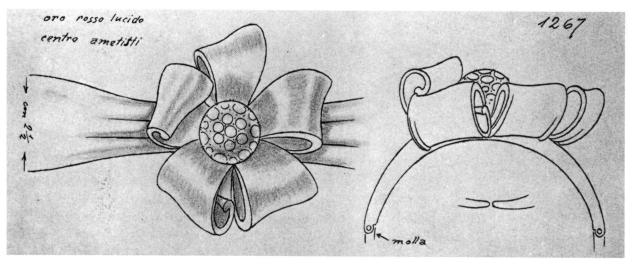

Detail. Illario (Valenza).

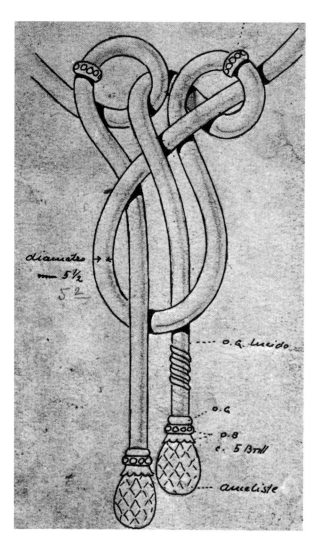

Necklace in gold and brilliants.
Bulgari (Rome).

Design for a 'gas-pipe' necklace in gold.
Illario (Valenza).

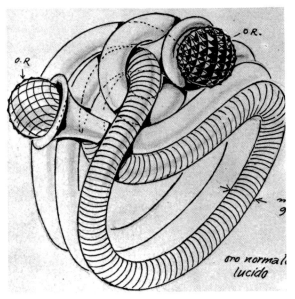

Design for a gold 'gas-pipe' bracelet (1946-48).
Illario (Valenza).

Jewellery in the U.S.A.

There was abundant production of jewellery in the United States during the period of the Second World War. The forms were recognisable and precisely similar to those of European design, although more aggressive and more richly decorated with precious stones.

1950 — The End of the Period of Crisis

One could ask why 1940s jewellery had such a short life, and, above all, why the specimens which have come down to us are so rare. The reasons for the ephemeral nature of this fashion period are the return of free circulation in Europe and the renewed import of precious metals and stones, which determined the decline of gold and a new enthusiasm for the precious stone, to the detriment of its metallic support. This rebirth in jewellery had as an initial consequence the destruction of most of the pieces in question.

What is more, gold jewellery was incontravertibly *nouveau riche*, and there was, from this point on, a concern to quickly get rid of this humiliating distinguishing feature by recourse to new forms and fashions.

Finally, once danger had been averted, investment jewellery was usually melted down, particularly when its owners were able to re-invest in property, industry or commerce.

'1940s jewellery', said Jean Mauboussin, 'was the jewellery of a period in crisis; it was logical that it should disappear when this came to an end.'

The return to better times was reflected in jewellery by the tendency to show off a maximum number of precious stones. With economic renewal, sumptuous pieces of jewellery, loaded with diamonds, were once more created and worn.

Jewellery is both a symbol and a reflection. It represents tangible proof of success. It is displayed with pleasure and ostentation, whatever the occasion (official reception, gala, première, night at the Opera). The 1950s marked the supremacy of gemstones to the detriment of mount and design. Brilliants were the undisputed masters of the field and reached their heyday at the approach of the 1960s.

Heavy mountings disappeared, now thought of as a sign of bad taste. They gave way to almost non-existent structures in platinum or white gold, deliberately designed to show off the stones. Gold jewellery continued nevertheless to play an important role, but in lighter, airier, almost transparent forms. This can doubtless be attributed to the abundant use of gold in the form of wire, whether alone, plaited or coiled — a new way of working gold which was to mark the 1950s generation of jewellery.

BIBLIOGRAPHY

Anni Trenta: Catalogo della Mostra del Comune di Milano Gennaio, April 1982.

Art Déco-Schmuck und Bucher aus Frankreich Sammlung, L. and B. Heuer and F. Marcilhac/Exhibition: Pforzheim, 1975.

Arwas, Victor: *Art Déco.* Academy Editions, London, 1980.

Bangert, Albrecht: *Jugendstil Art Déco.* Heyne, Munich, 1981.

Barten, Sigrid: *René Lalique.* Munich 1977.

Battersby, Martin: *La Mode Art Déco.* Flammarion, Paris, 1976.

Battersby, Martin: *The Decorative Thirties.* Studio Vista, London, 1971.

Black, Anderson: *Storia dei gioelli.* Instituto Geographico De Agostini di Novara, 1973.

Bossaglia, Rossana: *Il Déco italiano.* Rizzoli, Milan, 1975.

Brunhammer, Yvonne: *Le style 1925.* Editions Baschet, Paris, 1975.

Cartier, Louis: *Retrospective Masterwork of Art Déco,* 1982.

Charles-Roux, Edmonde: *Le temps Chanel.* Paris, 1979.

Cinquantenaire de l'Exposition de 1925. Musée des Arts décoratifs. Paris, 1976/1977.

Crespelle, Jean-Paul: *La folle Epoque.* Hachette, Paris, 1968.

Dewiel, Lydia: *Les bijoux du classicisme à l'Art Déco.* Editions Duculot, 1979.

Di Noto, Andrea: *Art Plastic,* Abbeville Press Inc, New York, 1984.

Falk, Fritz: *Art Déco, ein neueentdecker Kunstbegriff.* Blickpunkt, Pforzheim.

Follia Plastica, Esposizione di oggetti d'arte 1930-1940-1950. Edelktron, Milan, 1984.

Fouquet, Georges: *La Bijouterie et la Joaillerie modernes dans l'Orfèvrerie, la Joaillerie.* Editions du Chêne, Paris, 1942.

Fouquet, Georges; Sedeyn, Emile; Guérin, Jacques; Lanllier, Jean; Piel, Paul: *La Bijouterie, la Joaillerie, la Bijouterie Fantaisie au XXe siècle.* Paris, 1934.

Fouquet, Jean: *Bijoux et Orfèvrerie, Art international d'aujourd'hui, n°16.* Editions Charles Moreau, Paris, 1931.

Gabardi, Melissa: *Gioelli anni, 1940.* Giorgio Mondadori e Associati, Milan, 1982.

Gabardi, Melissa: *Gioelli: gli stili e il mercato.* Giorgio Mondadori e Associati, Milan, 1984.

Garner, Philippe: *Les arts décoratifs 1940-1980.* Bordas, Paris.

Garner, Philippe: *Encyclopédie visuelle des Arts décoratifs 1890-1940.* Bordas, Paris, 1981.

Gautier, Gilberte: *La saga dei Cartier (Rue de la Paix).* Editori Europei Associati, Milan.

Gary, Marie-Noël: *Les Fouquet, Bijoutiers et Joailliers à Paris 1860-1960.* Musée des Arts décoratifs, Flammarion, 1983.

Gregorietti, Guido: *Il gioiello nei secoli.* Mondadori, 1969.

Hughes, Graham: *5,000 ans de joaillerie.* Calmann-Lévy, 1973.

Kobal, John: *Movie Stars-Portraits of the Forties.* Dover Public, New York, 1977.

Lanllier, J.; Pini, A.M: *Cinq siècles de joaillerie en Occident.* Office du Livre, 1971.

Massobrio, G.P. Portoghesi: *Album degli anni Trenta.* Laterza Editori, Rome, 1978.

Menten, Théodore: *Authentic Art Deco Jewellery Designs.* Dover Publications, New York, 1982.

Menten, Théodore: *The Art Deco Style.* Dover Publications, New York, 1972.

Nadelhoffer, Hans: *Cartier.* Editions du Regard, Paris, 1984.

Raulet, Sylvie: *Bijoux Art Déco.* Editions du Regard, Paris, 1984.

Rolex Jubilé 1905-1920-1945. Roto Sadag S.A., Geneva, 1945.

Roselle, Bruno de: *La Mode.* Imprimerie Nationale, Paris, 1980.

Scarisbrick, Diana: *Il valore dei gioielli.* Umberto Allemandi, Turin, 1984.

Uckerman, P. d': *L'Art dans la vie moderne.* Flammarion, Paris.

Veronesi, Giulia: *Style 1925.* Editions Anthony Krafft, Lausanne.

Vever, Henry: *La Bijouterie française au XIXe siècle.* Paris, 1908.

Ward, Anne; Cherry, John; Gere, Charlotte; Cartlidge, Barbara: *The Ring.* Thames and Hudson, London, 1981.

Wolfers, Marcel: *Philippe Wolfers.* Editions Meddens, Brussels, 1965.